BEGINNING OF THE END

By the end of Day 9, the bombing of North Vietnam had taken an enormous toll. The planners were running out of suitable targets because the damage inflicted on most targets was higher than initially predicted. It became questionable whether those few targets remaining in the high threat areas were even of sufficient worth to continue attacking. The commander of the air force in the Pacific even suggested that it was time to look for targets in lower threat areas.

As on previous days, the TACAIR support effectively countered the enemy defenses. The few MiGs which had managed to get airborne were driven away by the American fighter patrols. Although up to 70 SAMs had been fired at the B-52's, the accuracy was noticeably poorer. The last desperate attempts to defend Hanoi were being made and it appeared the offensive was rapidly coming to a conclusion.

LINEBACKER:
The Untold Story of the Air Raids over North Vietnam

Karl J. Eschmann

IVY BOOKS • NEW YORK

Ivy Books
Published by Ballantine Books
Copyright © 1989 by Karl J. Eschmann

Library of Congress Catalog Card Number: 89-91317

ISBN 0-8041-0374-7

Manufactured in the United States of America

First Edition: November 1989

FOREWORD

The tremendous efforts expended by the people involved in the Linebacker operations showed the extent of the abilities of American military personnel when they are asked to support efforts of national importance. It only required the right reasons, a sense of dedication, and a "can do!" attitude. All were in good supply during Linebacker I and II. But the greatest reward for the men and women involved in the operation was the subsequent release of the U.S. prisoners of war and pride in having played a part for such an outcome.

This work is dedicated to the aircrews and those thousands of support personnel who worked the long shifts to keep the aircraft operationally ready. Their efforts were accomplished under stressful conditions along with shortages of manpower, spare parts, and experience. It is also dedicated to my friends and Aggie schoolmates, First Lt. Ron W. Forrester, U.S. Marine Corps, who flew a mission over North Vietnam in a Marine A-6A on 27 December 1972, but never returned to base, and Major David W. Stephens, who was one of the finest fighter pilots in TAC before his tragic fatal accident in February 1988.

I want to thank Owen Lock and Dan Cragg for their generous aid and encouragemment in the publishing of this book. A special thanks must go to my wife, Charlotte, and my children, Stephanie and Stephen, for giving me the family support I needed to put this effort together.

TABLE OF CONTENTS

LIST OF ILLUSTRATIONS

Figures

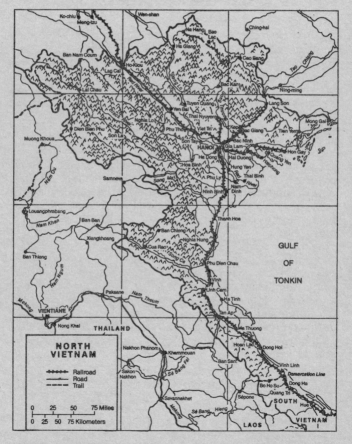

Figure 1. Map of North Vietnam

INTRODUCTION

Tactical Air (Tacair) is defined as "an arm organized from [military flying] units charged with Tactical Air Operations." For those involved in planning or executing military operations, Tacair is a collective term for tactical aircraft—fighters and fighter bombers—employed in the operations. The history of Tacair is filled with accounts of successful missions flown under extremely difficult conditions. The contributions of the airmen who flew the Tacair missions in the Vietnam War reflect credit on this history, yet little has been published regarding Tacair's superb support for Linebacker B-52 strike forces flying against heavily defended targets in North Vietnam (NVN) at night, and Tacair's role in playing both the strike and support roles during the day.

In the airwar over North Vietnam, Tacair fighter aircraft such as the F-4 Phantoms, F-105 Thuds, and A-7 Corsairs were used more in a strategic than a tactical employment against targets in North Vietnam. Likewise, in a role reversal, non-Tacair aircraft such as Strategic Air Command B-52s were used almost exclusively as tactical weapons for interdiction and support of the ground battle in South Vietnam except in the Linebacker II offensive.

This book tells for the first time the "untold story" of both the Tacair and B-52 strategic-strike accomplishments during the most intensive air operations conducted against North Vietnam during the war.

The significance of Linebacker II was summarized by

a Headquarters, Pacific Air Force (PACAF) report which described the unique aspects of the offensive:

Linebacker II represented an air campaign unique to the war in Southeast Asia (SEA). Its short duration with specific objectives and reduced operational restrictions provided the U.S. Air Force with an excellent opportunity to demonstrate the totality of its strike capability. During the twelve-day period, 18 to 29 December 1972, U.S. Air Force Tacair and B-52s flew almost half as many sorties in the northern areas of North Vietnam as were flown during the active previous six months of Linebacker I. The use of B-52s in large numbers was unprecedented, and the large-scale attacks on targets within ten nautical miles of Hanoi represented a dynamic change in the employment of air resources. Whereas Linebacker I was an interdiction campaign directed primarily at the North Vietnamese supply system, Linebacker II was aimed at sustaining maximum pressure through destruction of major target complexes in the vicinity of Hanoi and Haiphong.[1]

Although the focus of this book will be on air activities within the "Route Pack Six" sector of North Vietnam (see Figure 3), the operational area must be viewed in broader terms. Forces engaged in air operations over NVN originated from staging bases in Thailand, South Vietnam (SVN), and Guam, and from Navy carriers off the coast. Linebacker operations were begun early in May 1972 and included air strikes above the 20th Parallel in NVN. The original campaign, named Linebacker I, was started in response to the North Vietnamese invasion across the demilitarized zone (DMZ) into South Vietnam, which began in March 1972. With continuing interdiction missions being flown over NVN, SVN, and Laos, the situation had stabilized in the fall of 1972. Significant bomb damage was inflicted by U.S. air power, but the enemy's supply effort was not completely stopped; the strikes had blunted large-scale enemy activity and greatly diminished the severity of the offensive.

Linebacker I had excellent but temporary results. The concentrated use of basically tactical aircraft over NVN combined with the mining of Haiphong harbor had been aimed at reducing resupply of NVN from other countries, destroying internal stockpiles, and reducing the supply flow to the battle areas in the south. At least partially due to the air effort, the NVN offensive stalled and substantial proposals for negotiations were received from the North Vietnamese. In response, in October 1972, the U.S. bombing efforts were again restricted to targets in southern NVN, below the 20th Parallel, in an attempt to interdict the flow of enemy supplies into the south. The reduced effort was maintained through November and into December in anticipation of a ceasefire.

However, by mid-December it became obvious that peace was not really at hand. North Vietnam was using the bombing lull to restore its capability to carry the war to the south, further endangering the remaining 24,000 U.S. troops in Vietnam as well as the government of SVN. Furthermore, U.S. prisoners of war were still imprisoned, negotiations were at an impasse, and in the United States the activities of antiwar groups had not ceased. Delay in reaffirming U.S. resolve could only allow the situation to deteriorate further. Therefore, on 18 December 1972, following the unsuccessful peace negotiations and intelligence reports of continued NVN infiltration into SVN, President Nixon ordered the resumption of air attacks above the 20th Parallel.

The main difference between Linebacker II and previous air offensives was that for the first time in the air war it provided for around-the-clock air attacks against the North Vietnamese homeland. The operation's intent was to maintain a massive effort to strangle the North Vietnamese war-waging capabilities by shutting down the sources of their supply pipelines. The new offensive was also meant to provide the North Vietnamese with an incentive to return to the negotiating table.[2] The attacks were primarily targeted against electrical power and broadcast stations, railways and rail yards, and port and storage facilities around Hanoi and Haiphong. The USAF daily attacks were divided into two distinct, highly compressed operations: a daylight force comprised solely of Tacair F-4 and A-7 tactical-strike aircraft, and a night-time force that incorporated F-111 strikes with B-52 sor-

ties. The adverse weather conditions due to the monsoon
season called for the use of B-52s and F-111s with their
all-weather strike capabilities. These sorties were scheduled at night to prevent the use of optical or visual devices by the enemy SAM site crews and to reduce the
effectiveness of MIG fighter interceptor attacks.

The night B-52 strikes and daylight Tacair strikes included separate, complementary support packages. Naval Tacair strikes around Haiphong were coordinated with
USAF strikes. The F-111s were individually targeted as
single-strike sorties against airfields, surface-to-air missile (SAM) sites, power plants, and port and radio facilities. They entered the target areas at low level, made a
single high-speed pass and left the target area at high
speed, remaining at low level.[3] The F-111s used their
terrain-following radars for flying at these low altitudes
to slip into North Vietnam undetected to strike targets
accurately at night and in bad weather without warning.
These exceptional capabilities of the F-111 were used to
deliver bombs on selected SAM sites and airfields just
minutes before the arrival of the B-52 strike forces. Enemy defenses were thereby denied the preparation time
they normally had while awaiting the bombers to arrive.

The F-111 sorties struck throughout the night, bracketed by waves of B-52 strikes with their associated strike
packages. To properly protect against North Vietnamese
air defenses, each B-52 strike and its support had to be
precisely timed and executed. F-4s joined the B-52s to
provide escort; EB-66s established orbits to augment the
B-52 electronic countermeasures (ECM) effort; chaff
corridors were laid by F-4s escorted by other F-4 aircraft. Additional F-4s maintained MIG Combat Air Patrol (MIGCAP) positions, and F-105G Iron hand (SAM
suppression) aircraft on F-105G/F-4E Hunter-Killer
teams entered the area to ward off SAM attacks. The
B-52s struck storage areas, rail yards, SAM sites, and
power stations. As many as three waves of B-52s struck
in a single night. The support aircraft returned to their
home stations after the last B-52s departed, and were
resupplied to support the daylight Tacair missions, which
usually struck twelve hours after the nighttime force.

Daylight Tacair consisted of F-4 and A-7 aircraft with

delivery tactics and ordnance tailored to the specific target and weather conditions. F-4 Long Range Navigation (LORAN) equipped Pathfinders provided target acquisition during periods of limited or poor visibility for delivery of unguided bombs by non-LORAN equipped F-4 or A-7 aircraft. When target weather permitted, F-4s equipped with laser-guided bombs (LGBs) struck high-priority targets with pinpoint accuracy and little collateral damage. Support for the daytime strikes was similar to the support of the B-52 night strikes, varying in quantity and specifics of employment to adjust for changes in target types and strike characteristics. The fighter, bomber, tanker, support, and rescue aircraft were flown from widely separated bases to perform a very broad range of missions. The sorties were timed to achieve optimum results and were coordinated with U.S. Navy forces striking the Haiphong area from carriers, and Marine aircraft flying barrier combat air patrol (BARCAP) to protect the defenseless tankers, ECM, radar, and other support aircraft. The main difference between the BARCAP and MIGCAP missions was that the MIGCAP flights flew into the high-threat target areas with the strike forces, while the BARCAP orbits simply provided barriers between potential enemy forces and friendly high-valued air assets in stand-off positions from the battle areas.

The size of the Tacair support force required daily turnaround for many MIGCAP, Hunter-Killer, ECM, and escort aircraft. Tremendous efforts were required of all personnel involved to plan and coordinate the strikes and to provide aircraft and aircrews in support of the plans. The aircrews were required to fly daily combat missions under extremely hazardous conditions. Yet the hardships were worth the effort: the Vietnam cease-fire went into effect on 28 January 1973, exactly one month after the end of the Linebacker II operations.

Chapter One begins with a historical perspective of the use of Tacair prior to and during the Linebacker I air offensive over North Vietnam. The lessons learned and tactics derived from Linebacker I were important to the planning and execution of the Linebacker II offensive.

They are reviewed in great detail to lay the groundwork for the discussion of Linebacker II.

Chapter Two describes the air operations conducted within the period between the two Linebacker offensives. The primary emphasis at that time was to keep the pressure on the North Vietnamese below the 20th Parallel. With the introduction of the B-52s operating within North Vietnam, the air battles waged there resembled a miniature version of the situations faced by aircrews in the higher-threat zones of Route Pack Six. A number of significant lessons were learned that influenced the planning of Tacair support for the B-52s in Linebacker II, and those lessons will be discussed at length.

Chapter Three focuses on the planning and need for the Linebacker II operation. It highlights and describes the main players in the offensive: the enemy and the USAF strike- and support-force components. Also, the reasons why the B-52 strike required such extensive Tacair support over NVN will be explained in detail.

Chapter Four describes the execution of the first phase of Linebacker II and describes the day-by-day activities of the B-52 Tacair strikes.

Chapter Five outlines several hard lessons learned during the first three days of the offensive, and a phase-two effort that realigned the planned execution of Linebacker II to adjust to North Vietnamese defense tactics.

Chapter Six details the third and final phase of Linebacker II, characterized by the U.S. ability to refine strike tactics to new situations and the conclusive end to the most massive use of American air power since World War II.

Chapter Seven assesses the results and significance of the Linebacker II operations.

Chapter One

PRELUDE TO A SHOWDOWN: LINEBACKER I

Background: the North Vietnamese Invasion

The air war over North Vietnam can be characterized as two main campaigns, Rolling Thunder and Linebacker, with a $3\frac{1}{2}$-year bombing halt separating the two. Both campaigns had essentially the same objective—to reduce to the greatest extent possible North Vietnam's capability to support the war against South Vietnam. That was to be accomplished through three basic tasks: (1) the destruction of war-related resources already in NVN; (2) the reduction or restriction of NVN assistance from external sources; and (3) ultimately, the interdiction or impeding of the movement of men and materials into Laos and SVN. In each campaign air power was to be the prime instrument for the achievement of these objectives.[1]

Under the shadow of world disapproval and with the possibility of Communist Chinese intervention, Rolling Thunder was conducted between 1965 and 1968 under several, often crippling, constraints. To avoid the risk of major escalation, the U.S. followed a policy of gradual escalation, which, although politically prudent, imposed restrictions on operational commanders. The operations were controlled from the highest levels. Targets could be validated only by the Joint Chiefs of Staff (JCS) or higher authority. Even when validated, they could not be struck until authorized, and authorization often specified day, time, attacking force, and weaponry. At the operational level these restrictions hindered the achievement of the three stated aims. A thirty-nautical-mile radius ring around Hanoi and a ten-N.M. radius ring drawn around Haiphong were declared "no-strike" zones, thus providing the enemy with sanctuaries within which to protect war resources from air strikes. A prohibition against mining North Vietnamese harbors left the major ports open to foreign shipping, through which came approximately sixty-seven percent of NVN's external support.[2]

The northwest and northeast rail lines, the two main railways supplying Hanoi from Communist China, carried the bulk of the other supplies needed by NVN. These, too, were largely in sanctuary, as a thirty-N.M. buffer zone extended south of the Chinese border from Laos to the Gulf of Tonkin and was strictly off limits to air strike. This not only made the railways difficult to interdict, but also gave the North Vietnamese another advantage: since they knew that air power would not penetrate that airspace, they could concentrate their air defenses in the most likely strike zones.[3] The buffer zones and sanctuaries were readily apparent to the communists and they took full advantage of them. The buffer zone alone gave Hanoi thousands of square miles of territory it did not have to defend, allowing it to concentrate antiaircraft artillery (AAA) and SAMs in a far smaller area, increasing its ground-fire density tremendously. At the same time, the buffer zone reduced the flexibilities of the U.S. pilots by funneling approaches and departures into more predictable channels where the enemy could further concentrate his defense forces. Stereotyped operations, sanctuaries, and bombing pauses all accrued to the enemy's benefit. The U.S. concept of gradually increasing pressure gave Hanoi one more valuable factor, time— time to fully integrate its defense structure, with the SAM as the key.[4] These factors, coupled with the enemy's tenacity, allowed North Vietnamese and Viet Cong forces to build a formidable logistics base in Laos, Cambodia, and South Vietnam. The extent of this logistics base was not fully known until the 1968 Tet Offensive, when it became clear that the enemy had stockpiled more than enough stores to launch that ambitious undertaking.

Largely because of allied air power, the Tet Offensive turned out to be a disaster for the enemy, who suffered staggering losses. The communists required four full years to recoup to the point where they could again become a potent offensive factor.[5]

In November 1968 President Johnson ordered the total halt of bombing over the north, signaling the end of Rolling Thunder. It had accomplished but one of its three basic military tasks. Because of the constraints, it could not reduce external military assistance, nor could it destroy war materials in depth. It did harass, disrupt, and impede movement of men and materials through southern NVN, Laos, and SVN. It made the NVN effort more costly, time-consuming, and difficult, but it could not completely interdict the logistics flow.[6] The 1968 bomb halt permitted the intensification of enemy activities along his lines of communication (LOCs). Relieved of having to rebuild bridges, repair road and rail cuts, and the constant hazards of roving U.S. fighters overhead, the NVN began funneling men and supplies to the south. SAM sites were moved down into Route Package I (southernmost NVN adjacent to SVN), into the Demilitarized Zone (DMZ), and even into Laos. The continuing efforts against the enemy's lines of communication in the Laotian panhandle did not stop the infiltration; under cover of night, weather, and jungle canopy, the North Vietnamese constructed new roads, trails, bypasses, and truck parks. During the 3½-year bombing respite after Rolling Thunder, the enemy had little difficulty in getting enough supplies through to take care of not only their immediate combat needs, but also to provide a massive stockpile of equipment in caches in the south.[7] The reason for the continued stockpiling, even in the face of a de-escalating war and the withdrawal of American troops, became abundantly clear on 30 March 1972, when the Vietnamese conflict took on a new dimension: the North Vietnamese launched a full-scale conventional invasion of SVN.[8]

The reason for the attack probably related to the NVN perceptions of the building strength of SVN's military forces. During the latter part of 1971 the North Vietnamese had realized that if Vietnamization was allowed to

continue unchallenged, the south might prove capable of
defending itself without U.S. troops. It appeared to be
advantageous for the north to invade the south as soon as
possible before the South Vietnamese became too strong
and irresistible against armed force.[9]

By February 1972 the North Vietnamese had positioned thirteen divisions for a spring offensive into the
south. Timing this to coincide with the monsoon season
severely restricted U.S. air power due to rainfall, reduced visibilities, and low cloud ceilings.[10] On 30 March
the communist forces made three major thrusts into SVN.
The invasion started when two divisions supported by
armor and artillery moved through the DMZ into Quang
Tri province. Concurrently, a third division made an
easterly push toward Hue, ninety kilometers below the
DMZ. On the following day another division moved
against Pleiku in Kontum province, the Central High-
lands. By 4 April another drive was under way in Binh
Long province, only one hundred kilometers north of
Saigon. This effort was composed of two divisions supported by tanks attacking from Cambodia.[11] The South
Vietnamese were quickly overpowered by the weight of
the North Vietnamese Army onslaught, and it became
evident that U.S. support would have to play an important part in helping to stop the invasion.[12]

The invasion marked the first time that the allied forces
in SVN had opposed a North Vietnamese force equipped
with many first-line Soviet weapons. The weapons included a number of new tanks, heavy artillery pieces,
antiaircraft missiles, and antitank missiles. The NVA
used conventional tactics that were calculated to achieve
maximum shock effect against the South Vietnamese
forces, and they enjoyed a large degree of success initially.[13] As friendly forces fell back in panic, air power
was called upon to turn the tide.

U.S. Air Power Responds

The USAF response to the invasion was immediate as
B-52 Arc Light missions and Tacair attacks intensified
during brief respites in the weather.[14] Since the intensity
of the ground combat was high, it became clear that en-

emy forces would need replacements and supplies over and above those that had been positioned before the invasion. Thus, USAF planners felt that an aggressive, sustained air-interdiction program combined with close air support would have a decisive impact.[15]

The North Vietnamese may have made several errors of assumption in launching the invasion. It seems apparent that the NVN government had underestimated the vulnerability of massed infantry to air power, where Tacair is most efficient. It also seemed evident that they did not believe that air power, previously deployed out of the combat area, could respond and redeploy back into the combat arena so rapidly. Enemy lines of communication were stretched to the point where one must believe that the NVA predicated a major portion of its campaign on the assumption that its logistics flow would remain unbroken. They must have believed that the U.S. would not resume bombing the north, much less mine its harbors.[16]

As never before, the required massing of forces dictated by conventional war opened the NVA to the massive application of air power in the form of tactical and B-52 strikes. Following the 30 March invasion, President Nixon recommitted F-4 squadrons which had already left Southeast Asia; he augmented the B-52 forces at Guam and U-Tapao, Thailand, and redirected U.S. Navy carriers that were returning to the United States. As more U.S. Navy attack carriers rejoined the line, more B-52s were deployed to Southeast Asia, and more fighter aircraft arrived in Thailand to supplement Tacair, the NVA invasion stalled out with heavy combat losses.[17] In the overall assessment of the situation in South Vietnam, the rapid response of tactical air power combined with incessant bombardment by B-52s played the major role in blunting the communist drives into SVN and in supporting the successful drives by South Vietnamese forces to retake lost positions. Air power allowed the friendly forces to recover from the initial enemy assault and return to the battlefield with a counteroffensive.[18]

The invasion was checked, but the war was still going on, and with their stockpiles and an unbroken logistics system, the North Vietnamese might have carried it on for long time. A strong response was needed, not only to stem the immediate threat, but to allow Vietnamization to proceed unhampered. The beginning of that response was Operation Freedom Train, begun almost immediately following the invasion. It opened the southern part of NVN once again to allied air strikes against petroleum, oil, and lubricants (POL) storage, lines of communication, truck parks, military storage areas, artillery installations, and SAM/AAA concentrations from the DMZ to the 20th Parallel and from the NVN coastline to the Laotian border. During Freedom Train operations between 6 April and 9 May, over 2500 USAF and Navy attack sorties, together with eighty-nine B-52 sorties, were launched against targets in the north.[19] Throughout April attack sorties continued to increase and Tacair assets were built up throughout Southeast Asia to support close air-support missions in South Vietnam and interdiction missions over NVN. Increased numbers of Tacair craft were deployed to Southeast Asia (SEA) from Japan, Korea, and the Continental United States (CONUS). Figure 2 portrays the locations of the SEA bases. See Table 1 for a comparison of the Tacair buildup between 30 March and 13 May 1972.[20]

Freedom Porch Bravo

Although the basic guidelines for Freedom Train restricted targets to those south of the 20th Parallel, several key strikes were made farther north, including one highly significant coordinated operation code-named Freedom Porch Bravo, conducted within the Hanoi/Haiphong area on 16 April. On 10 April the Joint Chiefs of Staff (JCS) had sent a message to the Commander-in-Chief of Pacific Forces (CINCPAC) requesting a "coordinated plan . . . for an intensified one-day strike with combined Tacair and B-52 resources against key logistic targets in the Hanoi and Haiphong complexes." The plan would consist of a four-hour Tacair attack against air-defense and logistics targets, with concentration on enemy defenses that threatened the B-52s.[21] The plan's purpose and concept was explained in a 13 April message from CINCPAC as follows:

Situation: Continued aggressive action by the enemy clearly indicates that protective-reaction strikes in NVN in the past have had minimum effect on the Hanoi government's capacity or desire to continue a major offensive in South Vietnam.

Mission: Conduct one-day strikes by B-52, USAF, and USN Tacair against enemy defenses and logistics targets in the Hanoi and/or Haiphong areas in order to emphasize our determination to stop the Hanoi government offensive in South Vietnam.

Concept: The Haiphong and Hanoi areas are significant centers of the NVN logistic structures. The numerous lucrative military targets in these areas and the ability of all friendly forces to execute effective air strikes with minimum exposure to enemy air defenses affords both a tactical and psychological opportunity to reemphasize our dedication to stopping NVN attacks into South Vietnam.[22]

The first wave of Freedom Porch Bravo strikes began in the predawn hours of 16 April. With what was to become a forerunner of future B-52 operations in coordination with Tacair support, the strikes achieved respectable success over what was considered to be the highest threat areas within NVN. Fifteen Navy A-6As struck SAM sites in the Haiphong area and 20 Air Force F-4s laid a chaff corridor to screen the B-52s' entry into the threat zones. With 7th Air Force and Navy aircraft providing MIGCAP, Iron Hand SAM suppression, and electronic countermeasures (ECM) support, 17 B-52s attacked the Haiphong Petroleum Products Storage (PPS) area.[23]

The second and third waves, composed of Tacair assets, followed up with attacks on ten other targets in the Hanoi/Haiphong areas, including the Hanoi PPS, two airfields, and numerous warehouse complexes. Enemy reactions to the strike penetrations were formidable but largely ineffective. Even though more than 250 SAMs were launched and heavy antiaircraft artillery (AAA) fire was reported, the defenses were degraded

Figure 2. Major Airfields in Southeast Asia

TACAIR ASSETS—30 MARCH 1972

BASE	SQUADRONS	NUMBER AIRCRAFT
Danang	3 F-4	50
Korat	2 F-4	34
	1 F-105	19
	1 EB-66	12
Ubon	3 F-4	47
Udorn	3 F-4	54
	1 RF-4	19
	Total	235

TACAIR ASSETS—13 May 1972

Danang	3 F-4	59
	2 F-4 (Marine)	27
	1 A-6 (Marine)	12
Korat	2 F-4	34
	1 F-105	31
	1 EB-66	20
Ubon	5 F-4	92
Udorn	5 F-4	90
	1 RF-4	19
Takhli	4 F-4	72
	Total	456

Table 1. The Tacair Buildup, March-May 1972

by the countermeasures employed by the strike and support forces. Since the majority of the SAMs appeared to be unguided, it seemed that U.S. jamming, chaff, and SAM suppression tactics were preventing NVN operators from attaining their targets. Despite the great number of SAM launches, only two Tacair losses occurred, an Air Force F-105 and a Navy A-7E. Meanwhile, the MIGCAP force kept the few MIGs that had become airborne on the defensive, shooting down three MIG-21s in the process. The MIGs never became a direct threat to the strike force, and no friendly aircraft were lost in air-to-air combat during the day.[24]

The 16 April raids destroyed half of the known POL

storage in the Hanoi/Haiphong area and gave notice to the North Vietnamese that the U.S. was not going to employ a "slowly graduated escalation" strategy, as it had during the Rolling Thunder air campaign.[25] As an example of the success of the mission, the following bomb-damage assessment was reported and verified through photo reconnaissance:

Complex 35 percent destroyed.
30 21-metric-ton tanks damaged
6 large vertical tanks destroyed (POL burned)
50 percent POL drum storage destroyed
One 92-foot vertical tank heavily damaged
One 70-foot vertical tank heavily damaged
18 POL railroad cars destroyed
4 POL railroad cars damaged
7 rail cuts

Although Freedom Porch Bravo did accomplish some limited success, its results may have had a significant detrimental influence on Strategic Air Command (SAC) planners and staffs. The operation had proven that a co-ordinated surprise strike could effectively overcome enemy defenses. However, the fact that no B-52s were lost during the first-wave attacks may have promoted some overconfidence in planning for future B-52 tactics over the highly defended Hanoi/Haiphong areas.[26] The effects of this overconfidence would not be felt until the Line-backer II attacks in December 1972.

Linebacker I Begins

Even with the renewed U.S. effort over NVN, the flow of personnel, supplies, and materials to support the north Vietnamese invasion did not diminish. Therefore, in early May 1972, President Nixon decided that U.S. forces would counter the NVN invasion by launching an unprecedented effort to deny the enemy the means to wage war. On the morning of 9 May, Saigon time, the mining of NVN ports was begun for the first time in the Vietnam conflict. On the same day, commanders in the field were directed to initiate a coordinated campaign by air and naval forces to destroy and disrupt the enemy's war supporting resources in the north.[27] In his address to the nation, the President announced the reasons for these actions against North Vietnam:

> Five weeks ago, on Easter weekend, the communist armies of North Vietnam launched a massive invasion that was made possible by tanks, artillery, and other advanced offensive weapons supplied to Hanoi by the Soviet Union and other Communist nations. . . .
>
> As I announced in my report to the nation twelve days ago, the role of the United States in resisting this invasion has been limited to air and naval strikes on military targets in North and South Vietnam. As I also pointed out in that report, we have responded to North Vietnam's massive military offensive by undertaking wide-ranging new peace efforts aimed at ending the war through negotiation. . . .
>
> In the two weeks alone since I offered to resume negotiations, Hanoi has launched three new military offensives in South Vietnam. In those two weeks the risk that a Communist government may be imposed on the seventeen million people of South Vietnam has increased, and the communist offensive has now reached the point that it gravely threatens the lives of sixty thousand American troops who are still in Vietnam. . . .
>
> We now have a clear, hard choice among three courses of action: immediate withdrawal of all American forces, continued attempts at negotiation, or decisive military action to end the war. . . . What appears to be a choice among three courses of action for the United States is really no choice at all. The killing in this tragic war must stop. By simply getting out, we would only worsen the bloodshed. By relying solely on negotiations, we would give an intransigent enemy the time he needs to press his aggression. There is only one way to stop the killing. That is to keep the weapons of war out of the hands of the international outlaws of North Vietnam. Throughout the war in Vietnam, the United States has exercised a degree of restraint unprecedented in the annals of war.

That was our responsibility as a great nation, a nation which is interested—and we can be proud of this as Americans—as America has always been, in peace not conquest. However, when the enemy abandons all restraint, throws its whole army into battle in the territory of its neighbor, refuses to negotiate, we simply face a new situation. . . .

I therefore concluded that Hanoi must be denied the weapons and supplies it needs to continue the aggression. In full coordination with the Republic of Vietnam I have ordered the following measures, which are being implemented as I am speaking to you:

All entrances to North Vietnamese ports will be mined to prevent access to these ports and North Vietnamese naval operations from these ports.

Rail and all other communications will be cut off to the maximum extent possible.

Air and naval strikes against military targets in North Vietnam will continue.[28]

The effort to keep the weapons of war out of North Vietnam had three basic goals. Briefly stated, they were the same goals as for the Rolling Thunder campaign: (1) restrict the resupply of NVN from external sources; (2) destroy internal stockpiles of military supplies and equipment; and (3) restrict the flow of forces and supplies to the battlefield. Experience during past interdiction programs in NVN and Laos clearly indicated that the three goals were interrelated—a maximum impact on the enemy could only be gained through concerted efforts to achieve all three. The flow of supplies to the battlefield, for example, was strongly influenced by the ability to maintain external supply and by the degree to which stockpiled enemy supplies could be struck and destroyed. Attacks aimed at the flow of supplies through the enemy's logistics system in Laos and southern NVN could achieve the desired results only if conducted in conjunction with vigorous efforts to destroy stockpiled supplies in NVN while simultaneously restricting the flow of new supplies into NVN.[29] Mining the NVN ports supported the objectives of task number one, while Tacair attacks would achieve tasks two and three. For the first time in the air war against NVN, a serious effort would be made to destroy the sources of the enemy's massive logistics pipeline.

The decision to mine the NVN ports was an appropriate first step in an interdiction program in NVN. It forced the NVN to rely on land transport as their major source of resupply and their primary means of transporting supplies to the south. Thus began Linebacker, a coordinated air and naval campaign aimed at the destruction of the enemy's war matériel and the disruption of his logistics system throughout NVN. More than ever before, an air-interdiction program without the many restrictions of earlier NVN operations could become a decisive factor in the outcome of the Vietnam conflict.[30]

On 9 May 1972, orders were sent to the field by the JCS:

Conduct a continuing Tacair interdiction effort, augmented by B-52 sorties as required, to destroy and disrupt enemy POL and transportation resources and LOCs in NVN, for example, POL storage and pumping stations, rails and roads, bridges, railroad yards, heavy repair equipment, railroad rolling stock and trucks. Utilization of resources to neutralize defenses is also authorized.

Initial efforts should give priority to POL storage facilities as well as rail LOCs in the area between the Chinese Buffer Zone and Hanoi; Hanoi and Haiphong areas, and LOCs leading out of the Hanoi/Haiphong complex to the south. Also, strike remaining lucrative targets in route packages One, Two, Three, and Four.[31]

The areas of responsibility, or route packages, were assigned to subordinate commands, just as they had been during the Rolling Thunder campaign (Figure 3).[32] Route Pack (R.P.) One, the first package to the north of the DMZ, was the responsibility of the Military Assistance Command, Vietnam (MACV), since it was considered an extension of the ground battle zone in South Vietnam.[33] To take advantage of the close proximity of naval carrier forces operating in the Gulf of Tonkin, the Navy was given primary responsibility for R.P.s 2, 3, 4, and 6B.

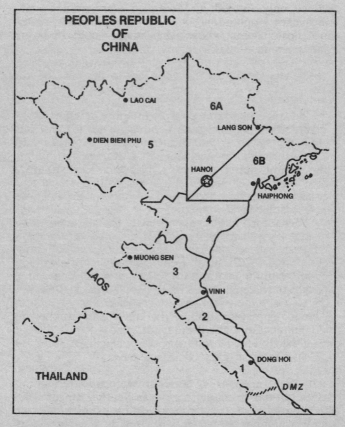

Figure 3. Route Package Areas of Responsibility

The Air Force was assigned operational responsibilities within R.P.s 5 and 6A.[34] Most of the important targets were in those areas, and enemy defenses were strongest there. To give it a prominent dividing line, R.P. 6 was divided between the Air Force and Navy along the northeast rail line.[35] The summary of Linebacker I activities in this book is primarily concerned with operations conducted within the RP 6 areas.

Since only limited air resources were available for Linebacker I operations, strikes were allocated against only those targets whose destruction would have the greatest impact on the enemy.[36] Therefore, a system of priorities guided the application of USAF and Navy resources in RP 6:

1. Interdict rail bridges along the N.W. and N.E. Railroads and maintain the waterway minefields.
2. Interdict highway bridges to preclude truck transshipment around downed R.R. bridges and inhibit truck traffic in general.
3. Destroy power generating facilities throughout the area.
4. Strike targets which directly support the enemy's logistic movement capability, e.g., vehicle storage and repair facilities, warehouse facilities storing truck and tank parts, POL storage capacity, and R.R. rolling stock.
5. Destroy SAM capability by continued employment of antiradiation missiles against sites threatening strike forces.
6. Degrade the NVN air-defense capability by continued aggressive use of our air-defense aircraft in conjunction with strike missions.
7. Destroy enemy command and control facilities, as authority permits.[37]

Although Linebacker operations were free of many of the restrictions that had encumbered earlier air interdiction programs, the airmen were still required to operate within a number of ground rules which remained fairly uniform throughout the Linebacker campaign.

1. Areas where JCS approval was required prior to adding targets within them to the JCS target list were called controlled areas. They included the Chinese buffer zone (25 to 30 miles within NVN, following the Chinese border) and all territory within ten miles of the centers of Hanoi and Haiphong.

2. "Restricted targets" were those generally off limits. The following fell into this category:
   (a) dams, dikes, locks, and other targets specifically restricted by separate directives.
   (b) watercraft that were obviously fishing boats or appeared to be engaged in fishing.
   (c) clusters of sampans or houseboats in populated areas.
   (d) watercraft/aircraft outside the twelve mile limit of NVN coast, unless hostile intent against U.S. air or surface craft was apparent.
   (e) third-country shipping.

3. Attacks could be made against all airborne enemy fighter aircraft, but not helicopters and transports. Aircraft engaged in immediate pursuit were authorized to pursue enemy fighter aircraft into the Chinese buffer zone, but in no event closer than twenty miles to the border.

4. Antiradar missiles could be employed, but tactics were to be used to avoid having the missiles fall in Chinese territory.

5. Military airfields could be attacked, unless third-nation aircraft were present.

6. Targets, munitions, and strike tactics were to be selected to minimize risk of collateral damage to civilian population, possible POW sites, or target categories not authorized for strike.[38]

During Linebacker, JCS approvals were often given to strike important rail and storage facilities within the controlled areas. For example, the enemy's most critical and vulnerable road and rail targets were clustered within the buffer zone, where the rugged terrain made road and rail bypasses very difficult to construct or repair.[39] Those areas had been off limits during previous air offensives, and the new rules provided a chance to severely impair the enemy's resupply efforts. This was a significant change from the previous rules followed during Rolling Thunder, where these areas had become virtual sanctuaries for the North Vietnamese. In the absence of the previous political and military restraints, the major obstacle that faced U.S. forces in these areas was the heavy concentration of integrated NVN air defenses.

The NVN Air Defense System

During 1972 the North Vietnamese possessed what was considered to be one of the best air-defense systems in the world. Among its strongest features were excellent radar integration of SA-2 SAMs, MIGs, and antiaircraft artillery. The NVN air-defense system could counter our forces from ground level (small arms and AAA) up to nineteen miles in the air (the SA-2 SAM effective range). MIG fighters were positioned for ready alert on the ends of the runways and, after takeoff, were vectored by ground-control radar to intercept U.S. aircraft.[40]

It was no secret that the enemy was almost always able to learn the strike-force structure as soon as the U.S. forces were airborne. There were approximately two hundred radars in the NVN defense system, with three major ground control intercept (GCI) sites at Bac Mai, Phuc Yen, and Kep (Figure 4).[41] The radar coverage included so much overlap that it was virtually impossible to jam all of them at once. The NVN were always able to provide good positive GCI control of their interceptors regardless of U.S. efforts to use countermeasures throughout Linebacker.[42] The radar operators were also quite adept in assessing the intent of U.S. strike forces as they entered North Vietnam. The use of chaff flights ahead of the strike force usually meant that a major Linebacker mission could be expected. The chaff flight and escorts were easily identified by radar because they always flew in a straight-line penetration flight path. Once the chaff flight had finished its run, the NVN personnel could count upon fifteen or twenty minutes before the strike force would arrive, since the chaff had to have time to dispense over the area properly. So the enemy could usually distinguish the outline of the approach and de-

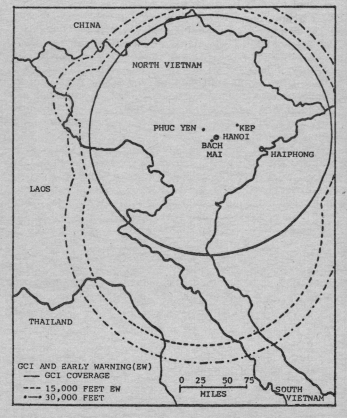

Figure 4. North Vietnamese Radar Coverage

parture corridors, the expected time of arrival of the strike force, and the probable target.[43] That helped the NVN forces set up their MIGs, SAMs, and AAA assets.

THE SAM THREAT

The strongest SAM reactions were reserved for defense of the most vital targets in Route Pack Six. During the initial strikes into the Hanoi/Haiphong area, it was not unusual for a U.S. strike force to be met by barrages of over a hundred missiles.[44] While the sheer number of SAM firings was in itself a problem, Linebacker I aircrews also had to cope with the added threats posed by refinements and variations in enemy launch tactics and modified equipment.[45]

Enemy SAM forces increasingly maintained strict emission control of their SA-2 ground guidance radars (codenamed Fan Song), employing radar radiation against U.S. targets for a minimum period and then only within the most effective portions of the SAM performance envelope. That decreased the effectiveness of the antiradiation missiles used by the Iron Hand F-105Gs, and reduced the warning time provided by "radar homing and warning" (RHAW) equipment.[46] In conjunction with emission control, the enemy employed the ripple firing of guided SAMs, a tactic devised by Soviet technicians after studying U.S. RHAW equipment from captured downed aircraft.* The technique involved sequential launches of at least two SAMs. The first SAM, fired high, would cause the target to take evasive action, and its transponder would provide tracking information useful to guiding the second missile, launched seconds later. The target, having lost maneuverability by avoiding the first missile, became vulnerable to the second missile, fired lower than the first.[47]

Another tactic widely used by the enemy during Linebacker I was the employment of barrage firings of *unguided* SAMs. This technique resulted from an enemy

---

*Recent newspaper releases from the Soviet Union have also revealed that Soviet air defense troops manned a number of the SAM sites, as well as providing training to the NVN crews.

reluctance to expose their sites to SAM suppression teams and the problems of tracking and guiding missiles because of U.S. jamming and chaff support. Barrage firings were used to distract and harass aircrews during the final stages of the strike mission. The tactic was also used to divert the attention of aircrews while MIGs positioned themselves for rear attacks of the friendly aircraft.[48] Its success was demonstrated on 11 May 1972, when a F-105G was shot down—a barrage of six SAMs diverted the attention of the Iron Hand flight while MIGs attacked from the rear.[49]

The introduction of modified SAM equipment added to the difficulties of countering the varied tactics of the SAM forces. In late April optically-guided missiles were employed by the enemy. During periods of clear weather, optical tracking of U.S. aircraft limited RHAW indications and made on-board electronic countermeasures (ECM) equipment useless. To make matters worse, the NVN forces began using an improved SA-2 beacon transmitter—used to tell the operators the missile's position—that was more difficult to jam than in the older systems.[50] On top of the improved SAM capabilities, the SA-2 was a mobile system, and the crews could take them from a mobile configuration to a firing configuration in less than an hour. Once they had fired, they could be packed up and gone inside of thirty minutes. The launchers were extremely difficult to find. The battle against SAM defenses involved constantly changing tactics, and these will be discussed in more detail later in the chapter.

THE MIG THREAT

North Vietnam's MIG defenses posed a formidable threat to renewed U.S. strike operations. At the beginning of Linebacker I the NVN Air Force had 204 MIGs on seven airfields (Table 2).[51] In the early phases of Linebacker as many as 15 to 40 MIGs would oppose U.S. strike forces. Following a heavy loss of MIG fighters on 10 May, where U.S. counter-air forces downed eleven, the NVN began reducing the size of their MIG reactions. From that point on they employed a variety of clever tactics designed to minimize the risk to attacking MIGs while placing U.S. aircraft at a maximum disadvantage.[52]

A favorite tactic was the coordinated employment of different types of MIGs at their optimum engagement altitudes in a high-low attack profile. MIG-21s would be vectored at medium or high altitudes to attack friendly aircraft. The U.S. aircraft would react by either breaking or engaging the hostile aircraft. Either choice could distract the attention of U.S. fighter pilots, making them more vulnerable to attacks by MIG-19s trailing at low altitude. Most of these attacks took place as single, high-speed passes while firing Atoll heat-seeking missiles behind U.S. aircraft formations. They were difficult to counter since U.S. GCI and radar-warning capabilities were not as capable in the RP 6 area due to their long standoff range.[53] Since the reverse situation was true for the enemy, NVN GCI radar could accurately predict U.S. ingress and egress times over the target zones and could schedule their MIG on-station times accordingly.[54] This was explainable, since the GCI tracking of U.S. tankers and fighters would provide roughly forty-five minutes of warning to the enemy defense system. Thus, MIG attacks could be executed just when U.S. aircraft were heavy with fuel and ordnance during ingress, or low on fuel during egress.[55]

MIGS

AIRFIELD	MIG-21	MIG-19	MIG 15/17	TOTAL
Bai Thuong	2			2
Dong Suong			12	12
Kep	46	1		47
Kien An	12			12
Phuc Yen	8		49	57
Quan Lang			3	3
Yen Bai	25	32	14	71
Totals	93	33	78	204

Table 2. NVN MIG Order of Battle, 10 May 1972

By the end of June the growing MIG aggressiveness and the advantage inherent in the enemy tactics had begun to work in the enemy's favor. During June seven USAF aircraft were downed; only five MIGs were shot down in the same time period. The unfavorable loss ratio continued through early July, when, by mid-month, the U.S. had suffered four more losses, while only three MIGs were shot down. Similar periods of unfavorable exchange ratios had been encountered during the Rolling Thunder (1965–68) operations, as the enemy perfected its GCI intercept techniques and introduced larger numbers of MIG-21s. Yet problems facing Linebacker forces were even greater, with more experienced NVN pilots, many more MIG-21s, increased radar and GCI control capabilities, and a more integrated defense system.[56] U.S. measures to correct some of these problem areas will be discussed later in this chapter.

THE AAA THREAT

The North Vietnamese had an active inventory of over 4000 guns ranging in size from 23mm to 100mm, over 2000 deployed in the Hanoi/Haiphong area alone. For the enemy the main advantages about AAA were that the weapons were highly mobile and the logistics of restocking AAA ammunition at the sites was less a problem than was the case for SAM defenses (each SA-2 missile was 27 feet long). Due to the great numbers of AAA, U.S. attacks against them were limited to sites posing an immediate threat to the strike force.[57] The rate of U.S. losses to AAA remained fairly low during Linebacker I because of the introduction of laser-guided bombs. The new weapons were delivered from high altitude, and their great accuracy reduced the number of strikes necessary to destroy specific targets, thus reducing exposure to AAA.[58]

THE COMBINED ENEMY THREAT

North Vietnam's greatest asset was the increasing integration of its air-defense resources. This integration was made possible through the enemy's extensive command

and control network, including dispersed command and control centers and the early-warning/ground-controlled intercept radars. The overall control of NVN air defenses was directed by an air defense command and control center located at Hanoi's Bac Mai airfield.[59] As the enemy's ability to counter U.S. strikes grew, for each of their defensive threats, it was the combination of these air-defense elements that together posed the greatest threat to friendly aircraft. The enemy's dense AAA network was able to prevent low-level operations, and when U.S. aircraft operated at high altitudes, SAM/MIG tactics were integrated. Often, an attack by one of the systems was intended to distract the aircrews, thus facilitating attack by the other system. A good example of this occurred during a 3 September Linebacker mission in the Phuc Yen airfield area. According to a message to the Commander, 7th Air Force:

The Iron Hand flight (Eagle) estimated that 24 SAMs were fired during 12½ minutes in the target area. Twenty of the SAMs were directed at the Iron Hand aircraft and they also received some very heavy AAA. The SAMs were fired from known sites as well as two previously unknown locations. The Iron Hand representative reported visual tracking was used extensively by the SAM sites. He commented that he had never seen SAM operators use such persistent tactics as on this mission. Once the sites came up, they stayed up, and fired even with the Iron Hand aircraft attacking. Eagle 02 sighted an Atoll missile heading toward Eagle 01 as they were working SAM sites on the north edge of Hanoi and called an Atoll Break (01 and 02 were F-105Gs). When Eagle 01 broke right, he visually acquired a light-blue MIG-19 low at his three o'clock, at approximately four thousand feet. The MIG continued to close and made a gunpass on 01. The MIG had a very high overtake [speed] and overshot. The MIG then barrel-rolled away from Eagle 01. Eagle 03, an F-4E in trail with 01 and 02, acquired the MIG. He followed the MIG through his escape maneuver, acquired a radar lock-on, and fired an AIM-7. Eagle 03 did not see the results of the missile, as he had to maneuver to evade a SAM. Shortly thereafter, Eagle 02 noted a smoking MIG spiral into the ground. Eagle 02 and 03 both observed a pastel-colored chute in the same area. Eagle 03 had previously dropped his Cluster Bomb Units (CBUs) on one of the active SAM sites, but missed as he had to maneuver to avoid a SAM shortly after starting his dive-toss pullout. Eagle 04 jettisoned his CBUs when the MIG was engaged.[60]

This example showed that SAM and MIG defenses were overlapped to provide mutual assistance. Although in this case a MIG was destroyed, the primary objective—destroying the active sites—was *not* achieved. It was this multiple-threat environment that dictated the use of very large support packages for escorting the strike elements into the RP 6 areas.

U.S. Strike and Support Forces

During the strikes into the RP 6 area, U.S. support forces were running at a ratio of about four to one.[61] The plan for all Linebacker force compositions centered around the type and degree of threat expected at the target area. As a rule of thumb, high SAM threat areas called for chaff, ECM, and Iron Hand aircraft. The support package grew larger when combat air patrol flights (MIGCAP) and escorts were added for protection against MIGs.[62] The exact number of aircraft varied with each mission, depending upon the targets, the extent of the threat, and whether common support aircraft could be used to cover separate missions with closely scheduled Time on Targets (TOTs). The mission sizes did not vary whether launched through Laos or the Gulf of Tonkin to allow flexibility for weather diversions.[63] A typical Linebacker I force was composed as follows:

Strike Force (20–28)		Support Force (65–79)	
8–12	strike F-4s with laser guided bombs	4	weather reconnaissance
12–16	strike F-4s with conventional ordnance	3	ECM EB-66s
		8–12	F-4 chaff bombers
		8	F-4 chaff escorts

32	MIGCAP F-4s
16–20	F-4 strike escorts
8–12	Iron Hand F-105Gs
4	barrier CAP F-4s
2	photo-recon RF-4s
2	photo-recon escorts

In addition, each mission had its usual search-and-rescue (SAR) forces, airborne-surveillance radars, and SAC tanker support.[64] A typical Linebacker I strike/support package is portrayed in Figure 5. Each of the strike/support elements will be discussed individually to describe its evolution and tactical use. To set the stage for the reader in these discussions, it might help to review the results of the first Linebacker mission conducted over RP 6 on 10 May 1972.

The primary targets for the initial strike were the Hanoi railroad/highway bridge (Paul Doumer) and the Yen Vien railroad yard. The strike tactics called for guided "smart" ordnance on the bridge, because of the precision needed on that type of target and also because of the requirement to minimize collateral damage. However, since the rail yard was an area target, unguided "dumb" bombs were selected as the proper ordnance. The mission plan consisted of a small strike package supported by chaff, Iron Hand, escort, and MIGCAP sorties. The weather-recon, SAR, combat air patrol (CAP), and barrier CAP elements preceded the main force. The eight chaff aircraft dispensed chaff to form an ingress/egress corridor for the strike force. Hidden from the searching NVN radars within the chaff corridors, the first wave of strike aircraft attacked the Doumer Bridge with laser-guided bombs. Five minutes later the second strike wave hit the Yen Vien rail yard with MK-82 500-pound gravity bombs. As the last strike aircraft left the target area, two photo-recon aircraft made a high-speed sweep, collecting battle damage assessment (BDA) photography. During the entire time the forces were in the high-threat area, a search-and-rescue force—one HC-130, two HH-53 helicopters, and two A-1Es—were on station over Laos. The results of this mission were later summarized:

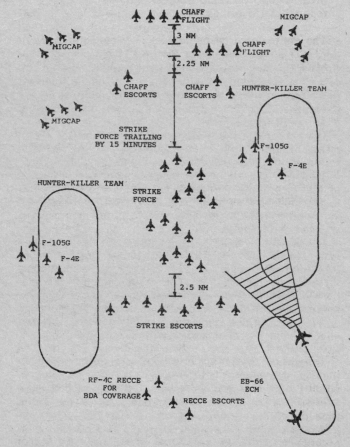

Figure 5. Typical Linebacker I Strike/Support Package

22 guided bombs were delivered on the Doumer Bridge, causing one full span to drop into the river.

184 MK-82 bombs were dropped on the rail yard, cutting tracks, damaging boxcars, and destroying warehouses.

19 AGM-45 and 6 AGM-78 antiradiation missiles were fired by the Iron Hand force as suppression against 42 reported SAM firings.[65]

The entire force encountered heavy concentrations of 23/37/57/85mm AAA over the target area. In addition, 9 MIG-19s and 7 MIG-21s were observed. Three of the MIG-21s were downed after the F-4s fired one AIM-9 (infrared homing) and 12 AIM-7 (radar-guided) missiles at the enemy fighters. The USAF Tacair losses were 2 F-4s downed by MIG-19 cannon fire.[66] Both crew members on one of the F-4s were killed when the aircraft exploded; on the second F-4, the backseater managed to eject safely, but the pilot died when the aircraft blew up seconds later. The same crew had chalked up 2 MIG kills during the previous week. The backseater was able to evade capture by North Vietnamese searchers for twenty-three days before a combat-rescue team could pick him up.[67]

Linebacker missions were "fragged" (scheduled) daily after the first strike on 10 May and were flown as weather permitted. Refinements were made in composition and tactics to obtain the best possible results with minimum losses. To better understand the process, each of the force elements will be discussed in some detail.

THE STRIKE ELEMENT

Throughout May and July 1972 the strike force remained at about eight to twelve bombers per mission. Laser-guided bombs (LGBs) were primarily used because of their high accuracy and success against point targets. Because of their great accuracy, LGBs allowed higher release altitudes for weapon delivery, thus providing for great survivability in high-threat areas. The accuracy of LGBs allowed the use of fewer aircraft to destroy targets

than was previously possible using conventional ordnance, which of course exposed fewer aircraft within a
high-threat area.[68]

The LGB consisted of three standard inventory items
mated into one system—the MK-84 general-purpose
2000-pound iron bomb, the AGM-45 Shrike control ac-
tivator, and the KMU-351/B laser seeker. In operation
one aircraft would designate a target with a laser beam
which, reflected by the target, created a ''cone'' or ''basket'' in the sky. The striking aircraft simply dropped its
bomb into the cone, then the seeker and guidance systems would home onto the designated spot.[69] One of the
most important LGB modifications on the F-4 aircraft
was Pave Knife, which provided a gimbal-mounted designator pod so that a flight leader could illuminate a target for himself and the rest of the flight simultaneously.
Prior to Pave Knife, the flight leader had been required
to fly precision circles around the target while the remainder of the flight dropped its bombs one by one. This
procedure had two disadvantages: exposure to air-and-
ground defenses was increased because of added time
over the target; the total strike effectiveness was reduced
since, with the rigid designator, the leader could not drop
bombs himself. From the beginning of Linebacker, the
USAF used Pave Knife effectively in the high-threat areas. As the leader rolled in on his target, the remainder
of the flight timed their roll-ins so that all could drop
their LGBs into the basket at the same time. The flight
then departed immediately, thus reducing their exposure
time to the enemy defenses.[70] The accuracy and destructive firepower of LGBs was demonstrated on numerous
occasions during Linebacker operations. For example, on
10 May the USAF knocked out five bridges on the northwest rail line with laser strikes using only 24 bombs.
Over 2000 bombs would have been expended to do that
by the conventional method.[71] It was primarily LGBs that
accounted for the rapid demise of the NVN rail system.
This allowed strike forces to attack the next-higher priority targets—the power plants, industrial targets, repair
facilities, POL and pumping stations, and other targets
requiring pinpoint accuracy and large destructive force.

The extreme accuracy allowed first-time attacks against vital targets located near populated or restricted areas.

The strike element changed during August, when higher headquarters directed an increase of strike sorties to no fewer than forty-eight per day. To meet the new minimum, because of the shortage of Pave Knife pods, the LGB bombers had to be supplemented by conventional unguided ordnance. Pinpoint targets were still attacked primarily by LGB means, but area targets such as rail yards, barracks areas, truck parks, and airfields were fragged for conventional ordnance. Since the northeast monsoon season was approaching, the skies over North Vietnam were expected to be overcast, with cloud decks from 4000 to 12,000 feet beginning in late August and September.[72] Because that kind of weather restricted both laser and visual deliveries, the 7th Air Force commander directed the use of long range navigation (LORAN) delivery to obtain an all-weather capability which, otherwise, did not exist in the RP 6 areas.[73] The LORAN system used electronics to fix an aircraft's position precisely. Master and slave stations at different locations emitted signals that arrived at a given position at a specific, microsecond exact time. Measurement of the time difference (TD) between the emission and arrival of the signal at the target point gave the distance between the two points. The use of two emitting stations permitted the determination of the target's exact coordinates. Once those were recorded, LORAN-equipped aircraft could reuse the information and relocate the target at a later date. The advantage was simply that from that point on, the target no longer had to be acquired visually. Bombing accuracy was limited only by the accuracy of the original time-difference calculations and external factors, such as wind velocity and aircrew technique.[74] But before LORAN could be utilized in RP 6 areas, several special preparations had to take place—the most important of which was target location. Existing maps and charts of North Vietnam were not sufficiently accurate for LORAN use. Therefore, every validated target had to be measured and located in time differences (TDs) from the LORAN stations in Thailand. As General Vogt, the 7th AF commander explained:

. . . it was apparent to me that when the monsoon season came in full force, we had to come up with good precision bombing on those rail yards, keep those lines interdicted, and certainly be able to hit those high-value targets. So we started a campaign to develop an all-weather capability. We started this when the weather was still good, and we scheduled the missions so that one flight—even on a good weather day—was compelled to drop on LORAN each time. We loaded that flight with 1000-pound bombs and delayed fuses so that the photo interpreter could pick his bombs out from the 500-pounders, so that we could score the bombing on each one of these targets [and place a correction factor to refine the TDs]. . . . [75]

The reconnaissance squadron at Udorn Royal Thai Air Force Base (RTAFB) used a LORAN-equipped RF-4 which simultaneously marked the film with the true TDs. Although several problems—such as system "break-locks" due to signal degradation and thunderstorms—were evident, the LORAN system gave Tacair the flexibility to execute missions when weather would have prevented visual bomb delivery. In a number of cases LORAN missions were carried out that would have otherwise been canceled.[76] For example, poor weather conditions caused a decrease in LGB strikes from 111 sorties in September to 22 sorties in October. To offset the LGB cancellations, two LORAN missions were planned per day, each with a minimum of 24 strike aircraft, to maintain the 48 strikes per day as directed by the JCS.[77]

During September the strike force was enhanced by the deployment of 48 F-111s to Takhli RTAFB. The F-111s added a new dimension to Linebacker. It was then possible to have night all-weather strikes using low-level attack techniques.[78] Thus, twenty-four hours of continuous pressure against NVN targets had become possible. The F-111s penetrated the NVN heartland without requiring the use of tankers or other support aircraft. High speed, low-altitude ingress over the mountains of Laos and NVN provided terrain masking from enemy radar. The F-111s terrain following radar (TFR) furnished automatic altitude control at a preset level, while an excellent terrain-mapping attack radar integrated with a weapons-release computer provided for automatic bomb release without visual acquisition of the target. The F-111 frag rate steadily increased, until 24 sorties per night were reached on 13 October. By using a progressive sortie buildup and initially selecting targets into the low-threat areas, a gradual movement into the high-threat area of RP 6 was possible as crews gained experience.[79] That was to prove invaluable for the Linebacker II operation later in December.

THE SUPPORT ELEMENTS

In order to protect the very limited number of strike aircraft equipped with Pave Knife laser-designator pods and LORAN systems, increased numbers of aircraft were required in the support packages for missions into the high-threat areas. The large size of the support packages, coupled with the limited air resources available for Linebacker operations, held the USAF to only one or two Linebacker missions in North Vietnam per day.[80] The basic support package was composed of weather recon, barrier CAP (BARCAP), chaff support, strike/chaff escort, MIGCAP, Iron Hand, and ECM, as well as photo recon, tankers, airborne surveillance, and SAR forces.

WEATHER RECON

Standard Linebacker weather reconnaissance procedures required a report of target and refueling-area weather $4\frac{1}{2}$ and $2\frac{1}{2}$ hours before time on target (TOT). This was usually accomplished one of two ways: two flights of two F-4s with each covering one of the time periods; or one flight covering both periods by using air refueling.[81] As the campaign progressed it became increasingly apparent that weather deserved a prominent place in the planning of any mission. Even in the best of periods over North Vietnam, weather was not a respecter of target priority, and the planning staffs realized that. The results of the early-morning weather-recon flights had a strong role in the daily target selections. Based upon recon, one of four decisions would be made:

1. The mission would be launched as fragged.
2. The launch would be delayed because of adverse weather and a new TOT would be assigned.
3. The mission would be diverted to alternate targets found to be favorable by the weather recon.
4. The mission would be canceled because all targets were unfavorable and forecast to remain so.[82]

BARRIER/TANKER CAP

The primary mission of the combat air patrols was to protect the tanker and SAR forces from the MIGs. Initially this mission was performed by four F-4s from Udorn RTAFB, but in July Marine F-4s from Nam Phong Air Base took over. The BARCAP flight was stationed near the Laos/NVN border for missions entering from the west. The Navy provided BARCAP protection for missions entering from the Gulf.[83]

CHAFF SUPPORT

Chaff was used extensively during Linebacker operations, as all strikes into high SAM-threat areas required protection from acquisition radar. ALE-38 chaff dispensers gave eight F-4 aircraft the capability to produce a continuous chaff corridor five miles wide and 105 miles long, sufficient to cover the entire ingress and egress routes within the NVN heartland.[84] The chaff effectively degraded the performance of SAM Fan Song guidance radar, E band AAA, and Barlock GCI radar frequencies. During August the chaff bombers began carrying six chaff bombs in addition to the ALE-38 dispenser. The bombs were filled with chaff that fell rapidly and established a vertical column to shield the strike aircraft.[85]

The provision of chaff corridors in high-threat areas was successful in limiting the loss of strike aircraft to SAMs, but not without a price. The employment of chaff required the fragging of the special chaff-dispensing aircraft at Ubon RTAFB, which made necessary additional escort, ECM, and Iron Hand support. These additional support craft themselves became prime targets of the NVN air-defense system. Thus, while the employment of chaff diminished the risk to the strike force, it increased the loss of support aircraft.[86] The chaff elements were particularly vulnerable to MIG stern attacks because the chaff bombers were required to fly straight and level from their initial point (IP) to the target zone. At first chaff was dispensed from an eight-ship line-abreast formation. But, besides being difficult to escort properly, this restricted maneuverability to avoid SAM and MIG attacks. Later missions allowed two flights of four separated by approximately three miles, with the trailing flight dispensing chaff to the side of the lead flight and ready, if necessary, to counter MIG attacks while the escorts protected the trailing flight.[87]

When reliable MIG warning was available, the chaff-flight lead could use one of several anti-MIG tactics. One was to perform random 360-degree turns, occasional racetrack patterns, large zigzags, and other such maneuvers to interrupt the MIG's intercept geometry. A 180-degree turn into the attack was generally effective if the chaff flight had sufficient warning. Another successful tactic was to give each chaff flight a MIGCAP call sign. The two flights would enter the target area using MIGCAP procedures, then would turn outbound over the target and dispense chaff along the strike route.

A highly qualified and experienced aircrew was required for duty as chaff lead. Not only were they responsible for establishing proper chaff corridor and the protection of the flight, but they were usually responsible for determining whether the target was workable. If the weather prevented target acquisition, valuable time could be saved and unnecessary exposure to attack could be prevented by diverting the force to alternate targets. As the chaff lead was normally the first over the target, he could divert the force before entry into the high-threat area. The importance of the chaff element was highlighted by the number of MIGs and SAMs committed to them, and by the fact that no USAF aircraft were shot down during Linebacker I by SAMs while protected by the chaff corridor.[88]

CHAFF/STRIKE ESCORTS

The escort element was the inner perimeter for MIG defense. Its primary mission was to protect the chaff and strike flights from MIGs that had evaded the outer perimeter MIGCAP defenses. The standard configuration for escort F-4 fighters was three external fuel tanks, two or four AIM-7 Sparrow missiles, four AIM-9 Sidewinder missiles, and two ECM pods.

Initially the chaff element was not escorted because the MIGs did not pose a threat. Beginning in June, however, MIGs attacked the chaff flights. As discussed in the preceding section, the chaff flights were extremely vulnerable to rear-hemisphere MIG attacks. As a result, the chaff-escort fighters were added to the Linebacker forces. Two escort flights normally accompanied the chaff aircraft, each positioned slightly to the outside of the chaff flight's flanks between two and 2½ miles to the rear. If only one escort flight was used, then it split into two elements of two aircraft each positioned in roughly the same location relative to its chaff flight. The chaff escorts remained with the chaff-dispensing aircraft until they left the high-threat area.

The strike escort flew a more variable and flexible formation than the chaff escort since strike flights were not as rigid in their formation style. The strike escorts would normally position themselves 2½ nautical miles behind and about 1000 to 2000 feet below the strike force. If the strike force approached at a relatively slow airspeed, the escort would perform an element weave behind it. An element weave was a formation in which the members of an element continuously cross each other's flight path, normally in the horizontal plane, to increase their visual coverage of each other's rear area as well as allowing them to keep pace with the slower airspeeds of the heavily loaded strike force aircraft ahead of them. When MIGs evaded the CAP flights, the escorts would turn into the MIG's direction and fire an AIM-7 or AIM-9 missile. This tactic often halted the MIG attack, but frequently there was insufficient time to achieve a radar lock-on or the proper launch parameters to result in a kill. The primary purpose was to defeat or degrade the enemy's abil-

ity to successfully shoot down the strike-force aircraft,
not to rack up MIG kills by waiting for correct launch
parameters prior to firing the missiles. The escorts were
also responsible for calling MIG or SAM breaks to flights
under attack.[89] An example of their value was described
in a message to CINCPAC on 23 August:

> The chaff escort flight (Pistol) engaged and destroyed
> one MIG-21. Two MIG-21s were attacking Pistol flight
> when Red Crown alerted them. Pistol flight was in an
> element weave pattern behind the chaff flight when Pis-
> tol 02 visually acquired the MIGs and called for a left
> break. The break by the F-4s confused one MIG and
> caused him to overshoot. Pistol 03 was able to maneu-
> ver the MIG and obtain a radar lock-on. He fired two
> AIM-7s and they both guided. The first impacted the
> MIG-21 and the pilot ejected.[90]

MIGCAP

MIGCAP comprised flights of four F-4s assigned to
defend the strike and chaff forces from enemy aircraft by
acting as a blocking force. Usually each flight was assigned a geographical position and station time rather than
specific orbits. This aided control facilities to maintain
positive identification and control of the MIGCAP apart
from the rest of the mission package. To provide continuous MIG protection, the MIGCAPs arrived on station
prior to the strike force and remained until all U.S. forces
had left the area.[91] Since—unlike the various escort
flights—the MIGCAP flights were not tied to the attacking force, they were able to engage the enemy aircraft
before the MIGs could attack the strike force.

The most important single action taken to improve
the counter-air capability of the MIGCAP was the introduction of F-4Ds equipped with Combat Tree equipment—electronic devices that could monitor the IFF
(Identification, Friend or Foe) signals emitted from the
MIGs for use by the North Vietnamese GCI control system.[92] The ability of the MIGCAP flight to monitor enemy IFF confirmed that unidentified aircraft belonged to
the enemy, and indicated the position of the MIGs rela-

tive to the friendly aircraft. Due to the small number of
Combat Tree F-4Ds available in 1972—eight originally,
but combat losses reduced this to five—they were con-
solidated within the 432nd Fighter Wing at Udorn
RTAFB.[93] The F-4s at Udorn were assigned the primary
counter-air role in support of all Linebacker missions.
The optimum composition of a MIGCAP flight was three
F-4Es with internal 20mm guns and one Combat Tree F-
4D.[94] The intercept capabilities of the MIGCAP forces
was greatly enhanced by close coordination with U.S.
command and control systems providing MIG tracking
and warning information. These systems will be discussed in a subsequent section.

IRON HAND

Iron Hand support, which involved the suppression of
the SAM threat through the use of F-105G Wild Weasels
equipped with antiradiation missiles, was another important element of the effort to degrade SAM defenses. Wild
Weasel support was believed to be a significant factor
contributing to the low losses of strike aircraft to SAMS.
During the initial phases of Linebacker I, the Iron Hand
operations consisted of four to eight F-105G Wild Weasel
aircraft, each armed with one AGM-78 and two Shrikes.
These antiradiation missiles (ARMs) were designed to
home in on enemy radar. To prevent attacks on their sites,
SAM operators often turned off their radars or used their
guidance radar only for brief periods. These practices
severely degraded the SAMs' effectiveness. But the SAM
operators quickly became more adept at tactics designed
to foil the effectiveness of the Iron Hand F-105Gs. Since
the ARMs needed a constant signal to home on, the SAM
operators would turn on their radar at the last moment
after the launch of an unguided SAM. The last-moment
turn-on was just long enough to guide the SAM missile,
but not long enough for the ARM missiles to establish a
site lock-on.[95] By turning on a decoy site then turning on
a number of real sites simultaneously after ARMs were
launched, the enemy tried to get the Wild Weasels to
waste ARMs. The AGM-45 could be drawn off target by
two or more simultaneous signals.[96] In any event, even

if the ARM succeeded in acquiring a good lock-on, the missile usually destroyed only the radar vans in the center of the site, leaving the SAMs themselves untouched. Spare radar vans could then be dispatched to the site, and in a relatively short time it would become operational again.

A new concept to improve the anti-SAM mission was implemented during Linebacker I. This development teamed two F-105Gs with their ARMs and two F-4Es loaded with Cluster Bomb Unit (CBU) munitions. The new creation was called Hunter-Killer team, and it increased the Iron Hand effectiveness in several ways. If the ARM missiles succeeded in destroying the radar van, then the SAM site would be marked by the destruction and the launchers would come under attack by the CBU-armed F-4Es. If adequate ARM guidance lock-ons were not acquired by the F-105Gs, but the SAM sites had radiated long enough to reveal their positions to the sophisticated equipment in the F-105G Hunter, then the F-4Es could be directed to attack the site with CBUs.[97] This capability became especially important when the Fan Song optical-tracking capability became operational, and the first radar warning of an active SAM site might occur after missile launch. The availability of CBU ordnance also gave the Iron Hand flights the capability of planning strikes against GCI/SAM/AAA sites, or attacking targets of opportunity such as airfields, rail rolling stock, or trucks.[98] Additionally, the F-4s played a role as the team's MIGCAP and would jettison their ordnance when the MIGs threatened.[99] The Hunter-Killer tactic was considered to be highly successful, and was acknowledged to be so by the enemy. The NVN SAM units were frequently forced to relocate, to improve their camouflage techniques, and to apply ever stricter emission controls. A side effect of the teams was the degradation of SAM equipment caused by the frequent moves.[100] The effectiveness of the Hunter-Killer concept was dramatically portrayed on 6 October. The events were described in a message from the Commander, 7th AF, to the USAF Chief of Staff on 13 October, as follows:

The Iron Hand flight (Condor) expended an AGM-

78 against VN-159 [SAM site designation] with a possible kill; one AGM-78 against VN-142 with a confirmed kill; two AGM-45s against VN-159, which was a preemptive launch; two AGM-45s against VN-243 with a confirmed kill; two CBU-52s and two CBU-58s were delivered on VN-263 for a possible kill. The Iron Hand flight (Goose) had no RHAW indications of the two SAMs fired at Cedar flight. Two SAMs were fired at Goose, which missed by approximately one mile at their six o'clock position. They fired two AGM-45s at VN-159 and VN-005 with no results. Eight CBUs were expended at VN-243 and VN-142, which resulted in both sites being destroyed. Numerous fires and secondary explosions were observed. One SAM was observed cooking off in VN-142. The Iron Hand flight (Cardinal) expended two CBU-52s and two CBU-58s on VN-159, and two CBU-52s and two CBU-58s on VN-005. Smoke in both target areas prevented Battle Damage Assessment (BDA). One SAM torched off in VN-005.[101]

The flexibility of the CBU-equipped F-4Es was displayed on the Linebacker mission of 29 September. A message sent to 7th AF after a Linebacker conference at Udorn RTAFB described the event:

The Iron Hand flight (Condor) reported two SAMs launched from VN-159 directed toward Condor 01. Condor 01 and 02 expended four AGM-45s on two Fan Song radars. Condor 03 and 04 [F-4Es] expended CBU-52s on Phuc Yen Airfield and reported visual BDA of one MIG-19 and two MIG-21s on fire and four MIG-21s damaged.[102]

ECM SUPPORT

Active ECM activity was conducted by EB-66 aircraft orbiting close to the threat area. Specific orbits were established for each mission to optimize ECM coverage during ingress and egress of the strike forces. Three EB-66s were normally on station during a mission. Two would perform active ECM functions, and the third was an airborne spare orbiting over Laos or the Gulf of Ton-kin to provide contingency support.[103] The EB-66 ECM support was supplemented with Marine and Navy EA-6s whenever possible.[104] During the latter stages of Line-backer I the North Vietnamese moved SAM systems be-neath the western orbits of the EB-66s, which caused the EB-66s to move farther from their desired operating ar-eas. As a result, the effectiveness of the EB-66s declined, because the farther away they were from the signal to be jammed the less powerful was their own jamming signal in relation to it.[105] Often EB-66 ECM support was with-held from Linebacker I missions because of the vulner-ability of the EB-66s and because of the size of the effort required to protect them from MIGs.[106] Thus, on many strike missions, ECM protection was primarily afforded through the combination of the chaff corridors and the employment of ECM pods on board strike aircraft (the pods were mounted on the forward AIM-7 launcher po-sitions).[107] The pods provided jamming over a wide se-lection of frequencies and were designed to inhibit the SA-2's ability to track targets. When flights were grouped into elements of four aircraft, the overlapping protection gained from the pods provided satisfactory results and, often, attacking SAMs "went ballistic" and lost their guidance capability.[108]

PHOTO RECON

The photo reconnaissance RF-4s from Udorn RTAFB provided pre- and post-strike bomb damage assessment (BDA) as well as photography to support the LORAN time-delay locations within North Vietnam. In high-threat areas, two recon RF-4s were escorted by two air-to-air configured F-4s. This formation usually flew in at low altitude after centerline fuel tanks were jettisoned. If SAM, AAA, or MIG threats were imminent, outboard wing tanks would also be jettisoned.[109] The escorts were for protection from MIGs and the flight of four provided what was thought to be the best possible means for mu-tual ECM protection against SAMs.[110] The Tacair recon-naissance elements provided important detailed target information for scheduling strikes and evaluating their results. It also provided both point and adjacent-area coverage of immediate value in making decisions for re-striking targets.[111]

TANKER SUPPORT

Coordination between the tanker force and the Tacair force was a critical factor because approximately eighty to one hundred aircraft required pre- and post-strike re-fueling. Two tanker tracks were used over the Gulf and *nine* over Laos. Whenever possible, mission planners would place aircraft with similar tasking within the same tanker cells to retain the integrity of the strike and escort forces during drop-off times. During the latter stages of Linebacker I, tanker cells of six KC-135s were used on all tracks, with vertical altitude separations of three thousand feet.[112]

Coming back from missions over North Vietnam, most of the fighters required another air refueling. Aircraft that had used a high fuel consumption over North Vietnam often just barely reached tankers with a "bingo" (low level) fuel state. Just as often, tanker crews would fly farther north than authorized into Laotian airspace to re-spond to the calls of fighters in need of fuel. Fighters returning with more adequate reserves would take on five thousand pounds of fuel to provide a reserve in the event of traffic delays at recovery bases.[113] The tankers pro-vided the basis for U.S. Tacair operations over North Vietnam. American air supremacy in Southeast Asia al-lowed the tankers considerable freedom of movement at comparatively small risk. This very same air supremacy was made possible by the additional fuel provided by the tankers to the multitudes of tactical aircraft flying over the theater of operations. Without the KC-135s it would hardly have been possible to conduct operations even re-motely resembling the Linebacker offensives.[114] In short, without the refueling supplied by the tanker force, the whole character of combat in SEA would have taken an entirely different form.

AIRBORNE SURVEILLANCE AND CONTROL

During the first few months of Linebacker I, U.S. forces over North Vietnam were highly vulnerable to surprise MIG attacks. This was due to the limited U.S. radar-warning and control capability in areas north and west of Hanoi, especially at the lower altitudes. To correct that deficiency, a new early-warning system, codenamed Teaball, was established at Nakhon Phanom RTAFB to provide positive control and near real-time MIG warnings for the strike forces. The Teaball weapons control center (WCC) used a combination of radar and "all-source" information down-linked from airborne platforms to a weapons controller. A number of supporting assets, including Combat Apple RC-135Ms, Olympic Torch U-2s, Red Crown ships, and Disco EC-121s, provided Teaball with one geographical position per minute on both USAF Tacair and MIG tracks (Figure 6).[115] The Combat Apple RC-135Ms flew twelve-hour orbits over the Gulf or Laos and collected electronic intelligence, paying special attention to indications of SAM Fan Song radar signals and to the enemy air order of battle.[116] The Olympic Torch U-2s provided similar support to the Teaball system. Another important surveillance asset for Tacair forces was the MIG tracking and warning information provided by Red Crown, a U.S. Navy radar-equipped cruiser on station in the northern Gulf of Tonkin. The Red Crown control center tracked hostile and friendly aircraft and provided MIGCAP forces with information such as the type, airspeed, altitude, heading, and relative position of MIG aircraft. Its ability to provide MIG warning to friendly aircraft was generally good, but it was limited when MIGs operated at low altitudes or when the number of friendly and enemy aircraft was so large as to saturate its tracking capabilities.[117]

Disco EC-121s were USAF airborne radar warning-and-control aircraft and were the closest command posts to the operations in RP 6. Disco had the responsibility for controlling intercepts, issuing MIG alerts, warning pilots of potential border violations with China, and—at times—issuing SAM warnings.[118] Initially Disco had maintained orbits over Laos to supplement Red Crown

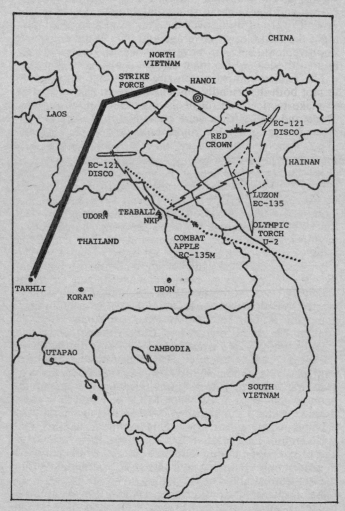

Figure 6. USAF Command and Control System

MIG tracking coverage as far into NVN as possible. An orbit over the Gulf was established after July, when, by staying at a low altitude, MIGs eluded detection by Red Crown and were able to shoot down two U.S. aircraft.[119] The EC-121s orbiting over the gulf were able to supplement the Red Crown coverage and offer some degree of improvement, but their coverage was still limited at medium altitudes, where most of the air battles took place.

The Teaball control system used all-source information to plot both the friendly and enemy positions, as well as to make tactical control decisions based on these plots. Disco and Red Crown were backups for Teaball in case of equipment problems, and a radio relay C-135 aircraft (LUZON) acted as a relay for the entire warning network. The results derived from the Teaball network were evident almost immediately after July. Between February and July 18 Tacair craft were lost to MIG attacks while the U.S. forces destroyed 24 MIGs. After Teaball became operational, U.S. losses between August and October numbered only 5, in comparison with 19 MIGs shot down.[120]

SEARCH AND RESCUE (SAR)

During Linebacker operations SAR forces continued to live up to their outstanding traditions by rescuing numerous aircrew members shot down over North Vietnam. The typical rescue force was comprised of two HH-53C "Jolly Green Giant" helicopters, one HC-130P Hercules refueling aircraft with special modifications to refuel helicopters, and six A-1 fighter escorts. The A-1s were Korean War vintage, single-engine propellor aircraft codenamed "Sandy." While supporting helicopter rescues, the slow speed and long loiter capability of the A-1 suited it better to operations in marginal weather, such as during the monsoon seasons, than the jet fighters. A description of one of the more interesting rescues will be covered in order to provide an insight into SAR operations within the high-threat areas of NVN.

As described earlier in this chapter, the first Linebacker I strike force on 10 May consisted of 32 F-4s launched against the Paul Doumer Bridge and the Yen

Vien railroad yard near downtown Hanoi. The North
Vietnamese strongly defended these targets, firing a large
number of SAMs and sending 41 MIGs to intercept the
U.S. attackers. After shooting down a MIG-21, one of
the F-4D MIGCAP aircraft was shot down by one or
more MIG-19s near Yen Bai, NVN. The aircraft, Oyster 1, was observed to be on fire during descent, and im-
pacted the ground in a ball of fire. No chutes were seen
or beepers heard from either the pilot, Major Robert
Lodge, or the backseater, Weapon System Officer Capt.
Roger Locher. Nothing was heard from either of the crew
members for three weeks, until an F-4 on a 1 June mission reported a beeper and voice contact with a downed
crew member in the vicinity of Yen Bai, NVN.[121]

Immediately SAR forces supporting a Linebacker mission in progress were diverted to the area. The A-1s
reached the area first and established radio contact with
the downed WSO, Captain Locher. Minutes later the HH-
53s arrived in the area. By this time enemy-defense reactions had intensified and the A-1s were receiving heavy
AAA fire from the flatlands around the Red River. Soon
after, one of the F-4s providing air cover over the recovery zone received a direct hit by a SAM. Luckily, the
F-4 crew managed to fly the aircraft back to Thailand,
where they bailed out over friendly territory.

Since the A-1s had been unable to locate the survivor,
the helicopters, which were equipped with electronic location finders (ELFs), attempted to pinpoint his position.
At this point a MIG-21 made a high-speed, low-altitude
pass at the helicopters. Within minutes there was another
MIG pass. The heavy MIG activity, coupled with the fact
that the SAR force was low on fuel and had been unable
to locate the crew member's position, prompted suspension of the SAR effort for the day. During this first day,
rescue operations had centered in an area only about
seven miles from Yen Bai Airfield, NVN.

Due to the long period of time that had passed since
the loss of Oyster 1, the unlikelihood that a survivor could
have evaded enemy troops for so long in such a heavily
populated area, and the fact that the survivor had been
so calm during the initial radio contact, there were sus-
picions that a captured POW was being used by the North

Vietnamese to lay a trap for SAR forces. If it was a trap, its location had been skillfully chosen, with a major enemy airfield only a few miles away and heavy SAM and AAA defenses located throughout the area. Despite the possibility of a trap, the SAR operation continued on the second day. If even a remote possibility existed to rescue any downed airman in Vietnam, the effort was always made a top priority.

In fact, Roger Locher had walked about twelve miles from where he had parachuted and had kept himself alive on wild fruit and weed shoots. The many streams in the area had provided him a plentiful supply of fresh water. On 1 June, he heard the whoosh of a SAM missile launch, and determined that U.S. aircraft had to be flying nearby. It turned out that the F-4 crew that heard him on the guard channel as he called on his survival radio was coincidently also using the callsign "Oyster" on that day. Soon after, another F-4 flight established a better contact with Locher, and the SAR effort went into full swing.

Operations on the second day began with a diversionary strike against Yen Bai Airfield. LGBs were used to cut the runway, then CBUs were dropped to limit the use of the field by enemy aircraft. Other Phantoms were used to hit AAA gun positions in the area. The rescue package and the bombers, plus the attendant array of F-4 escorts, EB-66s, F-105G Weasels and KC-135 tankers totalled 119 USAF aircraft. More aircraft were used to rescue Captain Locher than had been involved in the original 10 May attack on Hanoi when he was shot down (which had totalled 117 USAF aircraft). As the helicopters entered the rescue area, they picked up strong ELF signals from the survivor. The A-1 escorts, however, were receiving heavy and accurate AAA fire from positions between the helicopters and the airman. The A-1s called in F-4 strikes against the guns, while the SAR force headed around the guns toward an area northwest of Yen Bai and north of the Red River. At one point the force passed within four miles of the enemy airfield. To avoid the SAMs and MIGs, the SAR helicopters flew at an altitude of about fifty feet. As they neared the survivor's position once more, they began taking ground fire from the many villages in the area. The helicopter gunners used rapid-fire

miniguns to suppress the ground fire as they moved closer
to the pickup zone.

The ELF equipment proved to be particularly valuable
during this part of the rescue. After the helicopters
reached the general recovery area, the ELF signals
guided them directly to Captain Locher and greatly reduced the time it would have taken to search for him
visually. Captain Locher was hiding on the side of a ridge
with a forty to fifty degree slope, within sight of a village
at the base of the ridgeline. As the choppers began to
hover for the pickup, they took fire from the village,
which was then strafed by the A-1s. The A-1s also laid
a smokescreen to protect and hide the helicopters from
nearby AAA positions. As soon as the downed backseater got on the rescue helicopter's jungle penetrator at the
end of the cable that had been lowered the chopper made
a vertical ascent at maximum power. It was not until
Captain Locher climbed on board the helicopter that the
SAR force was sure that the rescue had not been a trap
planned by the North Vietnamese.

As the SAR force headed away from the heavily populated rescue location toward the Red River, it continued
to receive ground fire from villages in the area, which
were too numerous to avoid. Additionally, the HH-53
gunners traded fire with a number of trucks and military
compounds on the way out. At their exit point over the
Red River, the SAR force spotted a train that had stopped
exactly at their crossing point. As the A-1s passed overhead, guns mounted on several of the train's cars opened
fire. The helicopters returned the fire as they passed over,
damaging several of the cars. The A-1s strafed and
bombed the train, blowing up the engine and leaving
many of the cars burning.

When the rescue force crossed over the Red River, it
encountered yet another problem. Throughout the actual
rescue pickup they had been unable to contact their
MIGCAP support, and were then informed that the
MIGCAP was refueling with a tanker. Just as they were
starting to head for the Laotian border, a MIG-17 was
spotted approaching the SAR force. One of the A-1s
turned into the attacker, which then broke off the attack.
By now the helicopters were running short of fuel, but

they were met inside NVN by a refueling tanker just before their engines flamed out. After refueling was completed, they returned to base. This outstanding exploit added another brilliant chapter to the record of SAR forces in Southeast Asia. It was the ingenuity, perseverance, and dedication of those units that gave the aircrews the ability to don their flight suits each and every morning to fly the very unfriendly skies of North Vietnam. No matter what, the U.S. crews always knew that a maximum effort would be made to get them back to safety if they were ever shot down.[122]

Linebacker I Results and Lessons

BATTLE DAMAGE ASSESSMENT OF LINEBACKER I

The Rail Network. After the closure of the NVN ports by mining, the rail lines from China became the most efficient means of NVN resupply from external sources. Accordingly, interdiction of the rail lines became the first priority of the Linebacker operations. Thus, a concerted effort was made by Tacair to incapacitate the NVN railways by the destruction of the key railroad bridges. Within two weeks of the beginning of the air offensive, a relatively small force of F-4s equipped with LGBs had all but shut down the NVN rail system. Numerous bridges had been destroyed, the most notable of which was the Thanh Hoa Railroad and Highway Bridge.[123]

The Thanh Hoa Bridge, which, it was said, "would never go down," went down with a splash on 13 May 1972, under the impact of LGBs. It was first attacked during Rolling Thunder on 3 April 1965. Subsequently, it withstood three years of severe pounding from over one thousand USAF and Navy strike sorties. The bridge had highly emotional as well as military significance. Emotionally, pilots found it frustrating to put so much ordnance on one bridge without dropping it. Militarily, it was a key link in the NVN highway and rail systems leading down the NVN panhandle. The 56-foot-wide, 540-foot-long bridge was of steel through-truss construction with two spans, a massive center concrete pier, and concrete abutments. In the first Rolling Thunder strike,

79 F-105s dropped 638 750-pound bombs, fired 32 Bull-pup missiles and 266 2.75-inch rockets. Although the bridge was hit several times, it failed to drop. In this first raid the USAF lost an F-100 flak-suppression aircraft, an RF-101 recon plane, and three F-105s. One of the F-105s was lost to ground fire, while the other two were shot down by MIG-17s, the first U.S. aircraft to be lost to North Vietnamese fighters.[124]

Contrasting this and the many subsequent attempts to destroy the Thanh Hoa Bridge with the strikes on 13 May 1972, points out the dramatic advances in weaponry. In Linebacker II flights of F-4s carrying 24 LGBs, and one flight armed with conventional MK-82 500-pound bombs, struck the bridge and left it unusable. No aircraft were lost.

Constant emphasis on closing key bridges and tunnels enabled the USAF to keep the rail lines unserviceable. The effective interdiction of the railways, coupled with the closure of the ports and harbors, forced the enemy to place primary reliance on the less efficient road network for moving the supplies from China.[125]

The Road Network and Truck Facilities. The NVN road/truck system represented a formidable obstacle for the interdiction program. The North Vietnamese had demonstrated a great deal of resourcefulness in moving large quantities of supplies over considerable distances despite heavy attrition from air attacks. Nonetheless, a strike effort against targets associated with the enemy's road network had to be attempted if the interdiction program was to succeed. Otherwise, enemy movements of supplies via the roads between Hanoi and China could easily surpass the amounts received at North Vietnamese ports prior to the Linebacker operations.[126] The USAF did manage to slow down trucking activities at times; however, the enemy continued to move vast quantities of combat-essential materials between China and Hanoi. After hundreds of attacks against truck convoys, it became obvious that the efforts were not reducing the enemy's ability to keep himself supplied. So throughout most of the campaign, air attacks were concentrated primarily against the enemy's vehicle and repair centers to inhibit their use.[127]

POL Facilities, Equipment and Stockpiles. Prior to Linebacker I, over ninety percent of North Vietnam's petroleum, oil, and lubricants (POL) came from the Soviet Union by tanker, and virtually all of it was offloaded at the port of Haiphong. From the Haiphong area the NVN had constructed an efficient pipeline network to move POL all the way down to their base areas in the Laos/South Vietnam border regions. While the pipeline itself was relatively immune to disruption by air strikes, several associated elements of the line and the POL distribution system were more vulnerable. The destruction of key pumping stations disrupted the flow of the POL, while attacks on storage facilities destroyed large quantities of POL awaiting movement through the pipeline. By the end of May about ten percent of NVN's POL stocks and storage capability had been destroyed by air strikes and another fifteen percent had been consumed to support the greater reliance on the trucking transportation system.[128]

Power Facilities. One of the most notable accomplishments of Linebacker I was the successful targeting and destruction of the high-valued power facilities. Many of these facilities could not be struck during previous campaigns because of their proximity to populated areas or prohibited targets. Yet during Linebacker operations, due to the employment of the highly accurate guided bombs, these facilities were successfully attacked and destroyed with minimal collateral damage.

Electric power was an important factor in NVN's economy, with ninety percent of all power generated for industrial, rather than private, consumption. That the success of attacks against NVN power-generating targets hinged upon pinpoint accuracy was illustrated by a strike against the Lang Chi hydroelectric power plant (HPP) in the Red River Valley. This facility, the largest known power-producing plant in NVN, was sixty three miles up the Red River Valley from Hanoi and was considered capable of supplying seventy-five percent of the electricity for NVN's industrial needs. The target was a difficult one because the dam associated with it was off limits. Pilots reported direct hits in the transformer yard and to turbines and generators in the main building, while the dam itself and the spillway were not breached.

By mid-June strikes against NVN power plants had disabled over seventy percent of the country's power-generated capacity. Enemy attempts to rebuild the destroyed plants and to restore at least partial generating capacity were nullified by additional strikes as required. This continued incapacitation of most NVN power facilities forced the enemy to place heavy reliance on small, dispersed generators, a less efficient source of power which could meet only his most essential needs.[129]

RESULTS OF THE OPERATIONS

Throughout the period during Linebacker I the North Vietnamese willingness to enter into substantive discussions at the peace talks seemed to ebb and flow with the tide of the ground battle in the south. But in September, when the South Vietnamese recaptured the city of Quang Tri and continued to push against the NVN forces, Hanoi's willingness to negotiate increased.[130] By mid-October, as the Paris peace talks entered a new phase of fruitful discussions, the JCS issued new orders that restricted offensive air operations to below the 20th Parallel once again.[131]

The effects of Linebacker I definitely influenced the North Vietnamese to return to negotiations. The mining had closed the main ports to external means of supply by shipping, which greatly reduced the influx of replacement war-related goods. The closed ports meant a greater dependence upon supplies transported by rail from China on the northwest and northeast railways. Since daily Tac-air missions continuously interdicted the bridges both north and south of Hanoi using the LGB technology, the NVN had to resort to using the less than optimum means of transportation—an undeveloped highway system.[132] The destruction of vast quantities of POL resources along with truck repair and storage facilities kept constant pressure on this highway system. The bottom line was that less than twenty percent of the enemy's previous supplies were reaching front-line units engaged in combat.[133]

The effect on the enemy was dramatic. At the beginning of the enemy offensive key bases in South Vietnam had come under fire, receiving five to six thousand rounds a night. With reduced ammo supplies, the North Vietnamese forces were forced to curtail such heavy attacks, and the South Vietnamese were able to follow through with increased counteroffensive measures. The effects were evident by the statements of captured NVN soldiers. Many had not eaten in several days, and they were down to only one clip each for their AK-47 sub-machine guns. One young NVN lieutenant captured at Quang Tri had been told that he would be issued his sidearms when he got into the city. There weren't any available. When he arrived, he discovered that the issue consisted of finding a weapon from a dead body.[134]

LESSONS LEARNED

As in any complex operation, many problems developed during Linebacker I. To identify and resolve these problems, 7th Air Force held daily Linebacker critiques, including representatives from all the tactical fighter wings, the planners, controllers, and tanker-support people who had participated on the mission. In that way workable solutions could be achieved for specific problems, and each member was aware of other units' problems. Resolved problems were immediately incorporated into new Linebacker procedures.[135]

Significant actions identified during these meetings included:

Need for MIG Warning. NVN radar-controlled MIG attacks between February and July 1972 resulted in unacceptable USAF loss rates. A real-time warning system was needed because MIG engagements occurred within minutes after MIG takeoff. The Teaball Weapon Control Center was established to provide this warning.[136]

Chaff Delivery Systems. Chaff flights were extremely vulnerable to MIGs. The introduction of the ALE-38 chaff dispenser allowed an improved protective chaff formation. The enemy threat was negated further by use of deception tactics, such as simulating MIGCAP flights and laying chaff while flying away from the intended target, as opposed to into the target. Caution was necessary to prevent stereotyping the procedures.[137]

The SAM Threat.   SAM site destruction was needed in addition to SAM suppression measures. Hunter-Killer teams were formed consisting of two F-105G Hunters and two F-4E Killers. Once the SAM site was located by the F-105Gs, the F-4E Killers would strike the site with CBUs to destroy the missiles, support equipment and trained personnel. When occupied SAM sites could not be found, authority was granted to expend CBUs on airfields, AAA sites, or targets of opportunity.[138]

All-Weather Bombing.   Action was taken to introduce an all-weather bombing capability over North Vietnam by use of LORAN. A large number of priority targets were validated over the NVN heartland in anticipation of possible air operations over NVN during the monsoon season between September and April.[139]

Chaff Support.   Chaff was used heavily, in conjunction with ECM, in an effort to degrade the SAMs' Fan Song radar performance. The use of effective chaff corridors was essential for survival of the strike force in a concentrated SA-2 and radar-directed AAA environment.

Attaining Air Superiority.   In weighing the overall threat according to losses incurred by Linebacker I forces, one would list MIGs, then SAMs, and last, AAA. Throughout the operation, heavy support was retained for the chaff and LGB flights because it was felt that MIGs represented the greatest threat to those two forces. The countering U.S. tactics included a combination of MIGCAP escort aircraft aided by Teaball, Disco, and Red Crown.[140] MIGCAP forces met the MIGs far out from the target area in order to prevent the MIGs from engaging the chaff/strike force. This tactic did much to hold strike losses to a minimum (only three strike aircraft were lost to MIGs) during Linebacker, although exposed support forces suffered twenty losses to MIG attacks.[141]

Specialization of Resources. Linebacker I highlighted the requirement for specializing Tacair assets. The primary reasons for specializing the F-4 squadrons were the limited availability of resources and the efficiency of weapon-system operation. The illuminators (''Pave Knife'' pods) for the laser-guided bombs and the chaff dispensers were in critically short supply and were located at only one base, Ubon RTAFB. The Combat Tree F-4Ds, equipped with special devices to monitor and track enemy IFF, were all assigned to Udorn RTAFB, where the counter-air mission was the primary F-4 role. The combat air patrol and escort missions required a high proficiency and considerable cross-talk to be effective. From the viewpoint of combat effectiveness, it was undesirable to alternate aircrews between the various missions.[142] Specialization also was the reason for high Hunter-Killer team proficiencies at Korat RTAFB.

F-111 Penetration Profiles. Flying the F-111 profile into North Vietnam during Linebacker I caused some unique problems. Planners observed that stereotyped routes had caused the North Vietnamese to move defenses into the general areas over which eighty percent of the F-111 night missions were flown. Allowing flight crews to plan their own missions removed the tendency toward stereotyping.[143]

Support ECM. The NVN moved SAM systems into the orbit areas of the EB-66s, forcing them to move farther from their desired operating areas. As a result, EB-66/EA-6B ECM support was not as effective as it would have been if orbit areas could have been maintained closer to the target areas.

POSTSCRIPT ON LINEBACKER I

Although the President had ordered the stand-down of all offensive air operations in North Vietnam above the 20th Parallel, a substantial air interdiction effort continued in the route package areas south of that line. The battles that were waged between the NVN air defenses and the attacking U.S. strike forces in this area greatly resembled, in miniature, the battles fought within RP 6. This continuing effort, which served as a prelude to the Linebacker II offensive, will be covered in Chapter Two.

Chapter Two

SETTING THE STAGE: LINEBACKER II

"Peace Is at Hand"

As the aerial interdiction of military supplies during Linebacker I took effect, the North Vietnamese suffered one defeat after another in the battles in South Vietnam. Once they were convinced that President Nixon would be reelected, a negotiated settlement of the war must have looked more attractive to the communists. The negotiations during October 1972 in Paris between Henry Kissinger and Le Duc Tho, the North Vietnamese negotiator, yielded agreements in several significant areas. The terms basically called for the eventual withdrawal of U.S. forces from South Vietnam. Since the North Vietnamese had never acknowledged the existence of their troops in South Vietnam, the agreements could not call for their withdrawal. However, the agreements did specify the closing of their logistical support routes through Cambodia and Laos, under international supervision. In addition, the U.S. would be allowed to replace worn-out U.S. equipment in the south on a one-for-one basis.[1] Also, all U.S. prisoners of war were to be returned immediately after the signing of an agreement. Since the South Vietnamese were not participants in the peace talks, Kissinger had to present the agreements to President Thieu of South Vietnam. President Thieu was reluctant to agree to any proposal that did not address the withdrawal of North Vietnamese forces, and American efforts continued

throughout October and November to convince the South
Vietnamese to accept the agreements.[2] Kissinger was op-
timistic on this point, and he announced on 23 October,
"We believe that peace is at hand. We believe an agreement is in sight . . ."[3]

Throughout the negotiations U.S. interdiction strikes
continued, with emphasis on targets within the RP-1 areas. During November alone, B-52s flew 848 sorties
against logistic and interdiction targets with heavy Tacair
support.[4] It is worth discussing these missions, as they
had some bearing on the tactics that would be used during the Linebacker II offensive.

B-52 Employment during October-November 1972

Operational command and control of B-52s continued
to be withheld from the Military Assistance Command,
Vietnam, and the Commander-in-Chief Pacific Forces
(CINCPAC), remaining under control of the Strategic Air
Command. Although targets in South Vietnam were
nominated by MACV and coordinated through the SAC
liaison division in 7th Air Force (located in Saigon), all
targets in North Vietnam were controlled by the Joint
Chiefs of Staff. The JCS would then task SAC to strike
all nominated targets using established B-52 bombing
tactics.[5] Since enemy MIG, SAM, and AAA capabilities
steadily increased in RP 1 and RP 2, 7th AF was required
to support all SAC missions with chaff, Iron Hand,
MIGCAP, escorts, and ECM assets for protective cover
over these areas.[6] The support force used tactics in much
the same manner as employed during the Linebacker I
strike missions over RP 6.

The B-52s flew in formation of three aircraft referred
to as a cell. Each cell was identified by an assigned call
sign, usually a color; that is, Red One, Two, and Three.
The aircraft flew in a trail with one mile between each
plane, with the formation stacked up to provide a 500-
foot-altitude separation from the preceding aircraft (see
Figure 7). If a target required greater firepower than three
B-52s could deliver, then a "wave" or "compression"
was formed by adding cells to get the desired number of
bombs on target. The lead aircraft in each cell normally

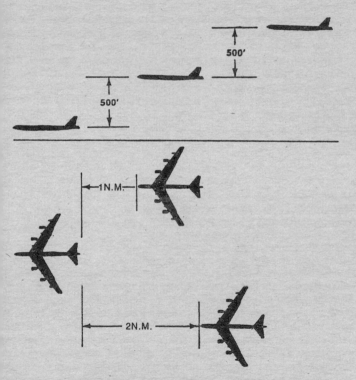

Figure 7. B-52 Cell Formation. The cell formation consisted of three aircraft in a two-mile trail. The second and third aircraft were stacked up to provide a 500-foot vertical altitude separation.

flew at the same altitude, and the remaining aircraft maintained their positions by using airborne radar for station-keeping.[7] These formations were used to increase the weight of the bombing within a target area and to provide overlapping ECM protection to the bombers. For the B-52, all jamming patterns were off the nose or the tail, the most power in-line with the fuselage.[8]

Between October and December the B-52 missions were steadily fragged toward higher-threat targets where major North Vietnamese supply distribution centers were located. During October most of the B-52 attacks were confined to RP 1 and the environs of Dong Hoi, a relatively low-threat area, although SAM activity sprang up sporadically throughout the RP 1 target areas.[9] Initially, B-52 missions were restricted to the low-threat areas, and if threats were encountered, the missions were usually diverted to alternate targets or canceled. During November the rules were changed because the North Vietnamese began to deploy small numbers of mobile SAMs near priority target zones, firing them to make the bombers divert. Because numerous diversions resulting from the SAM activations were reducing the bombers' effectiveness in impeding the vast flow of supplies, the new rule became "Press-On," and the B-52s continued to their targets despite SAM (or MIG) activities encountered or anticipated.[10] This gave increased importance in the use of Tacair support to protect the B-52 forces.

MIG Threats to the B-52 Missions

As the B-52 missions moved northward, the number of MIGs and SAMs encountered increased. The Press On missions required the same levels of protection afforded the Linebacker I strike forces.

The danger from MIGs was highlighted as early as 1971 to the B-52 aircrews. On 20 November 1971, a MIG-21 successfully intercepted a B-52 cell scheduled to strike a target near the Ban Karai Pass between Laos and North Vietnam. The MIG had taken off from a southern base and vectored directly toward the B-52s. A MIG warning was passed to the bomber cell along with a divert order. One minute after receiving the order, the lead B-52 began a left turn away from the area. While the cell was engaged in the turn, the MIG approached from behind, fired an Atoll missile at the cell, and returned to NVN. The number-three B-52 had observed the fighter on his radar at seven o'clock low, passing underneath his aircraft and heading for number two in the cell. The missile exploded about a hundred feet below and to the left of the number two B-52, which had been dispensing protective flares.[11] After this close encounter, all B-52 missions over North Vietnam were provided F-4 MIGCAP and escort forces.

SAM Threats to the B-52s

Protection from SAMs required the bulk of the support effort; targets in high-threat areas required the use of chaff corridors, ECM support, and Iron Hand SAM suppression flights. Initially ECM support was provided by a single EB-66 covering a single cell of B-52s. When the EB-66 was jamming radars from standoff orbit, its effectiveness was proven by the ineffectiveness of the SAMs. The jamming of the North Vietnamese radars denied SAM acquisition, and the delays afforded protection to the strike cell, while the ECM provided by the B-52 cell protected the EB-66 by preventing the NVN forces from pinpointing the exact positions of the jamming strobes emitted by the EB-66.[12] However, for mutual support to be effective, the EB-66 had to be within forty miles of the B-52 cell.[13]

During late October, to put more bombs on each target and to provide greater ECM support for the attacking force, SAC changed its bombing procedures from single cells to waves, with cells separated by two to five minutes. This change in tactics caused the suspension of single-ship EB-66 support because a single EB-66 could not remain in alignment with one cell, then get into position to support adequately the next. The EB-66s started to go in two- and three-ship flights, one supporting the first and third B-52 cells, another supporting the second and fourth cells, and an air spare giving additional support or providing a replacement for an aborted primary.[14]

One of the most frequent problems faced by the EB-66

crews came from SAC's changes in the attack plans. The EB-66s were flying established orbits just prior to B-52 entries into the target zones. But, often SAC changed time on targets, and sometimes diverted the B-52s to alternate targets, causing misalignments of the EB-66 orbits with respect to the B-52 routes. Because of the low airspeed of the EB-66, last-minute changes in target coordinates by SAC or the controlling agencies usually did not allow enough time for the EB-66 to get into proper position, which was hazardous for the EB-66 as well as the B-52s, since misalignments meant that the B-52s were providing ineffective ECM coverage of the EB-66. Lack of B-52 jamming would allow the NVN detection system to pinpoint the position of the EB-66 jamming strobes.[15] SAMs could then be fired using the less accurate, but often effective, "track-on-jam" technique, a method that did not require fire control radar (Fan Song) transmitting signals (which would have attracted Iron Hand attacks). In the passive track-on-jam technique, the SAM operator used the jamming strobes seen on the Fan Song receiver scopes to calculate the azimuth alignment (compass angle to the target) for the missile. The operators aligned the missile beacon (downlink) with the jamming strobes and let the missile's proximity fuse do its job. Using this method of target acquisition, range information was not required for the SAM. However, the launched missile required a long arc, and since the SAM-2 accelerated until it ran out of fuel, the missile's flight time was frequently so long that evasive maneuvers could be made by the EB-66 or any fighter aircraft subject to this kind of attack because the missile was flying too quickly to make sharp maneuvers.[16] B-52s are not as maneuverable as even the EB-66, so this method of attack had greater potential for success against them. For that reason, it was especially important that the B-52s maintain cell integrity for mutual ECM support, in addition to being provided with EB-66s and chaff protection. With overlapping ECM from the B-52s supplemented by EB-66 jamming and chaff, the North Vietnamese could not pinpoint individual B-52 jamming strobes on the scopes of the Fan Song receivers.

The danger from SAMs was further decreased by the

Iron Hand F-105G Wild Weasels which accompanied B-52 strikes. The Weasels arrived on station ten minutes prior to the B-52s' time on target (TOT) and searched for any threats to the B-52 cells.[17] Although the Weasels were aware of all possible threat locations, and their tactics protected the B-52s fully, last-minute changes occurred occasionally and threatened the safety of the B-52s. As in the case with EB-66 missions, changes in targets or TOTs by the SAC bombers required quick scrambling by the Weasels to get into proper positions to protect the B-52 cells.[18] This was especially critical when the B-52s resorted to wave attacks, where the relatively small Weasel force had to protect many aircraft in a short period of time within a greater area of coverage.[19]

To make matters worse, the NVN SAM operators began using new tactics which increased their effectiveness against the B-52 bombers. Fan Song signals often appeared for only a short time, rarely emitting long enough for accurate countermeasures by the Weasels. The SAM sites appeared to be toying with the B-52 and Iron Hand forces; when they launched missiles, the objective always seemed to be to divert the B-52s from the probable target, and the tactic was often successful.[20]

In November the B-52s were targeted into the Vinh area to destroy huge stockpiles of supplies in transshipment points. On 5 November four F-105G Weasels supported a B-52 cell in the Vinh target area. As the B-52 cell exited the area, a SAM was launched and exploded next to one of the B-52s, causing damage to its right wing. The curiosity of the incident was that the Fan Song SAM guidance radar was transmitting only after the missile was airborne and well into its flight. The signal was active only for fifteen seconds, but the missile was still guiding accurately.[21] No explanation could be found for the new development, despite the fact that the same procedure was used throughout the month. Finally, on 22 November, a SAM found its mark. A B-52D from Utapao suffered hits from a SAM that had exploded 150 feet off the wing, causing fires in both wings and the fuselage.[22] The crew managed to fly the crippled aircraft over a hundred miles before its engines flamed out only five miles to the Thai border. The B-52 was virtually a flam-

ing torch without power, but the crew chose to remain
on board and attempt to glide across the border. Just as
the aircraft crossed the Mekong River, the right wing tip
broke off and the aircraft started an uncontrolled turn;
the crew managed to eject near the U.S. base at Nakhon
Phanom. This was the first B-52 lost to enemy ground
fire in 7½ years of B-52 combat operations in Southeast
Asia.[23] Intelligence sources soon informed the Weasel
squadrons that the SAM operators had guided the missiles by tracking the B-52 jamming signals, then activat-
ing the Fan Song radar for a very short period as the
SAM neared the B-52.[24] An additional factor noted was
that the B-52 had not flown within the chaff corridor,
which could have moved beyond the intended track due
to high winds.[25] Two very important lessons were learned
from the first loss of a B-52: Sam operators could effectively counter U.S. SAM suppression and ECM measures
by using track-on-jam homing techniques and minimal
use of their Fan Song; the narrow chaff corridors became
ineffective and did not provide proper protection if winds
blew the chaff out of the planned B-52 tracks. These important lessons should have greatly influenced future
planned tactics for B-52 attacks into high threat areas.

Search and Rescue Exploits

Some of the most dramatic rescue efforts during the
long air war over Vietnam took place in the period between Linebacker I and II. One of the significant changes
in SAR was the replacement of the A-1E with the A-7D
for the "Sandy" mission. All of the A-1s were sent to
South Vietnam in October 1972, leaving the newly deployed A-7s at Korat RTAFB as the logical helicopter
escort. Just one week after taking over the Sandy job, the
A-7 pilots proved themselves capable of filling the role.

On 16 November a F-105G Wild Weasel with the call
sign Bobbin 5 was flying a night escort for a B-52 strike
near Thanh Hoa when it was downed by a SAM. The
pilot, Major Norman Maier, and his backseater, Capt.
Kenneth Thaete managed to eject from the burning aircraft.[26] One of the B-52 crew members who witnessed
the shootdown said:

It was a remarkably clear night at altitude with our cell attacking targets on a west to east heading. We had a F-105 Wild Weasel as escort, among others. He was flying off our left wing with another aircraft also in the area. Beneath them was a thick undercast. Suddenly a bright circle lit up on the ground as a SAM left its launcher. It slipped out of the overcast and moved toward the lead aircraft in our cell, but then missed as it passed in front of him. A second or two later I saw a second SAM light up the overcast almost directly below the F-105. It popped through the clouds and almost immediately struck the underside of the Thud. The ejection seats went out almost immediately, and I was surprised that I could see them fire at this distance. We continued the bomb run still straight and level and made our release.[27]

The two F-105 crew members drifted separately to earth, each unable to see the other. Captain Thaete landed in flatlands and rapidly made tracks for a nearby ridgeline where he could hide. Major Maier in the meantime came down near a road, where he immediately abandoned his gear and headed up a hill for cover. The local North Vietnamese troops knew that the airmen were hiding in the hills and tried to flush them out by shooting their guns every once in a while. But the high grass where the airmen were hiding made it very difficult for the enemy troops looking for them.

In the face of increasingly bad weather, a rescue plan evolved quickly. A SAR force that would eventually grow to about seventy-five aircraft was put together for an initial pickup attempt at first light the following morning. The force included A-7s for Sandy support as well as the usual EB-66s, F-4s, F-105Gs, HC-130s, EC-121s, and HH-53 helicopters. Selected to fly as the Sandy's on-the-scene commander was Major Colin A. (Arnie) Clarke of the 356th Tactical Fighter Squadron assigned to the A-7 354th Tactical Fighter Wing at Korat. Major Clarke, though never before having flown an SAR, had experience in rescues. He was himself shot down twice before while flying F-100s early in the war. In fact, in late August 1964, he became the first Air Force pilot to be downed in the war. In those early days there were no organized rescue forces, and KC-135 tankers were used to direct crews to the rescue.

The command post for this mission was a 56th Air Rescue and Recovery Squadron HC-130 "Kingbird," also from Korat. As in previous rescue efforts, the HC-130 role was to organize and direct the overall mission, making sure that the aircraft needed for a successful pickup were available and ready to go. At daybreak the next morning the Sandys rendezvoused with the Jolly Greens (from Nakhon Phanom) above a solid overcast along the Laos–North Vietnam border. Major Clarke looked for a break in the overcast for the HH-53s to let down, while the choppers orbited in place. He flew in from the west, checking over various approach points for a safe ingress route for the slower, more vulnerable helicopters. Just to the west of the planned pickup point, he noticed about ten trucks moving down a road. During his scouting mission he managed to pinpoint the exact locations of the two survivors on his projected map display. The A-7 computer system on-board accurately pinpointed the beacon-emitter locations for the downed airmen and allowed a direct return to the survivor when the helicopters arrived in the area for a pickup. The position of the downed airmen was passed via secure-voice radio directly to other aircraft involved in the SAR effort. This eliminated confusion in the SAR area and facilitated the pickup by quickly establishing a true location, when minimum exposure time in a high-threat environment is necessary for survival.

Escorted by an F-4, Major Clarke examined the area where the two crew members were hiding to get an assessment of the enemy forces in the pickup zone. Several of the A-7s accompanying him were hit by .51-caliber rounds. The weather, which had been steadily worsening, became a really serious hazard. Everything pointed toward an aborted mission, but Major Clarke also knew that the weather had been forecast to become even worse in the next few days. The helicopters, which couldn't venture above the clouds for fear of enemy MIGs, couldn't fly through the clouds because of the mountains hidden by the mist. They had planned to move underneath the cloud cover, but the low ceiling came right down to the mountains and, in some cases, into the valleys. To find a path for the choppers, Major Clarke flew up one valley after another until he found a way in. He then orbited within the designated valley—which was just barely wide enough to hold a two-G turn—until one of the Jolly Greens was able to home in on his position, about forty miles west of the pickup point. As his A-7 and the HH-52 approached the first pickup point, Major Clarke recalled, "Guns were twinkling right at me from near Bravo [the code name given to Captain Thaete]." He and his wingman kept fire on the guns while other A-7s fired smoke rockets to cover the area with a thick artificial mist. "Jolly came in dragging his back wheels through the grass. I just kept yelling at him to get lower, lower."

Meanwhile, awaiting pickup on the ground, Captain Thaete remembered his thoughts at the time. "They were shooting at the aircraft coming in on passes. Some sixty to a hundred rounds were fired at each—from pistols to eighty-five-mm guns." One .51-caliber gun sat on a ridge directly above the tall brush where Captain Thaete was hiding. Although the Jolly Green crew was unaware of the close proximity of the site, it appeared that the gun crew had also missed seeing the chopper as it taxied through the grass to pick up Captain Thaete. Captain Thaete was surprised when he was yanked by the pararescueman into the compartment of the helicopter. The crewman then swung a minigun into the doorway and opened up on the gun, as the adversaries finally had discovered one another. For several seconds the chopper had a gun duel against the enemy on the hill. The chopper won as the gun site disappeared under hundreds of the minigun rounds. The HH-53 next quickly picked up Major Maier at the bottom of the hill.

The Jolly Green then headed west and toward home at maximum power. All of the SAR force aircraft then withdrew without incident, except for Major Clarke's A-7. He had flown one last gun pass against several active enemy gun sites to cover the HH-53's escape. As Major Clarke explained, "They were firing at me, but the guns weren't coming too close—except the one that hit me."

He lost his instruments and electrical systems and pulled up into the clouds. As he broke out on top he was joined by other A-7s, and headed toward the sea in case he had to punch out. He was able to nurse the crippled aircraft to Da Nang Air Base in South Vietnam. It was discovered that a .51 caliber round had exploded one of his empty wing tanks, which blew in the side of the fuselage and bowed the underside of the wing. Later that day both rescued crew members returned to their home base at Korat after receiving minor medical treatment at Nakhon Phanom RTAFB (where the HH-53s were stationed). A large crowd of friends, as well as the many people who had tirelessly supported the SAR, greeted the two men as they departed the same HC-130 that had directed their rescue. Literally hundreds of personnel, from the aircrews to the maintenance people and other support agencies, had worked continuously to assure the success of the rescue. The 388th Wing Commander congratulated those who had participated, ''I know how much courage was involved. This was an example of everyone working together in what was probably one of the toughest SARs we've ever had here.'' For his part in the rescue, Major Clarke was awarded the Air Force Cross.[28]

Chapter Three

THE TALKS COLLAPSE

The Decision to Restrike the North

While Dr. Kissinger tried to convince President Thieu to accept the proposed agreements, the North Vietnamese had virtually reconstructed their air-defense network and facilities around Hanoi and Haiphong.[1] When talks resumed with the North Vietnamese negotiators at the end of November, a stalemate developed on some of the unresolved details of the earlier agreements. By December the North Vietnamese were rejecting most of the agreements and concessions made in October.[2] The North Vietnamese were probably reacting in this manner for two reasons: Congress was threatening to withdraw funds to support the war; quite possibly, the Hanoi government anticipated a resumption of bombing attacks in the Hanoi area, but believed that the impending onset of bad weather during the northeast monsoon would seriously hamper U.S. tactical-fighter attacks.[3] Hanoi probably least expected the use of B-52s for massive all-weather attacks against their valuable complexes. In any event, on 13 December the North Vietnamese walked out of the peace talks. It became clear to President Nixon that he needed to show Hanoi that continued negotiations would be preferable to continued hostilities.[4] Therefore, he decided to resume an intensive bombing campaign once again, above the 20th Parallel. Fearful of congressional and public condemnation of renewed bombing, he directed the execution of an intensive maximum effort against the NVN homeland while Congress was on

73

Christmas break. During discussions in the Oval Office, President Nixon told Kissinger:

> If we renew the bombing, it will have to be something new, and that means we will have to make the big decision to hit Hanoi and Haiphong with B-52s. Anything less will only make the enemy contemptuous.[5]

The President forwarded his decision to implement Linebacker II to the Joint Chiefs of Staff. On 15 December the JCS sent advance warning to CINCPAC and CINCSAC that they should prepare for a maximum-effort strike against targets in NVN.[6] Two days later, on 17 December, the JCS sent the following message to CINCPAC, CINCSAC, and 7th AF operational commanders:

YOU ARE DIRECTED TO COMMENCE AT APPROXIMATELY 1200Z, 18 DECEMBER 1972 A THREE-DAY MAXIMUM EFFORT, REPEAT MAXIMUM EFFORT OF B-52/TACAIR STRIKES IN THE HANOI/HAIPHONG AREAS AGAINST THE TARGETS CONTAINED IN [THE AUTHORIZED TARGET LIST]. OBJECT IS MAXIMUM DESTRUCTION OF SELECTED MILITARY TARGETS IN THE VICINITY OF HANOI/HAIPHONG. BE PREPARED TO EXTEND OPERATIONS PAST THREE DAYS, IF DIRECTED.

FOLLOWING INSTRUCTIONS APPLY:
A. UTILIZE VISUAL AS WELL AS ALL-WEATHER CAPABILITIES.
B. UTILIZE ALL RESOURCES WHICH CAN BE SPARED WITHOUT CRITICAL DETRIMENT TO OPERATIONS IN RUN AND SUPPORT OF EMERGENCY SITUATIONS IN LAOS AND CAMBODIA.
C. UTILIZE RESTRIKES ON AUTHORIZED TARGETS, AS NECESSARY. NORTH VIETNAMESE AIR ORDER OF BATTLE, AIRFIELDS, AND ACTIVE SURFACE-TO-AIR MISSILE SITES MAY BE STRUCK AS TACTICAL SITUATION DICTATES TO IMPROVE EFFECTIVENESS OF ATTACK FORCES AND MINIMIZE LOSSES.
D. EXERCISE PRECAUTION TO MINIMIZE RISK OF CIVIL-

IAN CASUALTIES UTILIZING LGB [LASER-GUIDED
BOMB] WEAPONS AGAINST DESIGNATED TARGETS.
AVOID DAMAGE TO THIRD COUNTRY SHIPPING.[7]

Early Planning Activities for a Maximum Effort

The order to use all available Tacair and all-weather
aircraft such as the B-52, F-111, and A-6 weapon systems, did not catch the planners by surprise. As early as
August targeteers had begun a detailed review to identify
targets against which all-weather bombing techniques by
B-52s and Tacair could be utilized.[8] Until late 1972 the
B-52, as the main U.S. strategic nuclear-weapons delivery system equipped with sophisticated ECM devices,
was considered far too valuable to risk over high-threat
areas such as RP 6. Losses over North Vietnam would
result in the recovery of secret on-board systems by the
Soviet Union, against whom they might have to be used
during nuclear war.[9] But the situation in late 1972 dictated a need to take the risks, because any meaningful
offensive would depend highly upon available all-weather
bombers. So the B-52s had to carry the weight of the
effort, since too few F-111s and A-6s were available to
produce the offensive's desired shock.[10] B-52s were to be
used for targets that were readily identifiable by radar or
sufficiently large to be attacked by a three-ship B-52 cell
with little likelihood that the bomb train would fall outside an established target box. SAC planners reduced the
list to targets ideal for strategic bombing. Targets that
met the criteria were airfields, railroad yards, petroleum-
storage facilities, power plants, large military warehouses, and transshipment points. By September the list
had been refined to approximately sixty targets.[11] The
initial planning for sustained use of the B-52 against targets in RP 6 was reviewed and approved concurrently by
CINCSAC and CINCPAC. The plan had a threefold purpose: to offset the effect of poor weather on Tacair strikes,
to destroy the North Vietnamese air-defense system, and
to destroy enough main supply and transportation facilities to halt the enemy logistic and war-supporting capabilities.[12] The resumption of the peace talks in October
had kept this plan on the shelf temporarily. But even dur-

ing October, refinements were continually added to the plans in the event such a maximum effort should be required.[13] A message to Air Force commanders in the Pacific from CINCPAC clarified further the planned use of a maximum effort:

> Linebacker priority targets require around-the-clock strikes in good and bad weather. We should utilize A-6s, A-7s, F-111s, LORAN-equipped F-4s and B-52s to the maximum extent under night and all-weather conditions in NVN. Allocation of air will vary from target system, route pack to route pack, and country to country. Such allocation will be oriented toward achieving the goals established for a twelve-day campaign cycle. A twelve-day cycle represents three incremental four-day target-planning periods established by 7th AF, and the current CVA [aircraft carrier] relocation cycles. Specifically, adjustments will be made as a result of enemy rebuilding efforts, bad weather, and the extent of target-system destruction.[14]

Thus, a maximum effort had been provided for if one was required. All that was needed to make rapid implementation possible was working out the actual tactics and establishing close coordination between USAF and naval Tacair and the SAC strategic-attack forces. During December 1972 505 Tacair aircraft were available from bases in Thailand and 206 B-52s assigned to Guam and Thailand (see Table 3).[15] These forces were expected to carry out missions against a formidable antiaircraft system in RP 6, which had been considerably rebuilt during the peace talks.

The Enemy Threat—December 1972

The air defenses that Linebacker II forces were called upon to penetrate were formidable. There were 32 operational SA-2 sites and 6 confirmed SAM operating areas in North Vietnam. These sites provided defensive coverage in and around the Hanoi/Haiphong complex as well as along the northwest and northeast rail lines. Defensive peripheries were also based in the Thanh Hoa,

TACAIR ASSETS—DECEMBER 1972

BASE	TYPE AIRCRAFT	NUMBER
Takhli	F-111	48
Udorn	F-4	99
	RF-4	18
Korat	F-4C (Wild Weasel)	6
	F-4E	24
	F-105G	23
	EB-66	17
	A-7	72
Ubon	F-4	111
Nam Phong	F-4 (Marine)	27
	Total	455

SAC B-52 ASSETS—DECEMBER 1972

BASE	TYPE AIRCRAFT	NUMBER
Andersen-Guam	B-52G	99
	B-52D	53
Utapao	B-52D	54
	Total	206

Table 3. TACAIR and SAC Order of Battle, 18 December 1972

Vinh, and Dong Hoi areas (see Figure 8).[16] Approximately 2300 SAMs and some 200 launchers were scattered within the Red River Valley area.[17] The North Vietnamese had replaced SAM assets expended during Linebacker I throughout October and November. Over two thousand SAMs had been photographed by reconnaissance arriving from China on the rail system.[18] The other major NVN air-defense asset was their 145 MIG fighters. Table 4 indicates their types and bases. The majority of the fighter aircraft assigned to defend the Hanoi area were located at Phuc Yen, Gia Lam, Yen Bai, and Kep airfields.[19]

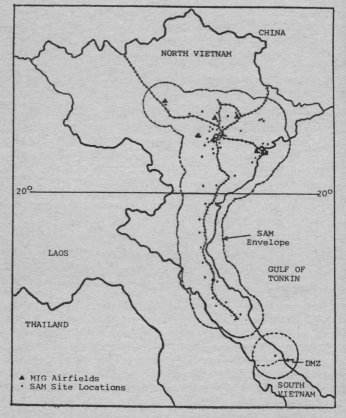

Figure 8. North Vietnam SAM Threat Areas, 1972

NVN MIG ASSETS—DECEMBER 1972

NVN BASE	MIG-21	MIG-19	MIG-15/17	TOTAL
Dong Suong	13			13
Gia Lam	4	2	5	11
Hoa Lac	2	3		5
Kep	4	3	27	34
Kien An			4	4
Phuc Yen	8	4	8	20
Quan Lang	1			1
Yen Bai	7	28	22	57
Total	39	40	66	145

Table 4. NVN MIG Order of Battle, 18 December 1972

The Linebacker II Plan

The planners of Linebacker II would have to overcome the formidable North Vietnamese air-defense system during both day and night bombing operations. The USAF daily attacks were divided into two distinct, highly compressed operations: a daylight force comprised solely of Tacair F-4 and A-7 strike aircraft, and a nighttime force that incorporated F-111 strikes with B-52 sorties. The night B-52 strikes and daylight Tacair strikes would include separate, complementary support packages.[20] Naval Tacair strikes around Haiphong were to be coordinated with USAF strikes.

The daylight Tacair strikes would consist of F-4 and A-7 aircraft with delivery tactics and ordnance tailored to the specific target and weather conditions. F-4 LORAN-equipped Pathfinders would provide target acquisition in limited or poor visibility for delivery of unguided bombs by non-LORAN-equipped F-4s or A-7s. F-4s equipped with laser-guided bombs were scheduled to accompany the strike force every day. Target weather permitting, the LGB bombers would strike high-priority targets with pinpoint accuracy to avoid collateral damage.[21] Support for the daytime strikes was to mimic that employed during Linebacker I. To optimize tactics and highlight problems during the new offensive, the daily

Linebacker conferences would be reinstituted by Tacair units.[22]

The B-52 tactics at night were to be basically the same as those used in Arc Light operations. To prevent optical or visual tracking by SAM sites and to reduce the effectiveness of MIG fighter attacks, all sorties were scheduled during darkness. The bombers would fly above 32,000 feet, to place the force well above the heaviest AAA concentrations.[23] Unfortunately, the SA-2 was specifically designed to shoot down aircraft at those altitudes. To minimize exposure to SAMs deployed in the target area, almost all of the routes approached from the west and northwest (Figure 9). These entry routes would take advantage of the high prevailing tail winds and coincide with two chaff corridors that would help blind the enemy radars. The actual axis of attack was based upon orientation of the target, availability of radar-bombing aim points, proximity of targets to population centers, and enemy defenses.[24] The B-52s would fly in the standard three-ship cells with two-to-three-minute spacing between cells. The bombers were grouped into three waves each night, with approximately four hours between waves to provide the psychological impact of a sustained bombardment. Each wave would enter and leave the target areas on approximately the same tracks every night.[25] After bomb release, each cell would make a steep 100-degree post-target turn (PTT) away from the target, to escape the area as soon as possible, and exit on a track to the west and southwest (Figure 10).[26] The B-52 aircrews were also ordered not to maneuver to avoid SAMs or MIGs from the initial point (IP) on the bomb run to the target bomb-release point, a period of about four to five minutes. Such maneuvers (called TTRs, for their effect against target tracking radars) were prohibited to ensure that the bombers maintained mutual, overlapping ECM support and to prevent midair collisions over congested target areas. The final reason for the restriction was political: it would permit maximum aiming time on the radar target, increasing the probability of target destruction and reducing the chances of civilian damage.[27]

The first night's sorties would consist of 54 B-52Gs and 33 B-52Ds from Guam, plus 42 B-52Ds from Utapao.

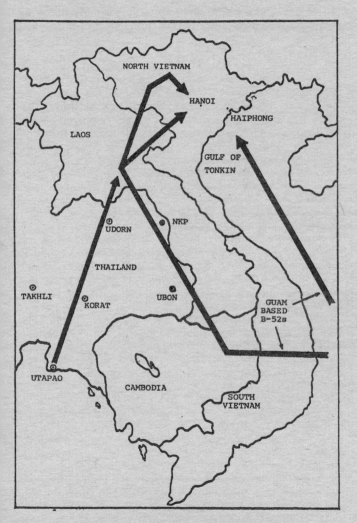

Figure 9. Linebacker II B-52 Attack Routes

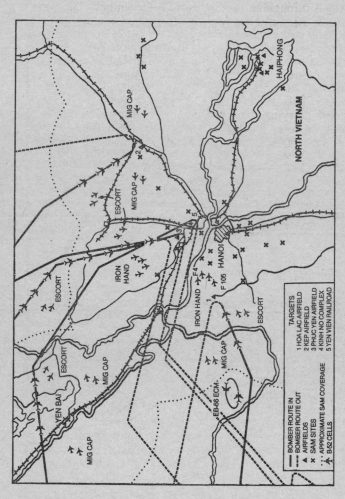

Figure 10. Typical B-52 Wave Attack, Days 1–3

The 129 aircraft were to attack military targets in three waves throughout the night of 18 December. The waves of 48, 30, and 51 B-52s, respectively, were divided into cells to strike individual targets. All B-52s operating from Utapao were D models, while Anderson AFB in Guam had both D and G models assigned.[28] The D models had undergone a ''Big Belly'' modification which enabled them to carry up to eighty-four 500-pound bombs internally. This modification, combined with the external bomb-carrying capacity on wing pylons, allowed it to carry a total of 108 500-pound bombs. The newer G models carried only 27 bombs internally.[29] All B-52 models were equipped with powerful ECM packages, but the B-52Ds and one-half of the B-52Gs had recently been modified with enhanced ECM equipment.[30]

To minimize B-52 losses, 39 Tacair craft would accompany each of the three waves.[31] Since the targets and bomber routes were selected by SAC planners, Tacair support had to be planned according to a known frag schedule. Therefore, to be effective, each B-52 strike and its support craft had to be precisely timed and executed. Eight F-4 chaff bombers would dispense clouds of radar-reflective chaff in planned corridors to mask B-52s from enemy radars during their bomb runs. Eight F-105G or F-4C Wild Weasels would accompany the first two waves of B-52s to detect and suppress enemy SAM sites attempting to bring their SAMs to bear on the strike force. Due to the Air Force's shortages of Wild Weasels and its inability to satisfactorily support a force stretched over twelve hours, Navy A-6As would provide SAM suppression for the third wave each night. ECM support was to be provided by three EB-66s which, from orbits west of Hanoi, would detect and jam enemy radar. Also, ten F-4 escorts would accompany the bombers through the threat area, and an additional ten MIGCAP F-4s would roam the areas of likely MIG activity to stop North Vietnamese interceptors before they could attack the bomber force. Finally, F-111s were to provide airfield suppression strikes against Yen Bai, Hoa Lac, Phuc Yen, Kep, and Bac Mai airfields just prior to B-52 strikes.[32] Throughout Linebacker II the F-111s were individually targeted and executed as single-strike sorties against air-

fields, SAM sites, power plants, ports, and radio facilities. They would enter the target areas at low level and
make a single high-speed pass while dropping a load of
twelve bombs. They would then leave the target area at
high speed, remaining at low level. The F-111s would
strike throughout the night, bracketed by the waves of
B-52 strikes with their associated support aircraft.[33]

Tacair Response to SAC Planning

Most of the personnel assigned to the Tacair bases in
Thailand did not even remotely suspect that a new offensive was being planned until the day before the first missions.[34] When the aircrews were notified, they reacted
on one hand enthusiastically in supporting an all-out
maximum effort against the North Vietnamese as a means
of bringing the war to an end and getting the POWs released. On the other hand, the Tacair aircrews had a sense
of apprehension, since they knew that the USAF attacking forces would be matched against a newly rebuilt and
capable air-defense system.[35] Throughout 17 and 18 December, the Tacair planners organized the forces to support the day and night efforts. One of the most difficult
aspects was the fact that the support aircraft used to cover
the B-52 strikes had to recover to their home stations and
then be regenerated to support the daylight Tacair
strikes.[36] A great deal of controversy also surfaced over
the intended SAC-planned tactics. Although Linebacker I had taught us to avoid stereotyped tactics which aided
enemy defenses, it became apparent that the SAC planners had not paid any attention to many of the lessons
learned during Linebacker I. The SAC tactics appeared
to violate two basic tenets of warfare: attacks would be
made piecemeal, by using three distinct waves over a
single target area; and, worse, they would originate from
the same points, since all of the B-52 cells flew basically
the same paths and altitudes.[37] These tactics gave advantages to the enemy since they would quickly note the
obvious, then adjust their SAM, AAA, and MIG defenses
to take into account known flight paths and altitudes of
the U.S. forces. A number of the fighter pilots assigned
escort duties were unhappy since they would share the

risks of repeatedly flying the same routes.[38] Their apprehensions were justified, as the execution phase of Linebacker II would show.

Tacair Preparations

Throughout 17–18 December intense activity took place at every Tacair base in Thailand to prepare for the new air offensive. Maintenance units brought as much equipment as possible to an "operationally ready" (OR) status by the 18 December deadline.[39] The Director of Operations staffs worked feverishly to match aircrew scheduling with the SAC frag. The tentative frag called for four complete strike/support packages per day (one Tacair day and three B-52 night attacks). This diverse schedule called for aircrews and flight leads to be continuously available for several days at a time.[40] The tactics sections at each tactical fighter wing quickly developed the necessary plans to support the B-52 waves. Planning for Tacair daylight support was easily resolved, since all missions would be flown using the same tactics as during Linebacker I.[41]

Support for the B-52s was tailored to minimize, as much as possible, the problems associated with flying at night and stretching the support capabilities over the long period of time required for the multiwave attacks. As mentioned earlier, support packages would consist of 8 F-4 chaff bombers, 8 F-105G/F-4C Wild Weasels, 10 F-4 escorts, 10 MIGCAP F-4s, and 3 EB-66s for the electronic role. In addition, 15 to 33 F-111 missions preemptive or pinpoint target strikes were planned for each night.

CHAFF SUPPORT

The 8 chaff bombers would sow two chaff corridors, each by a single flight of 4 F-4s (Figure 11). This would create an approach and departure corridor five to six nautical miles wide and forty miles long.[42] The chaff would be dispensed at 36,000 feet to correspond with the altitudes planned for the B-52 routes.[43] For maximum screening, the B-52 cells had to be within the chaff clouds both in azimuth and elevation as seen by the enemy ra-

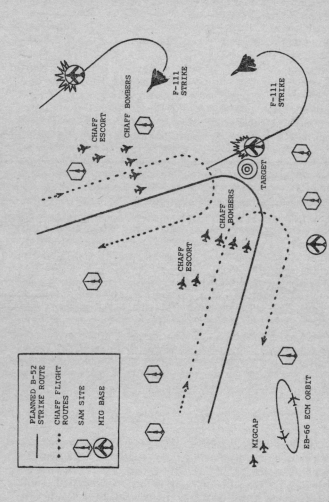

Figure 11. Typical Linebacker II Night Strike preparation effort. F-111 and chaff flights were flown about 10 to 15 minutes prior to B-52 TOTs

dars. A common misconception among aircrews was the assumption that aircraft could be screened either above or behind chaff clouds. This was not true, because chaff clouds are not solid targets; part of the radar energy penetrates the cloud and is reflected from an aircraft back to the radar. The aircraft and chaff must be within the same radar resolution cell in order to be reflected as a single target. Resolution is a measure of a radar's ability to separate targets into individual returns that are close together in some aspect of range, azimuth or elevation. A resolution cell is determined primarily by pulse width, or time between radar transmissions, and is the ability of the radar to separate two targets in close proximity (such as chaff clouds and aircraft). A pulse in free space occupies a physical distance equal to the time of the pulse in microseconds multiplied by the speed of light (984 feet per microsecond). If two targets are closer together than one half of this physical distance, then the trailing edge of a reflected pulse does not completely leave the first target before the arrival of the leading edge of the pulse reflected by the second target. This constitutes the area of a resolution cell, and any two targets within this area will register as only a single large target to the tracking radars. If the aircraft was greater than one radar resolution cell distance above the chaff corridor, it would be displayed on the enemy's elevation scope as a clean target above or behind the chaff.[44] For these reasons it was extremely important to know the exact planned tracks of the B-52 force, otherwise the narrow chaff corridor would not be in the positions required to screen the attacking forces.

WILD WEASEL SAM SUPPRESSION SUPPORT

Although the Wild Weasel Hunter-Killer teams worked extremely well under visual flight rule (VFR), daytime conditions, the same operations at night over undercast were, initially, not considered to be practical. The weather over the RP 6 areas during Linebacker II was expected to include thick undercast, ranging from 3000 to 8000 feet.[45] Since the most effective use of the Hunter-Killer teams required visual strikes on SAM sites, the thick undercast above the threat zones forced the 388th TFW planners to revert to the Iron Hand (F-105Gs or F-4Cs only) alternative for SAM suppression measures. Iron Hand was the code-name used to designate Wild Weasel flights of four F-105G or F-4C aircraft. The main difference between Iron Hand and Hunter-Killer teams was the inability of Iron Hand flights to follow-up Weasel anti-radiation missile attacks with Cluster Bomb Unit attacks of the SAM sites by F-4 aircraft. Subsequently, the procedure was developed wherein the Iron Hand aircraft would escort the B-52 strike forces in very close proximity with a great deal of premission coordination so that the Weasels could position themselves with regard to the known ground threat and the flight path and timing of the B-52s.[46] The Weasels set up an orbit racetrack-pattern alongside the route planned for the B-52s. The legs of the orbit were timed so that two Weasels would always be headed into the target area while two were outbound. So there were always Wild Weasels pointing toward the highest threat and ready to attack any SAM sites using radars to acquire the attacking forces.[47]

ESCORT AND MIGCAP SUPPORT

The F-4 escort formations from Korat and Udorn were to follow behind, below, and slightly offset from the B-52s; that is, in the position a MIG would have to reach for a successful Atoll launch.[48] The Soviet Atoll missile was an imitation of the U.S. AIM-9 Sidewinder infra-red seeking missile. The communists had stolen several copies of early AIM-9 missiles from friendly countries to which the U.S. had supplied them, and had virtually copied the design. The copies were reasonably effective, but shorter ranged than the U.S. versions. Its typical effective range was about a mile and a half from a stern attack position against a target with a jet engine exhaust. Since the B-52s were expected to fly between 35,000 and 40,000 feet, the escorts were to fly in radar trail, offset to the side at an altitude of about 25,000 feet. The escorts would fly five nautical miles in trail from the last B-52 in each cell to ensure against any possibility of an AIM-7 transferring to home-on-jam mode and homing in

on the B-52 jamming systems.[49] MIG attacks were anticipated as high-speed snap-up maneuvers from the rear.
To reach the Atoll envelope, the MIGs, in afterburner,
would have to position themselves in front of the F-4s,
making them very visible. The escorts could then launch
missiles on the MIGs. The escorts were assigned to protect multiple B-52 cells, following the first B-52 cell to
the target, then making a 180-degree turn outbound to
pick up and escort the next following cell to the target.
As was the case with the Iron Hand flights, this amounted
to an elongated racetrack orbit parallel to the B-52 run-
in.[50]

The tactics staff at Udorn decided that the best acceptable formations for the MIGCAP F-4s would be as flights
of two, with a Combat Tree equipped F-4 leading.[51] During November and December, new replacement aircraft
equipped with Combat Tree had arrived at Udorn, and
over twenty of the F-4s were available daily during Linebacker II.[52] In the two-ship flight the wingman would
attempt to fly a fighting wing position. The planners felt
that the wingman would help provide ECM coverage to
protect the flight, and his aircraft would provide a backup
fire-control system and missiles. If the wingman could
not remain in fighting wing at night, he would move back
to radar trail. If he lost the leader while in trail, he would
immediately leave the area and return to base. It was the
general feeling among 432d TRW aircrews that night
MIGCAP over North Vietnam against MIG-21s should
have been performed single ship with a Combat Tree aircraft. However, higher headquarters did not agree, because they did not want to risk the Combat Tree aircraft;
the decision to retain two-ship elements was upheld.[53]

EB-66 ECM SUPPORT

Since the EB-66s had only limited maneuverability to
avoid SAMs for self-protection, they were not allowed to
enter confirmed SAM-operating areas. Due to the two-
month bombing lull in RP 6, intelligence on SAM site
locations there was poor and inaccurate, so what had
been confirmed operating areas became suspect operating areas (the mobility of the SAM units allowed easy

relocation of any formerly confirmed sites). As the rules allowed the EB-66s to operate over suspected operating areas, three EB-66 aircraft were scheduled to orbit at a position forty nautical miles west of Hanoi to provide ECM support to the B-52s. Two of the EB-66s were to be primary, and the third would be assigned as a spare.[54]

Under the guise of an intense air effort in RP 1 and Laos, preparations to support Linebacker II continued until 18 December.[55] The disguise fooled hardly anyone involved in the preparations, since unusual security measures were in effect to prevent disclosure of the details of the planned operation. The fact that F-4 aircraft were being loaded with full complements of external fuel tanks and air-to-air weaponry pointed toward a renewed operation into the RP 6 areas.[56] Finally, on the afternoon of 18 December, the first sorties began launching from their bases in Thailand. Linebacker II had begun.[57]

Chapter Four

PHASE ONE:
THE FIRST THREE DAYS

The Bombers Go North Again—Day One

On the evening of 18 December 1972, the fighters scheduled for B-52 support rolled down the runways at Udorn, Ubon, Takhli, and Korat. The fighters took off at twelve-second intervals, until finally each base's commitment to the battle was reached. Additionally, Marine F-4s from Nam Phong took off and maintained an orbit over northern Laos to protect the tanker and EC-121 forces from MIGs. The tankers rendezvoused with the Air Force fighters over Laos to provide the extra fuel they needed to make it to Hanoi and back.[1]

At 1910 hours Hanoi time the first of sixteen F-111 fighter bombers scheduled to strike that night began hitting the five major MIG air bases scattered in the Red River Valley.[2] They penetrated North Vietnamese airspace using low-level high-speed dashes to their targets, relying on low altitude to evade enemy radars. The North Vietnamese had no warning of their attacks until the first bombs exploded on the runways. The surprise of the initial attacks was described by an F-111 pilot who flew on one of the earlier sorties on the night of 18 December:

The delta weather was way down, ceiling two hundred feet or thereabouts, and cloud piled up to 28,000 feet. The North Vietnamese, who long ago had turned the clock around, working at night and resting by day

91

because of day attacks, never expected anybody to hit them in such weather conditions. We came skiing down the mountains [crews called ground-hugging "skiing"] and plunged out into the open under the lower edge of the overcast, and it seemed to us the entire Hanoi valley was lighted up like Las Vegas. Hanoi was bright with neon and streetlights, and the port was aglow in the distance. On the roads leading out of town and on the mountain switchbacks to the south, truck headlights were blazing like strings of pearls. We happened to arrive about ten minutes to eight in the evening, Hanoi time. We were coming so fast, we were almost on release point before any of those lights started going out. Sections of the town blacked out one at a time, and we knew sirens were screaming and somebody down there was pulling master switches, even as the bombs left us.[3]

While the F-111s were busy attacking the MIG airfields, the rest of the support aircraft were taking up their positions. The EB-66s began orbiting in their assigned area while awaiting the arrival of the B-52s before turning on their systems. The EB-66 jammers would be turned on eight to ten minutes prior to when the first B-52 was scheduled to arrive over the target. This lead-time interval was considered sufficient to cover the in-bound B-52s and deny early enemy acquisition of the attacking force.[4] Similarly, the F-105G/F-4C Iron Hand flights and F-4 MIGCAP/Escort flights began flying their planned tracks to cover the B-52s (Figure 12). Approximately fifteen minutes prior to B-52 TOT, the Ubon chaff bombers began dispensing chaff at 36,000 feet to form the two chaff corridors. The aircrews observed numerous SAM firings in the target areas and reported tracking AAA that appeared to burst at the normal chaff-flight altitudes used on Linebacker I operations (15,000 to 16,000 feet). They also reported visual sightings of MIG aircraft using afterburners, which also appeared to be setting up their intercepts at the normal daytime chaff-flight altitudes.[5] It was apparent that the enemy was not expecting high-altitude B-52 attacks. At 1945 hours Hanoi time, the B-52s in Wave One began their attacks.[6] The first wave

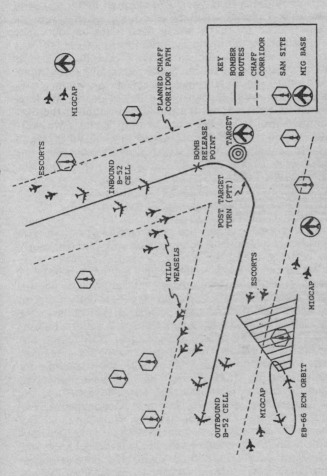

Figure 12. Typical Linebacker II Night Strike Package Plan (Days 1-3)

consisted of 48 B-52 aircraft targeted against the Kinh
No complex (18 B-52s), Yen Vien complex (9 B-52s),
Hoa Lac Airfield (6 B-52s), Kep Airfield (9 B-52s), and
Phuc Yen Airfield (6 B-52s).[7] Unfortunately, as the
B-52s entered the target areas, the prevailing 100-knot
northwest winds blew the chaff clouds out of the planned
corridors and the B-52s had to rely primarily upon their
own ECM to cope with the SAM threat.[8] That night, as
well as the following two nights, chaff was often not in
the proper position to protect the B-52 cells, due to vast
differences between the forecasted and actual winds encountered over the target areas.[9]

As the first wave of B-52s pressed on to attack the three
airfields at Phuc Yen, Kep, and Hoa Lac, history was
made by the gunner in Brown 03, a B-52D from Utapao.
For the first time in the war a B-52 gunner shot down an
enemy aircraft in combat. The gunner, SSgt. Samuel
Turner, described the engagement that night:

> It was a wild night, the sky was literally alive with
> SAMs. Just when we thought that we were back in a
> safe flying area, the electronic warfare officer said,
> "We've got something following us! It's a MIG!" I
> picked up the MIG-21 on my radar at about six miles
> back and closing fast. As the MIG closed in, I also
> locked on. While tracking the first MIG, I picked up a
> second enemy aircraft at 8 o'clock at a range of about
> 7½ miles. He appeared stabilized—not attacking us,
> obviously allowing the other fighter room to maneuver
> and complete his run first. As the MIG closed into
> firing range, I fired a burst, or what was really two
> quick bursts. I discovered later I had fired 690 rounds
> of ammunition at the MIG. There was a gigantic ex-
> plosion to the rear of our aircraft. I looked out the
> window, but couldn't see directly where the MIG would
> have been. Then, there was a secondary explosion and
> I lost the MIG's electronic signal and he had disap-
> peared from the scope. I knew I had hit him. Within
> fifteen seconds the remaining MIG broke away and I
> lost contact with him.[10]

Meanwhile, another attack was being made by the

B-52s from Guam against the Kinh No vehicle repair yards and the Yen Vien railroad yards. By then up to fifty SAMs had been fired at the attacking force, both in a barrage and guided mode. A B-52D, Lilac 03, was damaged by a SAM as it made its post target turn (PTT) after releasing its bombs over the Kinh No complex.[11] Major Billy Lyons, the aircraft commander and cell leader in Lilac 01, described the mission and situation over the target area:

At the aircraft, the survival gear, radios, and weapons were checked and double-checked. Our crew chiefs and ground-support specialists knew that something big was in the air. I thought I had seen maintenance troops hustling before to launch a sortie, but it was nothing compared to their efforts on this memorable day. As we taxied out, the crew chiefs of the aircraft on our parking row saluted and gave the thumbs-up sign as we passed by. After takeoff there was time to think about the mission—we were flying the first B-52 raid on Hanoi. Although we would penetrate far more known SAM sites than our crew did at Vinh, and be exposed to more MIG fighters, I had a great feeling of confidence that we would successfully accomplish our mission and return to Guam. We took on the scheduled 87,000 pounds of fuel from our first tanker and moved to our next tanker to fill out our 116,000 pound onload. We then flew across the northern part of South Vietnam and rendezvoused with the wave from Utapao exactly on schedule. From this point, we turned northwest and flew up the eastern portion of Laos before heading into North Vietnam. As we approached our initial point for the bomb run, we were able to hear a friendly radar site vectoring an F-4 against a MIG somewhere north of Hanoi. It was night by this time, and the F-4 pilot was relying on his radar and vectors from the ground radar site to get into firing position.

The sight as we turned over the IP inbound to our target is one I'll never forget. The red rotating beacons of the three-ship cell two minutes ahead of us stood out vividly against the dark night. We were entering the area of known SAM sites, and we started picking up visual [sightings of] SAMs being fired at our wave.

The F-111s were hitting the airfields, and our radar sites were picking up and informing us of the MIGs as they launched to engage the U.S. forces. The calls of visual SAM site guidance-radar lock-ons from our electronic warfare officer were almost constant now. The weather in the Hanoi area was overcast with low clouds, and we could see the bright glow through the clouds of SAMs being launched on either side of our bomb-run track. After the bright glow of the launch, the SAM would punch through the clouds and could be detected as a small, bright, pencil point of light as it approached our formation. Closer to the target area, a break in the clouds afforded us a view of the intense fire that was being thrown up at the aircraft over Hanoi. If you could take the largest Fourth of July fireworks display and multiply it one million times, you would have an idea of the scene as we approached the final portion of our bomb run. The SAM firings, although numerous, and in many cases in salvos of four at a time, had not presented a direct threat to our aircraft until about two minutes before bomb release. Suddenly my copilot yelled "Break left!" From having flown the Vinh missions with him, I knew he had a real reason for wanting me to break left. I rolled into a fifty-degree left bank and was able to move the aircraft just enough so that two SAMs headed directly at us in crossfire fashion from our right side missed us. After the SAMs passed by and exploded harmlessly some four or five thousand feet above our aircraft, I quickly returned the aircraft to our original heading while asking the radar navigator how our position was for release. The navigator and radar navigator downstairs seemed remarkably calm. They were unable to see outside the aircraft and view the spectacular fireworks. We discovered later that as we were evading the SAMs from our right side some two minutes before release, our number-three aircraft in the cell (Lilac 03) took a hit from a SAM from the left side that we never saw. Things were hectic after release as we broke to the west to head back to Laos. During the turn we were fired upon by several salvos of four SAMs at a time. Just as we would break in one direction to avoid a salvo, another firing of four missiles would come from the opposite side. The gunner who rides in the tail of the D-model was invaluable in directing our evasive action during and after the post-target maneuvers. He also reported that our number-three aircraft in the cell didn't make the post target turn to the west after bomb release but had continued south and was lost from the scope. After things settled down a bit we attempted contact with our number-three man. After several fruitless attempts by our cell and the wave leader, we could only assume he had been lost over the target area. Things were quiet as we headed south over Laos. Suddenly we heard a weak call from our number-three aircraft. They had taken a hit just prior to release and had been unable to make the post-target turn. The pilot informed us that all his fuel gauges were out and that they had taken a piece of shrapnel through the cockpit windows, resulting in glass in his left eye. His intention was to land at Utapao, which he did success-fully. We touched back down at Anderson AFB, Guam some 15½ hours after takeoff. Our mission to Hanoi on the first day of the ''Eleven Day War'' was my last mission as a SAC aircraft commander, and I can think of no more memorable way to have departed SAC.[12]

Meanwhile, just seconds to reaching the bomb-release point over the Yen Vien rail yards, B-52G Charcoal 01 was hit simultaneously by two SAMs. Less than a minute later the aircraft nosed down, crashed and exploded ten miles northwest of Hanoi. It became the first casualty of the Linebacker II operation. The crew had originally been scheduled to return home to Blytheville AFB, Arkansas, two weeks earlier. But due to a snowstorm, their replace-ment crew from Loring AFB, Maine, was too late in arriving to transition to a combat-ready status. So, in-stead of being safe at home, the crew of Charcoal 01 tragically met its fate over the skies of NVN. Lt. Col. Don Rissi, the aircraft commander, and MSgt. Walt Fer-guson, his gunner, lost their lives during the SAM deto-nation with their aircraft. The copilot, First Lt. Bob Thomas, is still listed as missing in action. The remain-ing three crew members—Major Dick Johnson (radar navigator), Capt. Bob Certain (navigator), and Capt.

Dick Simpson (electronic warfare officer)—successfully
ejected and became the first SAC POWs. Through the
course of the next eleven nights of combat, this crew's
fate would be shared in varying degrees by fourteen other
crews. [13]

TACAIR ACTIVITIES—WAVE ONE SUPPORT

In the meantime, the Tacair support aircraft were in-
tensely involved in defending Wave One. Judging the time
for their attacks on the scheduled B-52 arrival times
over their targets, the Wild Weasels expended all of
their AGM-45s preemptively against SAM sites and their
AGM-78s against active signals. [14] The numerous SAM
reactions against the B-52 forces saturated the Weasel's
capabilities, but they did succeed in warding off several
attacks. The lead Weasel flight provided this description
of the event:

> Tonto 01 (F-105G) led the force to the target via the
> land route from the southwest. There was heavy radar-
> controlled AAA in the area. Several SAMs were
> launched, and Tonto 01 expended a Shrike, thereby
> forcing the Fan Song [missile-guidance radar] to shut
> down in self-protection. The SAM, unguided after the
> Fan Song went down, harmlessly detonated away from
> the B-52s. Tonto 01 then returned to his initial point
> to escort in the second cell of B-52s. Again, as the
> B-52s entered the area, SAMs were fired. Again, Tonto
> expended a Shrike and protected the B-52s. [15]

The EB-66s providing jamming support in orbits forty
miles west of Hanoi were also experiencing problems.

> MIG warnings placed MIG-21s within five miles west
> of the flight, effectively pinning the flight between
> SAMs to the east and MIGs to the west. The flight
> remained on station and continued to provide ECM
> support for the B-52s while the MIGCAP tangled with
> the MIGs. The SAMs were a real threat, as the orbits
> were directly over a previously unknown SAM site. To
> provide maximum jamming support required straight

and level flight for a sustained period of time—[making the flight] an easy target for SAMs. Through the use of warning gear and visual sightings, a total of six SAM breaks were required by the flight that night.[16]

The F-4s assigned to provide escort coverage and make warning calls were also quite active. SAM launches were numerous, and the escorts reported that there was a tremendous amount of light from SAM booster engines, AAA tracers, and exploding warheads. As best they could, the escorts maintained their positions relative to the B-52s. As B-52 cells dropped their bombs and took up their departure headings, the F-4s turned back to cover the bombers' exit and position themselves to protect the next cell of B-52s. For up to fifteen minutes the crews held their positions while absorbing the intense SAM and AAA barrage. After the last bomber cell had safely released its ordnance, the F-4s finally departed.[17] Three of the escort flights reported MIG engagements. The first flight engaged two MIG-21 aircraft and fired two AIM-9Js. One of the AIM-9Js was believed to have struck one of the MIGs, but did not explode. A second flight engaged a single MIG-21 and was able to maneuver into a firing position with Red Crown vectors and Combat Tree equipment. The flight lead made four separate attempts to fire AIM-7s, but the missiles would not fire. Both of these MIG engagements took place at 15,000 feet or below. The third flight also engaged a MIG-21, but was unable to close to a firing position.[18]

ESCORT PROBLEMS

A number of problems surfaced during the Wave One attacks that were to be repeated throughout the offensive. The operation was characterized by the lack of initial planning and coordination with the SAC forces prior to the offensive. Rendezvousing and escorting the B-52s at night was made considerably more difficult for a number of reasons. The escorts were forced to maintain high altitudes at low airspeeds, where they could not effectively counter a high-speed MIG attack or have enough maneuverability to avoid SAMs.[19] Also, the exact B-52 approach routes were not always known, due to changes in TOTs. The only information provided to the escort aircrews was the B-52s' courses from the initial point (IP) to the target.[20] Therefore, the escort missions were flown based solely on timing, due to the fact that the crews were unable to maintain visual or radar contact with the B-52s at night. And, since the B-52s were jamming to defeat enemy radars, it was impossible for the fighters to use their on-board equipment to align themselves with the bomber cells. In many cases the visibility and the weather were such that it was difficult to maintain visual references off the B-52s, and then without very fine control from a ground-control intercept (GCI) radar, it was impossible to identify hostile aircraft that posed a threat.[21] But the friendly GCI controllers reported that the B-52 ECM activity also severely degraded their ability to guide the fighters to intercept North Vietnamese aircraft. The fact that the B-52s would turn off their IFFs prior to rendezvous and commence jamming activity very early in the mission, degraded the controlling agencies' ability to pass B-52 cell-position information to the F-4 escorts.[22] The B-52s did not use their IFFs, even though the escorts had identification equipment and could have identified them precisely at their rendezvous points.

Finally, the B-52s were not using the MIGCAP frequency, even though two ultra-high frequency (UHF) sets were available in the B-52s. This prevented warning them, calls that the "escorts were tied-on," and other coordination. The deficiencies were reported to SAC higher headquarters, but were answered with the comment that turning off the IFF systems and early jamming were valid requirements to reduce the B-52s' overall vulnerabilities.[24]

These procedures were also causing problems for the B-52 crews, which reported problems in knowing the exact locations of other aircraft in their cells and in determining if their escorts were in the proper positions. The tail gunners could not distinguish between friendly and enemy targets, and on two occasions escort F-4s were fired upon by B-52 gunners. The escorts attempted to solve the problem by staying out of the B-52 gun envelopes by avoiding the altitude at which the B-52s flew or whenever positive identification of the B-52 cells was possible.[25] Representatives from both the 388th and 432nd TFWs recommended that the escorts be discontinued and replaced with more MIGCAP flights. The requests were disapproved by 7th AF with the comment that Tacair would continue to provide escorts for the B-52s as per the agreement with SAC.[26]

DAY ONE—WAVE TWO ATTACKS

The Wave Two mission consisted of 30 B-52s from Guam targeted against the Kinh No complex (6 B-52s), the Yen Vien rail yards (18 B-52s), and the Hanoi rail yards (6 B-52s). The two Korat Iron Hand flights entered the threat areas and expended all their antiradiation ordnance, as was done for Wave One. The Ubon chaff flights and Udorn escorts reestablished the two chaff corridors, and six SAMs were fired at the flights without effect.[27] After midnight the second wave approached the target areas, using the exact same headings and altitudes as the first wave. One of the B-52G bombers in the first cell, Peach 02, was hit by a SA-2 just off the left wing as it performed its PTT maneuver after bomb release. A SAM site apparently was able to acquire a good lock-on of the bomber when all the aircraft in the cell presented a large radar cross-section to the site while performing the turn.[28] The Deputy Airborne Mission Commander in Wave Two that night, Lt. Col. Hendsley R. Connor, said:

I saw the SAMs as we came in closer to the target area. They made white streaks of light as they climbed into the night sky. As they left the ground they would move slowly, pick up speed as they climbed, and end their flight, finally, in a cascade of sparkles. There were so many of them it reminded me of a Fourth of July fireworks display. Just before we started our bomb run, we checked our emergency gear to make sure everything was all right in case we were hit. We would be most vulnerable on the bomb run, since we would be within lethal range of the SAMs and would be flying straight and level. We had been briefed not to make any evasive maneuvers on the bomb run, so that the radar navigator would be positive he was aiming at the right target. If he was not absolutely sure he had the right target, we were to withhold our bombs and then jettison them into the ocean on our way back to Guam. We did not want to hit anything but military targets. Precision bombing was the object of our mission. The crews were briefed this way, and they followed their instructions.

About halfway down the bomb run the EWO began to call over the interphone that SAMs had been fired at us. Four missiles had been fired. We flew straight and level. After bombs away, we began a right turn to exit the target area. Kaboom! We were hit. It felt like we had been in the center of a clap of thunder. The noise was deafening. Everything went really bright for an instant, then dark again. I could smell ozone from burnt powder, and had felt a slight jerk on my right shoulder. I called the lead aircraft to let them know we had been hit. He said he could tell we had been hit because our left wing was on fire and we were slowing down. I asked him to call some escort fighters for us.

The airplane continued to fly all right, so the pilot resumed making evasive maneuvers. We flew out of the range of the missiles, finally, and began to take stock of the airplane. The SAM had exploded right off our left wing. The fuel tank on that wing was missing along with part of the wing tip. We had lost number-one and number-two engines. Fire was streaming out of the wreckage they had left. Fuel was coming out of holes all throughout the left wing. Most of our flight instruments were not working. We turned on a heading that would take us to Utapao, Thailand. Two F-4s joined us and would stay with us as long as they were needed. One stayed high (to watch for MIGs) and the other stayed on our wing as we descended to a lower altitude. They called to alert rescue service in case we had to abandon the aircraft. Our first concern was to get out of North Vietnam and Laos. We did not want to end up as POWs. We knew they did not take many prisoners in Laos. We flew for about thirty minutes after we had descended to a lower altitude, and began to think we would be able to get the airplane on the ground safely. The fire in the left pod was still burning, but it didn't seem to be getting any worse. One F-4 left us. The other one said he would take one more close look at us before he, too, would have to leave. His fuel reserve was running low. He flew down and joined on our left wing. After a quick inspection, the F-4 pilot reported, "I'd better stay with you, friend. The fire is getting worse, and I don't think you'll make it." I unfastened my lap belt and leaned over between the pilot and copilot to take another look at the fire. It had now spread to the fuel leaking out of the wing, and the whole left wing was burning. It was a wall of red flame starting just outside the cockpit and as high as I could see. I said, "I think I'll head downstairs." [Lt. Col. Connor was riding in the jump seat behind the pilots, which was not equipped with an ejection seat. At that point the aircraft commander, Major Cliff Ashley, recommended that Connor should head downstairs for bailout.] The six crew members in the B-52G have ejection seats that they fire to abandon the aircraft. Anyone else on board has to go down to the lower compartment and manually bail out of the hole the navigator or radar navigator leaves when their seat is ejected [downward]. I quickly climbed down the ladder and started to plug in my interphone cord to see what our situation was. The red Abandon light came on. Bam! The navigator fired his ejection seat and was gone. The radar turned toward me and pointed to the hole the navigator had left and motioned for me to jump. I climbed over some debris and stood on the edge of the hole. I looked at the ground far below. Did I want to jump? The airplane began to shudder and shake, and I heard other explosions as the other crew members ejected. I heard another louder blast. The wing was exploding. Yes, I wanted to jump! I rolled through the opening, and as soon as I thought I was free of the airplane, I pulled the ripcord on my parachute.

I felt a sharp jerk and looked to see the parachute canopy above me. Everything was quiet and eerie. There was a full moon, the weather was clear, and I could see things very well. I looked for other parachutes. One, two, three, that's all I saw. Then I saw the airplane. It was flying in a descending turn to the left and the whole fuselage was now burning and parts of the left wing had left the airplane. It was exploding as it hit the ground.[29]

All seven members of the crew had successfully ejected near the Marine base at Nam Phong. The F-4 crew reported the coordinates of the bailout, and within twenty minutes all of the crew had been rescued by Marine helicopters. The next day all of the uninjured crew members were flown to Utapao and then on back to Guam.

The B-52 forces in Wave Two were fired upon by sixty-eight SAMs and had encountered heavy defensive reactions by numerous AAA sites. However, no MIGs were reported airborne during the wave. Cap. Kenneth Nocito, a B-52 EWO from Griffiss AFB, New York, recalls his vivid memories of the Wave Two strike:

The pre-IP was the point where we turned east into North Vietnam, started certain bomb preparation checklists, and picked up our fighter escort. It also was the point where we became vulnerable to the SA-2 and AAA sites. We could already hear the SAM launch calls from the aircraft that preceded us. Five minutes past this point my pilot said, "SAM launch, E.W. It's coming right at us." I had not picked up the radar signal yet, but I can guarantee that I put every possible jammer on the SAM frequency. It detonated in front and below us. Then I picked up the radar signal [of the active SAM site] as we saw more launches. We called our sightings to the other cells as they called theirs to us. The Hammer [Wild Weasel] aircraft were busy attempting to locate the sites and to fire their radar-homing missiles. Our gunner scanned the skies for MIGs. Except for the external SAM calls, I was oblivious to anything but my countermeasures systems. All of my jammers were active, but still they required constant tuning and monitoring.

We hit the IP about thirty miles from the target. At this point each of the three aircraft which were designated Cell Lead turned to head toward their target. As

Aqua 1, we led not only Aqua cell, but the two cells behind us, Red and Gold. As we looked down, there were fires everywhere. The cells ahead of us had already dropped their weapons or were in the process of doing so. And still the SAMs and AAA came. They were detonating all around us. I now had over fifty enemy radar signals on my scope. I had five different SAM radars up. At least one in each quadrant. The cockpit flashed each time a burst went off near us. I had more threat radars than jammers. And still they kept coming. Then the radar navigator called: "Five, four, three, two, one!"

Bombs away! Good! Stop release! Turn! We cranked into a sharp bank just as I picked up a SAM radar that was off my scope in intensity. The fighter escort called, "Aqua One, you have a SAM launch! You have three coming up!" [Note: Although the B-52 cells could not visually monitor their Tacair escorts, the escorts and bombers could communicate by radio, and certainly over the guard channel for SAM warnings.] We started evasive maneuvers in the turn and still they kept coming. The Hammer aircraft moved into position and fired his Shrike and still they kept coming! One passed below, but the other two streaked less than five hundred feet above us and detonated. Then all excitement broke loose as Hammer called "Lock-on! You got an Iron Hand, you got an Iron Hand!" He had destroyed the site. The SAM signals went off the air. We breathed easier. There were more SAM launches and AAA bursts, but we could now maneuver, and most important, we were heading home. As we passed the Terminate Countermeasures Point, I started to log the radars. Our wave had encountered sixty-eight SAMs, twenty-two against our cell. But we had survived. As soon as we landed, I would call home. I wanted them to know how much I missed them.[30]

Another significant problem surfaced during Wave Two: saturation of the primary B-52 SAC GCI frequency. Fighters and bombers were transmitting instructions without identifying themselves, which created confusion on the radios. Radio frequencies in the target area became saturated with transmissions concerning SAM, MIG, and AAA warnings.[31] The Brigham controlling agency recommended the use of the separate interplane frequency for other than necessary radio transmissions.[32]

DAY ONE—WAVE THREE

The third and last wave of Day One consisted of 51 B-52s (30 from Guam and 21 from Utapao). This wave was the largest raid of the first night, and the targets were Hanoi Radio (21 Utapao B-52s), the Hanoi rail yards (21 B-52s), and the Kinh No complex for the third time in a row (12 B-52s).[33] As in the previous two waves, the support packages performed their roles, with the only significant difference being that Navy Iron Hand aircraft had replaced the USAF Weasels for SAM suppression.

The 21 Utapao B-52s targeted against Radio Hanoi were within lethal range of 11 SAM sites. As a result, the formation came under the most intense SAM attacks of the first night, with at least fifty SAMs fired. No aircraft were hit until the last cell passed the target, when the cell leader, B-52D Rose 01, was hit while in a PTT at 38,000 feet.[34] The B-52, commanded by Capt. Hal "Red" Wilson, had not encountered any SAMs on the final approach to target. As the aircraft banked to the right during the PTT, Captain Wilson spotted two SAMs heading straight for the B-52. The first missile passed within feet of the aircraft but did not detonate, even though its proximity fusing was designed to do so at close-miss distances. However, the second SAM ripped a hole in the left side of the fuselage large enough for the radar navigator to see the fire on the number-three engine.

Despite the hit, the aircraft was still flyable. But the electrical system was knocked out, preventing Captain Wilson from getting a damage assessment from the crew. Meanwhile, a fuel line had ruptured in the forward part of the fuselage behind the cockpit and was dumping fuel into the crew compartment.

Electrical shorts from the ruined avionics immediately ignited the gushing JP-4 fuel, which burned rapidly out of control and spread toward the cockpit. Captain Wilson's first thoughts after the SAM impact had been to maintain control of the aircraft and to head toward the Gulf and out of the Hanoi area. But only thirty seconds had elapsed from the time of the hit to the raging fire in the bomber. The intense heat built up in the lower deck, where the navigator and the radar navigator (R.N.) were located, as well as the upper deck, where the communications gear was blowing up all around the E.W. Officer. The R.N. and EWO were apparently the first crew members to eject from the aircraft. As the flames reached the cockpit the pilots realized that they, too, had to leave. The copilot ejected first, but the low-pressure area caused by the blown hatch sucked the flames into the cockpit and burned Captain Wilson on the back of his neck and right side of his face. Four of the six crew members ejected safely, but the navigator and gunner were unaccounted for and presumed missing or killed in action. As Captain Wilson was free-falling in space before his parachute opened, he saw the B-52 explode into tumbling pieces. He and the other three members of his crew were taken prisoner soon after landing.[35]

Again it appeared that a post-target turn within radar "burn-through" range of numerous SAM sites contributed to the successful SAM engagement. Burn-through range is the point at which the SAM site's radiated power exceeds that of the aircraft's jamming power, and the site can "see through" the jamming and identify individual aircraft. Burn-through for a B-52 cell usually occurred at approximately ten miles, and was enhanced by the cells' increased radar cross-sections in the PTT maneuver, which turned the bombers broadside to the SAM radars.[36]

During the strike by eighteen B-52s from Guam against the Hanoi rail yards, B-52D Rainbow 01 was hit by a SAM just prior to bomb release. The cell was within burn-through range of six SAM sites at the time of the engagement. In spite of the damage, the crew pressed on to release their bombs. The aircraft successfully flew to Utapao and landed safely.[37] Wave Three had received the heaviest enemy opposition of the campaign, with at least 154 SAM firings and heavy AAA. In spite of the stiff opposition, only one aircraft was lost.

In the meantime, MIGs were active again during the Wave Three attacks. The F-4 MIGCAPs were having communication problems throughout the period with the controlling agencies on the primary MIGCAP frequency, and experienced difficulties with engaging the enemy. Mosby flight from Udorn had intermittent contact with Red Crown—the Navy cruiser providing radar surveillance from the northern part of the Gulf of Tonkin—but communications were good enough to allow Red Crown to give flight vectors on a MIG. The flight engaged the MIG, but due to further communications problems with Red Crown, the crews could not validate the radar target as hostile and were unable to fire when they got into position. The MIG turned and then fired at Mosby flight, disengaged, and then attempted an unsuccessful attack on an exiting B-52 cell. Spat flight, another Udorn F-4 escort element, also engaged a single MIG-21 using Red Crown vectors. The crews obtained a full system lock-on and fired four AIM-7 missiles. No hits were observed and the MIG escaped. Teaball control reported only one airborne MIG throughout Wave Three, and apparently both Mosby and Spat flights had engaged the same lucky MIG pilot.[38]

REFLECTIONS ON THE DAY ONE ATTACKS

The Day One B-52 attacks had revealed some serious weaknesses in planning and execution which would become even more evident in succeeding days. The overconfidence of the SAC planners to fly over the North Vietnamese air defenses in wave attack formations may have been due to their earlier successes over Haiphong during April. The lack of wider or more chaff corridors per wave prevented the B-52s from using the high tailwinds to their best advantage. The time required to support three consecutive wave attacks spread the chaff bomber and Iron Hand forces too thinly. The wave attacks also greatly aided the enemy air-defense system: the four-hour period between waves allowed the enemy time to reload SAM launchers and rearm MIGs. The high winds that aided the bombers to their targets were also blowing away their chaff protection, so that the B-52s had to rely primarily on their own jamming gear for protection. Furthermore, the steeply banked PTT put the B-52s head on into the hundred-knot winds, considerably slowing their retreat and diverting their main downward-directed ECM jamming beams away from many of the SAM radars. The diversion of the ECM patterns enabled those SAM sites with a broadside view of the B-52s to penetrate weak spots in the jamming barrage and lock-on to individual bombers within the cells. Even worse, the long bomber streams and the use of a single point for all PTTs in the attacking stream allowed the defenders to set up defenses on the turning point once it had been identified by the passage of the first cells.[39]

The North Vietnamese must have been incredulous as they watched each B-52 wave fly at the same altitudes, headings, and airspeeds into the target areas. Over two hundred SAMs had been fired at the attacking force, downing three B-52s and damaging two others, a $2\frac{1}{2}$ percent loss rate considered acceptable by SAC planners, who had expected even higher losses.[40] Of the first day's 129 planned sorties, 121 had been effectively flown over the major target areas. For these reasons, the raids planned for the second night were to be mirror images of the first night's attack.[41]

Some of the comments voiced by SAC crew members reflected the tension and excitement of the first night's air battle:

> . . . The straight scared reaction seemed more on the ground than on the way to the target. Once it really started happening and stuff started coming up at us, there was just no time to be scared. You were too busy all the way in.

> . . . Everything came so fast. We were in there, and it was really over with before we even knew it.

> . . . We were scared to death—especially when we saw the lines on the chart in Bomb-Nav on where we were going.

> . . . I didn't think we were going to lose any air-

planes, really. My first surprise was when they started calling for Charcoal 01 and couldn't raise him on the radio. We found out later he'd been shot down. We weren't so ready to go back the second night.

. . . Actually, a SAM is very pretty. When you see it—we were flying over a five-thousand- to six-thousand-foot cloud deck up there—you see a nice big red glow. Then you see a real bright white light, and you just follow the light.

. . . On the first night, the copilot had never seen any SAMs. We came driving down the bomb run and he reported one coming at us and told the pilot to maneuver. It turned out that it was just a star that had been up all along. The pilots kept seeing the damn thing and thinking it was a SAM, and it was just some star floating out there in space.[42]

The only Tacair casualty on Day One was F-111 Snug 40. The aircraft had been scheduled to strike the Hanoi International Radio Communication (RADCOM) Transmitter at 0853 hours, Hanoi time. The last radio-call contact was received by an orbiting Moonbeam C-130 command-and-control aircraft at 0854 hours after bomb release on target.[43] No trace was ever found of the aircraft, and the crew is still listed as MIA.

Day Two Attacks

DAY TWO—TACAIR STRIKES BEGIN

The weather over North Vietnam during the daylight hours greatly influenced the schedules for the Tacair TOTs. The vast majority of the daytime attacks were scheduled between 1200 and 1500 hours, because that was when the weather was most favorable to visual and laser-guided bomb operations in RP 6. There were no planned efforts to take advantage of brief periods of favorable weather at times other than scheduled, because LGB pods were still in short supply and the Tacair priority to support the night B-52 strikes limited the options for generating additional daytime sorties.[44]

On 19 December the Tacair strike force was composed of twenty A-7Ds from Korat accompanied by LORAN-equipped F-4s from Ubon. Their target was the Yen Bai Airfield. Whenever the weather allowed, the A-7s would attack visually throughout the campaign. If the weather was poor, the LORAN F-4s would drop their bombs and direct the A-7s to pickle at the same time. In addition to the main strike force of A-7s, F-4s from Ubon were scheduled to attack other targets simultaneously. Ten F-4 LGB bombers were scheduled against the Hanoi railroad station and thermal power plant. Thirty-two LORAN-led F-4s were scheduled to drop "dumb bombs" on the Hanoi RADCOM and Transmitter number-2 site.[45] The strike forces were accompanied by the same numbers of support aircraft, using the same tactics, as during Linebacker I. Due to the heavy overcast over the target areas, the LGB flights were canceled and all A-7 and F-4 bombers had to bomb using LORAN guidance. No battle damage assessment (BDA) was possible due to the poor visibility.[46] Despite the fact that the attacks were conducted over high-threat areas, the air-defense responses to the fighter-bomber attacks were negligible. It was obvious that the North Vietnamese intended to save their best efforts for the night B-52 attacks.

DAY TWO—B-52 OPERATIONS RESUME

For Day Two some minor variations were made in the B-52 tactics. Because of the heavy SAM reactions of the night before, B-52 base altitudes were lowered to between 34,000 and 35,000 feet, to better correspond with the chaff corridors laid by the F-4s at 36,000 feet.[47] A request by SAC to lay corridors at altitudes higher than 36,000 was rejected by the 8th TFW commander because the flights dispensing chaff at 36,000 feet were already 8000 to 10,000 feet above the F-4's service ceiling in the chaff configuration; this required considerable use of the afterburner, allowing easy visual contact of the chaff aircraft by North Vietnamese defenders.[48] Another change in tactics concerned TTR maneuvers during the bomb run. Several B-52 aircrews had performed evasive maneuvers to avoid SAMs on Day One despite orders to the contrary. On Day Two the SAC Wing Commander threatened to court-martial any aircraft commander who knowingly disrupted his cell's integrity to evade SAMs.[49] Although the B-52s in Day Two, Wave One followed this direction, the order was changed for all follow-on attack waves because analyses by targeteers had shown that not as much time was required as initially thought to make last-minute refinements during the bomb runs. Therefore, aircraft were allowed to perform target-tracking-radar (TRR) maneuvers from the IP to target, provided they maintained cell formation and were straight and level prior to the bomb-release point.[50]

On Day Two 93 B-52s were scheduled to attack in three waves of 21, 36, and 36 aircraft.[51] Thirty-three F-111s once again went in ahead of the B-52s, to attack MIG airfields and communications facilities.[52] The support packages were composed of the same forces as during the previous night.

DAY TWO—WAVE ONE

Wave One consisted of 12 B-52Ds and 9 B-52Gs out of Guam. The target was once again the Kinh No complex. During the attack, about sixty SAMs were sighted, but no B-52s were lost or damaged.[53] The 4 Udorn MIGCAP F-4s again reported poor communications on the MIGCAP primary frequencies. There were no MIG engagements during Wave One, but one MIGCAP flight reported 15 SAMs had been ripple-fired at them.[54] The Iron Hand F-105Gs were furiously engaged in combatting SAMs. Their efforts were described by Colonel McCarthy, who was in the lead bomber during the Wave One attack:

About ten seconds prior to bombs away, when the E.W. was reporting the strongest signals, we observed a Shrike being fired, low and forward of our nose. Five seconds later several SAM signals dropped off the air and the E.W. reported they were no longer a threat to our aircraft.

The BUFF [Big Ugly Fat Fellow, that is, B-52] began a slight shudder as the bombs left the racks. The aircraft, being relieved of nearly twenty-two tons of ordnance, wanted to raise rapidly, and it took a double handful of stick and throttles to keep it straight and level. After the release was complete and the bomb doors closed, Tom Lebar [aircraft commander] put the aircraft in a steep turn to the right. A second later a SAM exploded where the right wing had been. The turn had saved us, but the gunner and copilot reported more SAMs on the way.

We completed the turn and started our maneuver as the SAMs reached our altitude, but they did not explode. One on the left and another on the right seemed to form an arch over the aircraft. As they approached each other at the apex of the arch, they exploded. We saw another Shrike missile launched, and again some of the threat signals disappeared. Those F-105 Wild Weasel troops from the 388th Tactical Fighter Wing were earning their pay tonight.[55]

DAY TWO—WAVE TWO

The second wave of 21 B-52Gs from Guam and 15 B-52Ds from Utapao were targeted against the Bac Giang transshipment point and the Hanoi radio station. Over 58 SAMs were launched at the wave, and this time some scored hits.[56] Hazel 03, a B-52G, received damage from a SAM missile approximately thirteen miles from the bomb-release point. The cell was nine miles off its intended inbound track, had lost its cell integrity for mutual ECM support, and also possessed a number of inoperative jamming transmitters.[57] Despite all these factors causing a near shootdown, Hazel 03 ended up being the only G model to sustain damage and not be forced down.[58] Ivory 01, a B-52D three cells behind Hazel, experienced major damage approximately ten seconds after bomb release as it initiated its PTT. All aircraft in the cell had maintained good integrity throughout the bomb run, but during the PTT Ivory 01 was broadside to SAM site VN-549.[59] The SAM detonation caused aircraft control difficulties as well as engine malfunction. The aircraft was commanded by Major John C. Dalton, whose crew had led the first cell across the target the night before. Extensive damage, including fire in the number-six engine, forced the crew to shut down engines five, six, and seven. Major Dalton nursed the crippled aircraft back over Thailand and managed a difficult landing at the small Marine airfield at Nam Phong, Thailand. Major Dalton provided the following recollection of the mission:

> On our second night, our target was Hanoi Radio. The mission was going fairly smooth until approximately sixty seconds before bomb release. The EWO got a lock-on and then detected the SAM on its way about ten seconds after our release, which placed us in a forty-five-degree-bank angle post-target turn. No one on the crew saw the SAM until it detonated while we were still in the turn. The gunner estimated the detonation occurred at some fifty to a hundred feet off our tail. We experienced aircraft control difficulty as well as engine malfunction, and later learned that the rudder cable and right elevator-control cable had been severed, in addition to fragments and holes throughout the aircraft. Just after we rolled out of the turn, the gunner saw another SAM coming at us, which called for an evasive turn in the opposite direction—that one went well above us and detonated. Returning to level flight, we analyzed our equipment losses and did some praying on the way back. We had fourteen aircraft behind us, and it was a great feeling to know we had not lost anyone in that wave. Approximately eight hours after we had landed at Nam Phong, a C-130 picked us up and flew us back to Utapao.[60]

Major Dalton's crew was placed in crew rest and would fly again on the fourth night.

DAY TWO—WAVE THREE

The last wave mission on Day Two consisted of 36 B-52s, with 15 B-52Ds and 6 B-52Gs from Guam, and 15 B-52Ds from Utapao. The targets were the Yen Vien complex (9 B-52Ds) and the Thai Nguyen thermal power plant (TPP), thirty-one miles north of Hanoi (27 B-52s).

During this wave only a small number of SAMs were fired at the B-52s, and none of the attack forces sustained damage.[61] As in the case of waves One and Two, no MIGs were sighted or reported during Wave Three.[62] The light damage and no losses incurred during Day Two may have created a false sense of confidence to the SAC planners, and set the stage for a disaster on Day Three. Since over 180 SAMs had been launched at the Day Two forces without causing losses, the decision was made to fly the Day Three mission using the same attack plan as on days One and Two.[63]

Day Three Attacks

DAY THREE—TACAIR STRIKES

As on Day Two, a total of 20 A-7s were scheduled to strike Yen Bai Airfield at approximately 1230 hours Hanoi time. Due to poor weather conditions, no LGB bombers were scheduled. However, 54 F-4s from Ubon were assigned to strike the Hanoi transformer and Lang Truoc RADCOM facilities using LORAN guidance.[64] The Yen Bai Airfield was restruck due to its proximity to the inbound B-52 routes at night. The airfield was located seventy miles northwest of Hanoi, and it supported a number of MIG-17s and MIG-21s. The strikes were a virtual repeat of the previous day, and no battle damage assessment was noted due to undercast over the target areas.

Tactical reconnaissance support of Linebacker II began on Day Three. Although two RF-4C sorties had been scheduled for Day Two to obtain post-strike photography, the missions had to be canceled due to maintenance problems. On 20 December the mission was expanded to three aircraft to provide an airborne spare. Tactics used during Linebacker II were to be similar to those of previous missions into highly defended areas, with the one exception: for several reasons, the RF-4Cs would not be fragged with fighter escorts. The first was that the MIGCAPs had been quite successful in negating MIG attacks on the post-strike RF-4s; without their heavily loaded escorts, the RF-4s could operate at higher airspeeds and decrease exposure time; the other F-4s were being heavily tasked in supporting the rest of the Linebacker II frag, so reconnaissance aircraft were committed in flights of two RF-4s over the high-threat areas throughout the offensive. Nine daily missions were scheduled, and by the end of Linebacker II, the recces had flown eighty-one successful missions into the heartland of North Vietnam.[65]

DAY THREE—B-52 WAVE ONE

As on the previous two nights, the attack was centered around three waves of B-52s, for a total of 99 bomber aircraft. Wave One consisted of 18 Guam-based aircraft (6 B-52Ds and 12 B-52Gs) and 15 B-52D models from Utapao. Again, 33 F-111s were scheduled to strike airfields, RADCOM sites, and the Bac Giang thermal power plant. The initial B-52 target was the Hanoi railroad repair facility. Although the 6 B-52Ds from Guam assigned to bomb this target came within burn-through ranges of 11 SAM sites, only 4 SAMs were fired and no losses or damage were incurred.[66] Apparently the NVN forces were allowing the initial cells through to establish the stereotyped route for the wave. The 27 B-52s following the initial cells were targeted against the Yen Vien railroad yard and adjacent Ai Mo warehouse area, and they encountered very intense SAM firings. At least 130 SAMs were launched at the wave.

Quilt cell, which had two B-52Gs with unmodified ECM, led the attack and was engaged by sixteen missiles. Besides the handicap of their unmodified ECM equipment, Quilt 01 and Quilt 03 each lost two ECM transmitters just prior to the target run. Quilt 03 was hit by a SAM during the PTT and went down approximately five miles north of Hanoi.[67] Capt. Terry M. Gelonick, the aircraft commander, described the final mission of the doomed aircraft:

Our scheduled time over target was 2209 hours, local time in Hanoi. The weather was clear at our bombing altitudes of thirty-five to thirty-six thousand feet, but the ground was obscured by cloud layers, the tops of which were predicted at eight thousand feet. We turned in a northwesterly direction and entered Laos, paralleling the country of North Vietnam. While we were to maintain radio silence unless we needed fighter support, the activity in the target area was beginning to heat up. We could hear Red Crown issue numerous SAM and MIG warnings to friendly aircraft, and hear our fighter guys reply "engaged" each time an enemy aircraft was spotted. The only outside activity we could see was the rotating beacons on top of Quilt 01 and 02. Leaving these lights on as an aid to formation flying was recommended by pilots from days One and Two, since MIGs hadn't been a problem and the weather was low overcast. Naturally, in case of approaching MIGs, we would turn them off.

We turned east and entered North Vietnam just above the infamous Thud Ridge, heading southeast down the Red River Valley toward Hanoi. At this point we began to see several black explosions, indicating AAA, but none was close to the cell and [all were] considerably below us. So far, so good. Approaching the initial point, where we began our bomb run, we picked up the first SAM signals, reported by the E.W., Captain Craig Paul. At the direction of the cell leader in Quilt 01, all aircraft began a series of maneuvers, called "TTR" for their effect against the SAM target-tracking radars. Such maneuvers made the aircraft more difficult to track and also increased the crew's ability to visually spot SAMs. Bombers on the first two days of raids weren't allowed to maneuver after the IP and until the bombs were dropped—another change instituted after the first two days. The only time we had to be straight and level was about twenty to thirty seconds prior to release, for the bombing system gyros to stabilize and provide an accurate bombing platform. Past the IP now, we continued to maneuver while the R.N. and navigator calmly ran through their checklist, throwing switches, identifying aiming points on their radar scopes, and preparing to release our twenty-seven 750-pound bombs. So unhurried and calm were their voices on the interphone, one would have thought we were on a stateside practice mission. Both were truly professionals, doing a job they had been trained to do expertly. About halfway between the IP and target, the E.W. said that SAMs had been fired at us. I continued to maneuver as the bomb-bay doors were opened one minute prior to bombs away by the R.N., and then I saw them! Breaking through the overcast, the SAMs' rocket exhausts burned in a bright circle, and I could see three or four of them. Even though they generally zigzagged on their upward flight, we had been briefed that if a SAM was tracking our aircraft, it would maintain its same relative position on the cockpit windows. At least two were following this pattern, and I attempted to watch them as best I could while continuing to maneuver.

The R.N. piped up, "Pilot, we're thirty seconds out, maintain straight and level." I replied, "Roger, radar, I'm rolling out." At about fifteen seconds to go, a SAM streaked by just off our left wing, so close its exhaust illuminated the entire cockpit. For some reason its proximity fuse failed to detonate, because it certainly was close enough! The R.N. began his countdown as we continued to fly straight and level. "Ten seconds to go. Five. Four. Three. Two. One. *Bombs Away!*" The aircraft shuddered slightly as the bombs were released from their racks in the bomb bay. I rolled the giant aircraft into a hard right turn to depart the area as the R.N. closed the bomb-bay doors. We had been turning about ten seconds when . . . WHAANG! We were hit. The loud metallic bang of the exploding SAM hit us like a huge rock, accompanied by a bright white flash. The control column was thrown violently forward, but snapped back. We were still flying, and I was able to keep the aircraft in the steep turn. The smell of burnt powder was evident. A quick check of the instrument panel indicated all engines were still operating and so far we were maintaining altitude. While completing the post-target turn, I began talking on the interphone, "Crew, pilot, we've been hit but are still flying okay. Nav, check on headings to a safe area and everyone report damage."

"Copilot [First Lt. Bill Arcuri] is okay, but it looks like we have a fuel leak in the left main [tank]. All

B-52D being prepared for a mission over North Vietnam.

B-52D refueling from a KC-135 tanker. B-52s assigned to Guam had to fly 11–12 hours and refuel twice to attack targets in North Vietnam and return to base.

The F-111 swing-wing bomber used terrain-following radar to penetrate enemy airspace at low altitudes, then used radar-bombing techniques to accurately place bombs at night or in bad weather.

Aircraft of the 388th Tactical Fighter Wing. The F-4E (left) and F-105G (center) are a hunter-killer team. The EB-66 is an electronic warfare aircraft.

Armed with Shrike and Standard Arm radar suppression missiles, a hunter-killer team F-105G refuels from a Strategic Air Command KC-135 tanker, while other elements of the team await their turn.

The A-7 had limited all-weather capability and was an accurate bombing platform. This one is from the 354th TFW.

A 388th TFW F-4E loaded with 6 MK82 500-lb. bombs, 4 cluster bomb units on the center-line racks, and 2 AIM-7 missiles.

An EB-66 Destroyer, an electronic countermeasure aircraft.

EC-121 early warning aircraft worked with the Navy's Red Crown radar-equipped cruiser to vector US fighters against MIGs.

The author, Lt. Col. Karl J. Eschmann, then as a 2nd lieutenant and an F-4E maintenance officer in the 388th Tactical Fighter Wing at Korat RTAFB in 1972–73.

The A-1E's long loiter capability and numerous weapons made it ideal as escorts for Search and Rescue HH-3s.

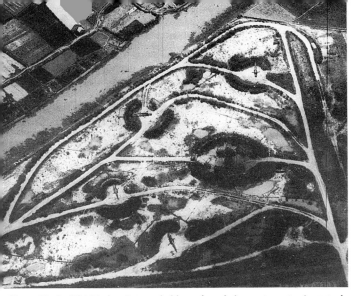

Above: Typical SAM site: 6 occupied launch pads in revetments. A central revetment contains radar and related equipment. *Below:* One of North Vietnam's 200 SAM sites, this one is empty and has been cultivated by an enterprising farmer.

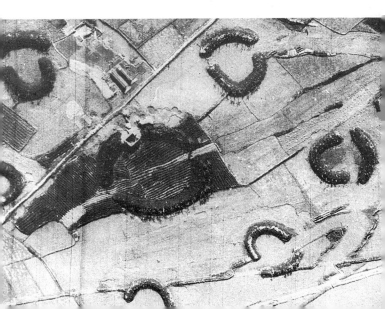

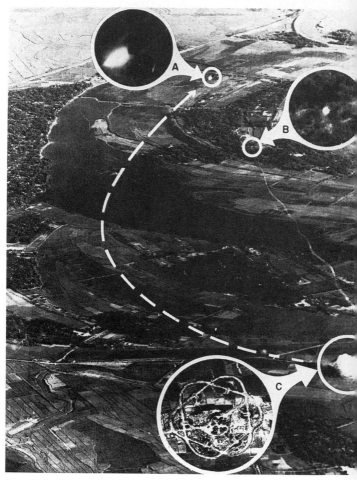

Two SA-2 missiles (A and B) fired from SAM site (C). Missile A is on a normal flight path; missile B has crashed in a populated area of North Vietnam.

SA-2 missile canisters at a SAM support facility.

SAM redeployment: (left to right) two SA-2 missiles in tow, a missile on a parked transporter, and a tracked vehicle used to tow missile equipment.

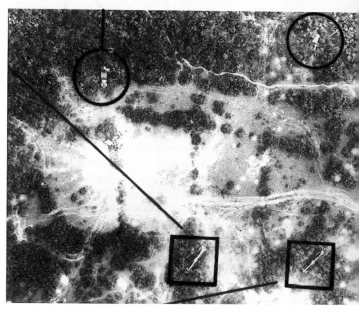

A SAM site 30 miles NW of Dong Hoi. Squares outline transporter-launchers, circles outline truck-tractors.

Same site as above, after airstrike by US Air Force, showing two burned-out SA-2s.

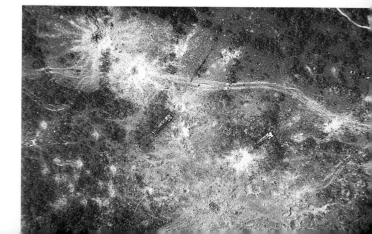

North Vietnamese AAA site with 8 gun positions, 5 occupied by 57mm guns. Radar and electronic equipment are located in the center of the battery.

A partially concealed AAA site is surprised by a low-flying reconnaissance aircraft. Note the figure in the upper left-hand corner running to man the equipment.

A MIG-17 concealed in a village 12 miles from its base.

Above: Five MIG-17s in revetments at Hoa Lac Airfield, west of Hanoi. *Below:* An A-7 pulling up after dropping bombs on the Hai Duong Railway Bridge during Linebacker I on 10 May 1972. This strike resulted in one span dropped and one severed.

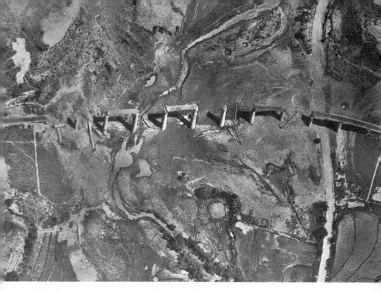

Six of eleven spans of the Lang Giai Railway Bridge were dropped on 25 May 1972 by F-4s using laser-guided bombs.

A view of the Hanoi POL storage area after the 18 May attack which destroyed five and a half million gallons of petroleum products.

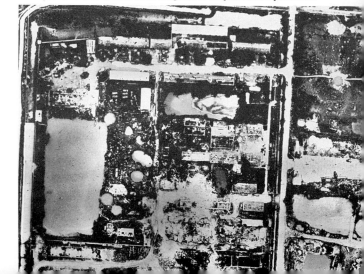

B-52s destroy the entire Ai Mo warehouse area adjacent to the Yen Vien railroad yard complex.

HANOI THERMAL POWER PLANT

BEFORE

16 NOV 72

HANOI THERMAL POWER PLANT

AFTER

22 DEC 7.

Above: The Hanoi thermal power plant on 16 November 1972. *Right:* The Hanoi thermal power plant as photographed on 22 December 1972, after F-4 attacks using laser-guided bombs. This target had earlier been off-limits because of the nearby civilian living areas.

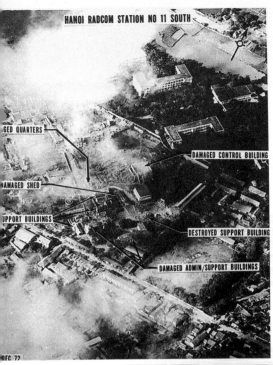

HANOI RADCOM STATION NO 11 SOUTH

GED QUARTERS

DAMAGED CONTROL BUILDING

AMAGED SHED

UPPORT BUILDINGS

DESTROYED SUPPORT BUILDING

DAMAGED ADMIN/SUPPORT BUILDINGS

DEC 72

GIA LAM RR YARD & SHOPS

18 PIECES ROLLING STOCK DAMAGED/DESTROYED

CRANEWAY DAMAGED

6 SUPPORT BUILDINGS DESTROYED

16 DAMAGED BUILDINGS

27 DEC 72

DAMAGED BUILDING
DESTROYED BUILDING
TRACK INTERDICTION

Above: Damage to Hanoi radio communications facility number 11, a result of 11 F-111 and 28 F-4 strikes dropping 325 500-lb. bombs. *Right:* Damaged areas in the Gia Lam railroad yard and shops. B-52s dropped 2371 bombs on this target.

HANOI RR STATION YARD/SHOPS

2 SIDE LOADING PLATFORMS DAMAGED AND 5 TRACKS INTERDICTED

ADMINISTRATION BUILDING DAMAGED

7 SUPPORT BUILDINGS DAMAGED

MAIN TERMINAL DAMAGED

SUPPORT BUILDING DAMAGED

WAREHOUSE DAMAGED

2 WAREHOUSES DAMAGED

SUPPORT BUILDING DESTROYED

11 PIECES OF ROLLING STOCK DAMAGED
10 PIECES OF ROLLING STOCK DESTROYED

Above: This damage to the Hanoi railroad station yard was caused by only 4 F-4s equipped with laser-guided bombs. *Below:* This composite photo of the Hanoi area taken in January 1973 on completion of Linebacker II demonstrates that there was no indiscriminate carpet bombing. Areas 1–11 (outlined in black) are military targets; areas outlined in white are accidental damage areas. Area 19, the Ha Lo POW camp ("Hanoi Hilton"), was not hit and is depicted only as a landmark.

HANOI

electrical systems operating, but cabin pressurization is lost.''

"Navigator and radar are okay. This heading is good to exit the target area."

"E.W. is hit and bleeding all over. There are holes in the side of the airplane by the gunner and he is unconscious.'' [The aircraft had sustained substantial damage, and four six-inch holes were blown in the fuselage next to the gunner, SSgt. Roy Madden Jr., shattering his leg. After his release as a POW, the leg was later amputated.]

I called Quilt 01 and told them we'd been hit, and then I noticed we'd began losing altitude. A quick check of systems revealed all hydraulic pressure to the rudder and elevator system in the rear of the aircraft was gone. I recycled the system and turned on the emergency backup, but still no pressure. The control column was all the way back in my lap, and we continued to descend rapidly. I appraised the crew of the situation and raised the air brakes, which slowed our descent some, but not much. After telling the crew to prepare for a possible bailout, I made a Mayday call to Red Crown. By this time we were in a rapid, high-speed descent at around twenty thousand feet and five hundred knots true airspeed. It was time to leave. I turned on the red Abandon light and said "bailout, bailout" over the interphone.

Woosh! The sound of one ejection seat as it left the aircraft. I rotated the ejection handles on my seat armrests, which exposed the firing triggers. Just before squeezing them, I looked over at Bill Arcuri, who was also preparing to eject, and he nodded his head at me.

Bam! I squeezed the triggers, which fired my entire seat up and out of the aircraft with a tremendous force and into the cold night air. Not knowing how high I was, I went ahead and opened the chute manually. Beginning my slow descent to the ground, I looked around for other parachutes, or the airplane, none of which I could spot. It was strangely quiet and eerie, with a bright moon. Occasionally I heard rumblings and sounds which seemed far away, and saw several SAMs break through the clouds and begin their upward chase.

When I hit the ground, I rolled slightly and the soft plowed ground made for an easy landing . . . there was an old man pointing a large rifle at me. I thought of the thirty-eight-caliber pistol under my left arm, looked at the old man's rifle, considered where I was . . . and slowly raised my hands.[68]

Four of the crew members had successfully departed the aircraft, but the R.N., Capt. Warren Spencer, and the E.W., Captain Paul, were killed in action. Their bodies were later returned by the North Vietnamese.

Four cells behind, Brass cell was experiencing similar difficulties. Like Quilt cell, this flight was composed of one B-52G with modified ECM, and two with unmodified ECM.[69] In addition, as a result of taking TTR evasive action against visual SAMs at the final turn point, Brass 01 was six miles in front of Brass 02. Both Brass 01 and 02 aircraft possessed unmodified ECM packages and both had inoperative jamming transmitters.[70] Brass 02 was struck by two SAMs during the PTT after bomb release. One SAM detonated under the wing and one under the fuselage. Although the bomber was seriously crippled with five engines out, the crew flew the B-52G back to NKP in Thailand, made successful ejections, and were recovered.[71]

The navigator on board, First Lt. Robert Clement, described the events of that night:

Our first contact with the opponent came shortly after we flew into Vietnamese airspace north of Da Nang. The E.W. began hearing the beeps and buzzes of the NVN early-warning radars. Our routing then took us northwesterly along the eastern edge of Laos. The F-4 fighter escort reported its position. Red Crown, a Navy radar picket ship operating in the Gulf of Tonkin, began issuing sporadic MIG warnings. It looked like the F-4s might have a busy night! Some of the MIGs were in our general area, but radio transmissions did not indicate any MIG-bomber engagements. Were the MIGs playing a cat and mouse game, waiting for the most opportune time to attack? Or were they relaying the headings and altitudes of the bombers back to the

SAM batteries, as was suspected on the previous nights? There wasn't much time to speculate; we were almost ready to start our southeasterly turn toward Hanoi. About this time numerous MIG and SAM warnings began saturating the radios. Suddenly, the high-pitched warbling of emergency-locator transmitters filled the radios. Someone had taken a hit and had bailed out. Who was it? How many ELTs?—I only heard two. [The ELTs were from the Quilt 03 crew as they escaped from their crippled B-52]

The MIG calls diminished as we started our right turn toward Hanoi and the target. The predicted jet stream was a reality, and the strong tail wind quickly boosted our ground speed to over six hundred miles per hour. About twelve minutes out from the target, the fireworks began. Brass 01 electronically detected SAM signals ahead and to the right of us. A few seconds later our copilot reported a visual sighting of SAMs coming toward the cell. For the next several minutes we were constantly TTRing as more SAMs were salvoed in our direction. Fear?—you bet! From the navigator team's windowless perspective, the SAMs exploding close to the aircraft resembled distant flashbulbs going off. Occasionally I could also hear the muffled explosions as the SAMs detonated. But for the most part I couldn't see much of what has been described as a "Fourth of July fireworks display." For the time being we were in the hands of God, our pilots, and our defensive teams. Voices were naturally higher in pitch, but there was no yelling or sense of panic. Increased concentration on the rapidly approaching bomb run caused me to lose count of visual SAM reports at number nine (the copilot later reported twenty-six SAMs fired at our cell, and fourteen were directed toward our B-52). Six minutes to bomb release! More SAMs and TTRs. Radar-scope interpretation became more difficult. While the aircraft was turning, the radar-scope gyros would "cage" and not provide stabilization to the radar video. This resulted in blank areas on the radar picture that were void of radar returns. Compounding the pacing problems was the high ground-speed from the strong tail wind. But Chuck [Major

Charles Archie], the R.N., appeared to have things well
under control. At two minutes to go he was on the final
aiming point, and a minute later requested, "Sixty
seconds to go. Center the FCI, pilot." [A "flight command indicator" to establish proper bomb run heading.] The pilot answered, "Twenty degrees right and
centering." I then called, "Doors." [Request for the
R.N. to open the bomb doors.] The RN replied, "Not
yet."

Now came the critical part of the bomb run. The FCI
was centering, and we would not maneuver until after
bombs away. The stabilization system for the bombing
computers needed this straight and level period to
"settle out" and properly solve the bombing problem.
I again called, "Thirty seconds; *doors*, Radar!" He
again replied, "Hold on, Nav!" It finally dawned on
me that the R.N. was delaying the bomb-door opening
so as not to increase the aircraft's radar cross-section
signature [open bomb-bay doors and their sharp edges
enhance the enemy's radar capabilities to zero in on a
target]. Finally, at fifteen seconds to go, he opened the
bomb doors. Then the E.W. reported: "SAM *uplink*!
3½ rings." The copilot verified with, "Got two visual
SAMs. Let's get the bombs out!" This was definitely
unsettling. Previous SAMs directed toward us were
ballistically fired and appeared to have little or no inflight terminal guidance. Uplink meant that the SAM's
controlling ground radar was providing guidance—and
at 3½ rings, strong guidance—signals to the missile.
These two SAMs were "locked-on" to us—and we had
degraded ECM and couldn't maneuver until bombs
away. The R.N. counted down, "Three, two, one,
bombs away, pilot!"

There was a slight aircraft shudder as the bombs rip-
pled from the bomb racks. When all the bombs were
gone, the copilot [Capt. Lawrence Casazza] called,
"SAMs one o'clock, *break left!*" We were supposed
to break right after bomb release, but with degraded
ECM, we would have been turning into the SAMs and
directing our ECM away from the threat rather than at
it. All I could do for the next few moments was pray
and sweat it out. The copilot continued to call out,

"Keep going left . . . (about fifteen seconds later) roll out! . . . They're still on us, *break right!* They're still coming right at us! *Roll out, Pilot, wings level!" Kaboom!* . . . Total darkness. Three seconds later, another sickening . . . *Kaboom!* My immediate thoughts were, My God, is this really happening? I sensed motion and grabbed my flashlight. First thing I looked at was the altimeter. I thanked God we were only in a slight descent and not plummeting out of the sky.

The pilot indicated that things were bad, but the plane was holding together and was flyable. For the time being, staying with a crippled but flyable aircraft was a more attractive alternative than being a POW. None of the crew reported any noticeable injuries. We continued to turn to the west in an attempt to egress the area. The nightmare continued as the copilot called out another salvo of five SAMs coming up behind us. Miraculously, these SAMs disappeared behind the aircraft and did not become a threat to us. I began cursing the now hundred-plus knots of head wind. The pilots had reported four engines out, so I estimated our groundspeed to be about 250 knots with the reduced thrust and strong head wind. At that speed it would be another ten to twelve minutes before we were out of range of the SAM defenses. I sure hoped the SAM batteries would be concentrating on the BUFFS inbound to the target and not trying to finish us off. My prayers were answered when the copilot did not report any more SAMs.

The situation was grim. We had taken heavy shrapnel hits from the two SAMs. The first SAM exploded slightly off the right wing area. The second missile detonated off the right side of the aircraft near the tail section. The first hit immediately knocked out engines one, two, five, and eight. Subsequent attempts to restart those engines were either unsuccessful or had to be abandoned because of fire indications. We also had lost all A-C power, cabin pressurization, and the aft battery. With no A-C power, we had no navigation instruments, heading system, directional gyros, radio, mach, or true airspeed indications. Within five minutes of the first SAM hit, the pilots had problems with two additional engines. Engine number four was shut down for a fire indication, and engine three showed a fire indication anytime the throttle was advanced past the idle position.

The second SAM detonation near the tail section disabled the aircraft's elevator and stabilizer-trim systems that control the pitch of the aircraft. This problem, combined with the reduced available thrust from only two engines, resulted in an initial descent of a thousand feet per minute. This descent rate continued for the first five minutes after being hit. Then the pilots began using the aircraft's air brakes to change the aircraft's pitch. By raising the air brakes, the nose of the aircraft would pitch up and thus slow our rate of descent. But this upward pitch also caused a loss of airspeed. When the airspeed diminished to about 250 knots, the pilots lowered the air brakes, which in turn lowered the nose of the aircraft and increased our airspeed. As the speed climbed to approximately 285 knots, the pilots would again raise the air brakes, and thus the nose of the aircraft, to slow the descent rate. Using this procedure of trading off airspeed for altitude and vice versa, our descent rate would average about six hundred feet per minute for the remainder of our "controlled glide." Partial use of the rudder allowed the pilots to turn the aircraft. The altimeters and indicated airspeed system were operating normally. Also, an emergency battery in the forward wheel-well area provided power to the crew interphone system. This allowed us to talk amongst ourselves inside the airplane, but we could not transmit outside the aircraft. The gunner [TSgt. George Schryer] would later disregard his own personal safety and broadcast Mayday distress calls, and our intentions, on a handheld survival radio. To help ensure that the messages would be heard, he got out of his ejection seat and stuck the antenna of the survival radio through a sextant-port opening on the top of the aircraft.

Once clear of the defensive threats, I plotted a course to NKP. Navigation and map-reading duties kept fear from preoccupying my mind. Yet I couldn't help thinking about our vulnerability. We had fallen out of position in the bomber stream and did not have any mutual ECM protection. In all probability we did not have any fighter escort either. (Unknown at the time, a B-52 in the following cell saw us get hit and stayed with us for a while. So did an F-4.) Although we were now safe from the SAM threats, our controlled descent had brought us into the lethal altitude range of AAA. Worst of all, with no electrical power, the EWO could not detect, let alone counter, any AAA or MIG threats. But our luck held out . . . Ahead was the Mekong River, the Thai border, the rotating aerodrome beacon at NKP—and safety! The pilot [Capt. John Ellinger] already had decided to bailout near NKP, and the red Abandon light would be coming on shortly. After a quick check of my survival equipment and a final tightening of my parachute straps, the bailout command came as we passed through 9500 feet. *Ka-phush!* The EWO was gone! I gave a quick nod toward the R.N. and hoped that the seat would work as I slowly pulled the ejection-control trigger ring.

Ka-phump. In what seemed like a split second, I sensed a downward motion, a quick blast of air in the face, one forward somersault, and then the tug of the parachute as it opened. The ejection seat and the parachute's automatic opening device had worked perfectly. Then I began looking to see if the others had ejected successfully. I didn't see any other parachutes, so I could only hope for the best. Suddenly, I heard someone shouting ''get out of the way!'' It was the EWO [Capt. Silverio Barroqueiro]. He had a ''Mae West'' parachute malfunction (lines over the top of the parachute causing unequal inflation of the canopy). He was spiraling down toward me, and ended up literally walking across the top of my parachute canopy. Then he disappeared into the darkness below. I knew he would be hitting the ground pretty hard, and hoped he wouldn't get hurt. I began hearing the faint whopping sound of helicopters. Looking around, I spotted the red rotating beacon lights of helicopters heading in our direction. But I also spotted other helicopter gunships firing machine guns just across the Mekong River in Laos. Thinking there might be some insurgents in the area, I decided to hide as soon as I hit the ground.

Once safely concealed, I would contact the rescue helicopters. I could now identify ground features, and began maneuvering toward a small clearing. Suddenly I heard a thunderous explosion which turned out to be our B-52 crashing into the jungle. Watching the explosion, I stopped maneuvering toward the clearing I had selected for landing. Next thing I knew, I was crashing down through a tree . . . I finally came to a dangling halt about thirty feet from the ground. I was upside down, entangled in shroud lines from the parachute, and somewhat confused, to say the least! I pulled out the survival radio and was happy to hear the rescue helicopters on frequency. They had already picked up the copilot and R.N. They finally saw me, and one of the para-rescue crew was lowered to my position on a jungle penetrator device designed to hoist people into and out of helicopters. The para-rescue man strapped me onto the penetrator and cut me free of the entangling shroud lines. I was hoisted up into the helicopter, and pleasantly surprised to see the copilot. He told me that everyone else had already been picked up and that they were in pretty good shape. Several minutes later I was at NKP undergoing a simultaneous debriefing of the mission events and a medical examination. I had survived the ordeal with only minor cuts and bruises—undoubtedly due to my tree landing. I asked the medic how the others were, and learned that the copilot and gunner were in the same general condition as I. However, the EWO had injured his knees as a result of the hard, spiraling landing caused by his parachute malfunction. Similarly, the pilot's left leg had rope burns and torn muscles. Apparently, his leg became entangled in some parachute lines after his parachute deployed. When the canopy inflated, the tautening parachute lines caused the injuries. The R.N. was in the worst shape, with a dislocated left shoulder. His left elbow had contacted the side of the hatch during his downward ejection.

The next day, we flew back to Guam on a KC-135. We debriefed the mission and strongly criticized the repetitious routing. Shortly after the debriefing, we were told we would be going home . . . On Christmas morning we left for home on a KC-135. Linebacker II was over for Loring crew Quilt-03. It was not over for the rest of the B-52 crews. Many more bombing missions over Hanoi and Haiphong would be flown—and several more aircraft and crew members would be lost.[72]

Three cells behind Brass, the three B-52Ds in Orange cell were approaching the target. Orange 03 was hit by two SAMs simultaneously just seconds before bomb release.[73] Both Orange 01 and 02 had already released bombs and were in the PTT, thus degrading the effects of their ECM coverage in protecting Orange 03.[74] The burning B-52D went into a flat spin, exploded, and crashed just north of Hanoi into Yen Thuong hamlet. Only the copilot, First Lt. Paul Granger, and the navigator, Capt. Thomas Klomann, were able to successfully bail out of the exploding aircraft. Both were captured immediately and became POWs; the remaining four crew members, including the aircraft commander, Major John Stuart, went down in the aircraft and are still listed as MIA.[75]

The supporting Tacair craft were busy coping with a number of airborne MIGs during Wave One. Two of the four Udorn MIGCAPs reported MIG engagements at the bombers' altitude. Raccoon flight engaged a MIG-21 with the assistance of Red Crown vectors. The F-4s were able to maneuver to a firing position, but then experienced communication difficulties on the MIGCAP frequency. Raccoon 01 requested clearance to fire from Red Crown, but did not receive any transmissions until they were relayed by Teaball. When he attempted to fire an AIM-7, the missile fell off the rails without igniting. The remaining missiles failed to launch. Hydra flight also engaged a MIG-21 in the vicinity of Hanoi, but was unable to obtain firing position. The MIG disengaged at the B-52 altitude with a split-S maneuver as it headed back toward Hanoi.[76] The MIGCAP flights reported that the MIGs were apparently being used to confirm B-52 altitudes to allow the enemy to fuse SAMs for the proper altitude. In each instance, the departure of the MIGs was followed by accurate SAM salvos against B-52 targets.[77] This was verified by Hammer flight (four Iron Hand

F-4Cs). One of the F-4C crews fired his AIM-7 at a MIG, with no observable results. When he tried to fire his second AIM-7, it would not launch.* The flight reported that there was no SAM launch activity while the MIGs were airborne in the vicinity.[78] It appeared that the NVN defensive elements were exhibiting the same excellent in-

*The constant problems associated with the reliability of the AIM-7 Sparrow missiles caused consternation among the aircrews. Time after time the F-4 crews would line up with a good radar lock on a MIG, only to find out that the missile would not fire or guide correctly. What was especially baffling was the fact that the missiles would check out perfectly on the maintenance/calibration test stands, with no apparent reasons for the failures. One of the reasons became evident to the F-4 maintenance officer (the author) at Korat in the middle of the Linebacker II offensive. He was sitting in his parked jeep awaiting the completion of several F-4s undergoing the final stages of preflight inspections so that he could sign them off as operationally ready. As a passing interest, he was watching the normal flow of vehicular traffic moving in and out of the flight-line area at the entry checkpoint. All of the traffic driving onto the aircraft parking areas were normally required to drive over a "Foreign Object Damage" shaker-and-catcher device set into the road. This device was a rectangular-shaped metal plate with welded steel bars which formed a series of bumps much like the old washboards. The intent was to shake loose any debris caught in the tire treads, such as rocks, wires, and screws. This kind of FOD debris would instantly cause severe damage to expensive jet engines if they were ingested off of the ramp area accidently.

This device was not meant to be used by vehicles pulling trailers with sensitive equipment on board, such as ordnance, aerospace ground-servicing equipment, etc. As the maintenance officer watched, he noticed a munitions tractor pulling a trailer full of AIM-7 and AIM-9 missiles directly over the FOD shaker. The missiles were literally bouncing in their holding fixtures as the trailer passed over the bumpy grillwork of the shaker. The officer immediately started his jeep and caught up with the tractor driver as he headed for the F-4 revetments. When he told the driver that driving over the FOD device could cause damage to the missile's internal components, the driver indicated that he had never been briefed not to drive over the shaker while hauling munitions (as obvious as that should have been). The officer called maintenance control on his radio and requested a recheck of the missiles prior to any loading up on the F-4s. The rechecks revealed that some of the fragile internal electronic boards had indeed become displaced and had caused damage to some soldered joints. While on the ground, damaged missiles would often still check out, but at higher altitudes and colder temperatures during flight, potential solder-joint breaks could occur due to contraction of the metal (basic high-school physics). There was no way to determine how many missile failures may have resulted from problems like this, but the driver had admitted to putting dozens of missiles through a severe vibration environment by driving over the shakers on numerous occasions. Immediate word was put out to all flight-line drivers with munitions trailers to avoid the FOD shakers when approaching the ramp area. Although this action would not solve all of the AIM-7's reliability problems at Korat, it at least eliminated one of the more obvious ways of contributing to their failure.

tegration of their resources that was displayed during Linebacker I. Several flights also reported coordinated SAM and AAA defensive efforts. The SAMs were fired to force aircraft to descend, then accurate tracking AAA was employed.[79]

The coordination of the North Vietnamese forces was further verified by the B-52 crews. Capt. Rolland Scott, the pilot in Gold 02, the fourth cell in Wave One, reported:

On the northbound leg over NVN we heard a good deal of fighter activity and numerous sightings were made of aircraft with lights on, presumably friendly fighters. There appeared to be no SAM activity. On the southeast leg approaching the IP, my copilot stated he saw a MIG-21 on the right wing of our aircraft. In mild disbelief, I stretched to see out his window, and sure enough, a MIG-21 with lights off was flying tight formation with us. I believe I could actually see the pilot. The approach of the fighter had not been detected by on-board systems. Shortly, after two or three minutes, the copilot reported the MIG had departed. Almost immediately I saw the same or another enemy aircraft flying formation to the left of us. After a brief period, less than a minute, it departed.

Our sighs of relief were short-lived, and we quickly learned what the MIG had been up to. We visually detected missiles approaching from our eleven and one o'clock positions. Several pairs of missiles were simultaneously launched from these directions. The E.W. reported no uplink or downlink signals with the missiles, as were reported on the night of the eighteenth. ["Uplink" is the missile guidance signal of the Fan Song, while "downlink" is the beacon frequency of the missile used by the site to identify the location of the missile in its flight path.] However, these missiles appeared to be a lot more accurate than on the eighteenth. They seemed to readjust their track as I made small turns. I waited for each to get as close as I dared, and then I would make a hard, although relatively small, maneuver in hopes of avoiding them. They arrived in pairs, just a few seconds apart. Some, as they pass, would explode—a few close enough to shake my aircraft. One exploded so close and caused such a loud noise and violent shock that I stated to the crew that I thought we had been hit. After assessing engine instruments and control responses, I determined we had not been hit, or were at least under normal control, and we continued the bomb run. Apparently the MIG-21 we saw was flying with us to report heading, altitude, and airspeed to the missile sites.

The missiles were no longer directed toward us in the latter half of the bomb run. However, I could see SAM activity ahead in the vicinity of the target. In fact, while on the run we saw a large ball of fire erupt some few miles ahead of us and slowly turn to the right and descend. I thought it was a BUFF and was sure no one would survive what was apparently a direct hit. I later learned what I saw was Quilt 03 going down in flames. Amazingly, four crew members successfully ejected.

We completed our bomb run and were in the middle of our post-target right turn when we again became an item of interest to the missiles. From our left and below were at least three missiles, perhaps four, approaching rapidly. I felt I had no chance to avoid them by either maintaining or rolling out of the right turn, so I increased the planned bank angle drastically . . . and lowered the nose. The SAMs passed above us from our left. I lost some altitude in the maneuver, and in the attempt to climb and accelerate on seven engines [one engine had quit] I lagged behind lead and was somewhat out of position. There were no further SAMs directed at our aircraft; however, there was apparently a lot of enemy fighter activity on our withdrawal, according to radio transmissions. We could see numerous fighters with lights on, and the gunner reported numerous targets on radar, one of which appeared to follow us, but not in the cone of fire. We saw no aircraft that appeared to be hostile, nor any hostile maneuvers [these were probably F-4 fighter escorts].

As we passed east of NKP on a southernly heading, we heard what was apparently a B-52 crew abandoning their aircraft over friendly territory. In the distance, toward NKP, we soon saw a fireball which we assumed to be a BUFF impacting the ground. It must have been Brass 02, and Captain John Ellinger and his crew were mighty lucky.[80]

DAY THREE—WAVE TWO

It was becoming obvious to the SAC battle staff that the B-52G models did not possess sufficient ECM power to successfully counter the SAM radar-guidance systems. The attacking force of 27 B-52s (9 B-52Ds and 18 B-52Gs from Guam) were targeted against the Hanoi rail yards, the Thai Nguyen thermal power plant, and the Bac Giang transshipment points. Due to the losses suffered by G-models over Hanoi, the 6 B-52Gs assigned to strike the rail yards were recalled by SAC. The remaining bombers resumed their attacks without damage or losses.[81] No MIGs were reported airborne during Wave Two.

DAY THREE—WAVE THREE

Wave Three consisted of 12 B-52Gs and 9 B-52Ds from Guam, and 18 B-52Ds from Utapao. The 9 D-models from Guam were assigned to bomb the Hanoi rail yard (the same yard that the recalled B-52Gs in Wave Two had been assigned.[82] Straw 02, the fifth aircraft in, took a hit during its post-target turn from a missile fired, most probably, by SAM site VN-549.[83] Straw cell was engaged by up to 18 SAMs during the bomb run.[84] Severely damaged, Straw 02 managed to keep airborne for thirty minutes as it flew toward Laos.[85] Capt. Vincent Russo, the navigator on board Straw 02, recalled:

We took off out of Guam for Hanoi and were six hours into our mission at 34,000 feet. We were transiting the densest air defense in the world, with Soviet SA-2 missiles poised for our squadron's flight path, which would put us over over target. Two seconds after releasing our bomb load, we got hit. The pilot had just started a forty-five-degree banked turn, and then everything went black inside the fuselage. We were the

second airplane in the cell when we were hit. We had
fire in the number seven and eight engines, and the
copilot [First Lt. James Farmer] hit the fire bottle.
Rolling out, the pilot [Cap. Deverl Johnson] said, ''It's
flying pretty good,'' and took an outboard heading using only Pitot-static (airspeed indication), the only instruments working. Flying without two engines, the
airplane was so damaged by the explosion of the missile that it looked like Swiss cheese. Because the aircraft lost electrical power, the crew could not transfer
fuel from one side of the plane to the other. As fuel
ran out in one tank, the bomber was losing its center
of gravity. The pilot called for bailout about thirty minutes after the missile hit.[86]

At 15,000 feet, Captain Russo exited the plane over
Laos in a downward ejection, tumbling several times before being jolted upright by his deployed parachute. He
watched the aircraft turn into a fireball as it struck a
hillside. After landing in a tree, Captain Russo waited
for twenty minutes for first light before lowering himself
to the ground. After a few minutes, he used his survival
radio to transmit a Mayday call. An F-4 crew responded,
telling him that help was on the way. An SAR A-7 eventually located him, after which a rescue HH-53 arrived
and he was hoisted to safety.[87] All of the remaining crew
was also rescued in the same manner, except for the radar
navigator, who was injured during the SAM explosion
and was not observed in a parachute.*

Not far behind Straw cell the B-52Gs began their attacks on the Kinh No complex. Unfortunately, Wave
Three was composed of too many B-52G models to allow
a recall of the bombers and still possess enough B-52s

---

*The search-and-rescue force could not obtain any reading of a survivor beeper,
and after an initial search, it was determined that the R.N. had probably gone
down with the aircraft. In 1981 a U.S. satellite, in a random pass over the same
area, photographed a jungle clearing in Laos. The isolated area showed that
someone had stamped the number 52 in the elephant grass, in numerals three
feet wide and fifteen feet long. It is possible that the R.N. had in fact ejected
successfully but may have had a defective locator. If this is true, then he was
tragically missed during the rescue effort.

to effectively cause the desired level of destruction of the vital storage area. Therefore, the decision was made to press on with the G-models against the heavily defended target. The lead B-52G, Olive 01, was hit by one of several SAMs while in a high angle of bank during the PTT. Only three of the seven crew members ejected successfully: Lt. Col. Jim Nagahiro, the pilot; Capt. Lynn Beens, the navigator; and Lt. Col. Keith Heggen, the deputy airborne commander of the attacking wave. Lieutenant Colonel Heggen died in captivity from wounds caused by the SAM explosion. The other two survivors were returned later; the remaining five crew members are MIA.[88]

Two cells behind Olive was Tan cell. Tan 03, an unmodified G-model, lost its bombing navigation system, became disoriented, and separated from the cell. When Tan 03 was about six miles to the side of its cellmates, a SAM exploded directly below the forward fuselage. The pilot, Capt. Randall Craddock, struggled with the aircraft after a brief dive and was able to regain control and altitude. A minute later the aircraft was hit by another SAM and the pilot lost complete control. Captain Craddock ordered his crew members to bail out, but the aircraft exploded before his orders could be carried out. The gunner, SSgt. James Lollar, was the only crew member who was able to eject successfully before the aircraft disintegrated. He was taken prisoner soon after he bailed out. The other five crew members on Tan 03 are still MIA.[89]

The last cell into Hanoi that night was Brick cell. As it attacked the Hanoi petroleum products storage area at Gia Thuong, it was attacked by four SAMs. Although the three bombers had maintained good cell integrity and all ECM jamming systems were operational, Brick 02 received damage from a SAM detonation as it entered the post-target turn.[90] The aircraft managed to limp back to Utapao despite numerous holes in its right wing.[91] The day's activities closed out with six B-52Ds from Utapao attacking the Bac Giang transshipment point. Twelve SAMs were fired at the two cells, with no hits. Day Three, remembered as the day with the greatest number of B-52 losses in the Linebacker II campaign, was finally over. Crew comments on the day's operations focused on the ferocity of the NVN air defenses:

> Coming in from the west again, we were near the end of the wave . . . driving in while the other aircraft began to bomb in front of us. Just watching all the SAMs was like watching a show, until you realized that as you got closer, they were starting to shoot at you. Then they let go a barrage of AAA that literally was like all the war movies you ever heard about. It was so thick you could get out and walk on it. That's exactly what it looked like. It was coming north of Hanoi and was just one big blanket. I could see it coming up, and it all went off at the same time.[92]

It was during this night that one of the B-52 EWOs, Capt. R. J. Smith, became a "legend in his own time." He was the first EWO to complete five hundred combat missions in SAC. Captain Smith always carried a whistle as a good-luck charm, and he would blow it at opportune times. As his B-52 ran through a gauntlet of SAMs during the straight-and-level phase of its bomb run, Captain Smith broke into the enemy GCI net, blew his whistle, and called, "Time Out!" For ninety seconds not a single SAM was launched by the NVN forces, giving the crew time to complete the bomb release and the PTT and to leave the area. Whether due to coincidence or fate, the brief respite from the otherwise continuous SAM barrage was welcomed by the B-52 crews in that particular cell.[93]

REFLECTIONS ON DAY THREE

The casualties sustained during Day Three were grim indeed: 4 B-52Gs and 2 B-52Ds had been shot down, with a third D-model sustaining serious damage. Over two hundred SAMs had been fired at the bombers, causing the greatest single loss of B-52s in the entire campaign.[94] Several significant factors were evident with relation to the 9 B-52 losses suffered on days One through Three. Six of the B-52s had been in their PTT maneuver, and five of the lost B-52Gs had unmodified ECM systems. One thing was known for sure by almost everyone who participated in Linebacker II: the SAC planners would have to develop a new battle plan if the B-52s were to continue their nightly attacks into the Hanoi area.[95]

Chapter Five

PHASE TWO: A NEW BATTLE PLAN EVOLVES

The Basis for New Tactics

Several significant factors were noted by the Tacair crews during the Day Three wave attacks. The MIGCAP flights reported that enemy SAM reactions were lighter during Wave Three and no MIGs were airborne. The enemy was firing either single SAMs or pairs of SAMs against individual B-52s. The SAMs appeared to be very accurate.[1] This was further verified by the Iron Hand flights. The Weasel crews knew that something was aiding the SAM operators besides their Fan Song missile-guidance radars, because the Weasels were not intercepting indications of valid guided SAM launches. Yet numerous aircrews had observed airborne SAMs that appeared to be guiding on the B-52 forces. It was surmised by our Wild Weasel crews that a modified target-data acquisition systems was being used by the North Vietnamese as a countermeasure against the support forces.[2]

On Day Three, several crews intercepted a new North Vietnamese radar signal on their ECM receivers that operated in both E and I bands. The new signal was code-named T-8209.[3] The T-8209 radar appeared to be a modified Fire Can gun-control radar, with a band-switching capability from E band (2000–3000 MHz) to I band (9000–10,000 MHz). T-8209 radar had initially been picked up in 1972 by RC-135 intelligence-gathering aircraft, but its use had remained unknown. EB-66 crews has been looking for it since August.[4] The EB-66s orbiting west of Hanoi also verified the use of T-8209 at a number of NVN SAM sites, notably the infamous VN-549 site which had apparently been responsible for a number of accurate SAM engagements with the B-52s. The North Vietnamese crews had been careful to hide T-8209 until it was really needed. The checkout and testing of the system had probably taken place during November near the Vinh area, and may have been responsible for the downing of the first B-52 on 22 November, which was described in Chapter Two.

Basically, the T-8209 was used to provide range information for the SA-2 SAM tracking system. Combined with the track-on-jam azimuth information available from the Fan Song radar, the normal missile-guidance information could be obtained and the straight point-to-point missile path could be used. This allowed a shorter time of flight for the missile and lesser time for defensive SAM breaks by the targeted aircraft.[5] The use of T-8209 explained the almost complete lack of active Fan Song signals reported during periods of numerous SAM launches. During the first two nights, the enemy had salvo-fired large numbers of SAMs, hoping to gain lucky hits using the SAM's proximity fusing. However, by the end of Day Three, it appeared that I band radar guidance allowed very accurate single and paired SAM launches. Since the technique used the passive, guided home-on-jam procedure and an odd frequency, none of the U.S. electronic countermeasures were designed to counter it.[6] The ECM experts at Korat began investigating possible methods to counter the new threat.

The effectiveness of the protective chaff corridors was a major concern during days One through Three. Only four of the 27 cells within the most dangerous areas around Hanoi had been protected by the chaff.[7] The narrow corridors sown by chaff flights of four F-4s, coupled with the high hundred-knot winds and long bombing periods, prevented chaff from significantly influencing the SAM radars in the most dangerous areas. For all B-52 losses, chaff was five to ten miles from the aircraft's location at the time of SAM engagements. The lack of chaff in the immediate vicinity of the target aircraft allowed the NVN to use the active radar modes.[8]

To address the deficiencies of the first three days, a special tactics panel was formed.[9] Until new tactics could be devised to compensate for the enemy's defensive tactics, the Guam-based B-52s were reassigned from missions over North Vietnam to flying the Arc Light operations over South Vietnam, which had been put on hold when all SAC B-52s were used to support Linebacker II.[10] The resumption of Arc Light missions gave aircrews recently assigned to Guam the chance to practice cell-formation procedures.[11]

After the first three days of operations it was evident that the North Vietnamese air-defense command had figured out the pattern the attacks would take. It was also apparent they were concentrating their efforts against the B-52s and not the support aircraft. The enemy's job was made easier for them since the B-52s came inbound to the targets every night on the same basic routes and made their post-target turn at a standard time after bomb release. The high angle of bank used in the PTTs degraded the ECM effectiveness at the planes' most vulnerable time, when the SAM radars could read through the ECM due to the aircrafts' proximity to the SAM sites. The enemy was obviously using the first aircraft cells over the target to determine the track and turn points. Defenses were then probably aligned and committed after approach routes and turn points were revealed by the initial strike on a target. SAMs were then salvoed into the bomb-release and turn areas. Furthermore, the single corridors of chaff provided axis-of-attack information to the defenders by defining the exact routes to and from the target areas. Thus, the enemy's ability to exploit the strike force's ECM tactics and operations required that we change our techniques.[12] The tactics panel worked with Tacair planners to recommend the necessary changes, which included varying the bombers' approach and departure routes, altitudes, and locations of post-target turns. In some cases the PTT would be eliminated entirely and attacking cells were to be routed to fly straight toward the Gulf of Tonkin after dropping their bomb loads.[13] By varying the attack approaches, the defender's ability to predict follow-on bomber-cell routes was degraded, reducing the effectiveness of their "ambush" defense tactics. In addition, the chaff bombers from Ubon would either create multiple corridors to confuse the enemy or devise an area or block chaff screen. Area chaff screens would eliminate the stereotyped corridors and overcome two problems: wind effect, and corridor placement.[14] The changes proposed by the panel were approved immediately and would become the basis for the raids on Day Five.[15]

Day Four Attacks

DAY FOUR—TACAIR STRIKES

To keep up the pressure on the North Vietnamese rail network, Tacair day strikes on 21 December were weighed heavily on several key rail yards. A total of 16 A-7s accompanied by LORAN-equipped F-4s were targeted against the Giap Nhi railroad yards, and 46 F-4 fighter bombers from Ubon were scheduled for attacks against rail yards at Giap Nhi, Trung Quan, and Duc Noi, along with the Hanoi railroad station, the Hanoi AM transmitter, and the Hanoi thermal power plant (TPP). All attacks would take place between 1305 and 1315 hours Hanoi time.[16]

The weather over the target areas was clear enough to perform more accurate visual strikes. The Ubon F-4s struck the Trung Quan rail yards first, but the bomb damage assessment could not be confirmed due to large amounts of smoke over the target. They were followed by a flight of F-4s which attacked the Giap Nhi rail yards. Several large secondary explosions were observed and portions of the yard were left on fire. The A-7s followed up with additional accurate hits which caused a large secondary explosion and the destruction of a number of tank and boxcar rolling stock. The main line was also severed at three points.[17] This damage hindered all rail traffic traveling south of Hanoi and overloaded other facilities north of Hanoi.

The Hanoi railroad station and thermal power plant

were attacked by F-4s with LGBs. The station was destroyed and major cuts were made on the adjacent main lines. The most significant BDA for the day occurred when the 4 F-4s with laser-guided MK-84 bombs attacked the power plant, knocking it out and disrupting power to the capital city. It would take over six months to repair the plant.[18] The last attack of the day took place when 12 F-4s bombed the Duc Noi rail yards. Three large secondary explosions left the yard in flames, with clouds of smoke reaching up to nine thousand feet. The only defensive reactions were from the AAA sites.[19]

DAY FOUR—B–52 STRIKES

Day Four marked the beginning of the second phase of the B-52 bombings. SAC was requested by the CINC-PAC to continue the raids on a reduced basis, 50 strike missions for the next four days were flown from Utapao and comprised only 30 B-52s in single-wave attacks.[20] With the missions all originating from Thailand, the coordination and conduct of the operations were greatly simplified. Two distinct advantages were apparent: all B-52D missions could be flown with full bomb loads without tanker support, and the D-models possessed greater ECM capability.[21] Even more important, the Tacair support force was nearly doubled to support a single-wave B-52 attack. Since Tacair support sorties were now required to protect only two major waves instead of four, it allowed a greater number of forces available to protect the strike forces for each day and night attack. For the first three nights, each wave had only 39 support aircraft. Now, however, no less than 58 Tacair craft were available for each nightly wave. The most significant changes were instituted to the chaff and Iron Hand flights, chaff flights increasing from 8 to 12 bombers.[22] The increase was necessary to create an effective block or area coverage of chaff clouds. In order to increase the chaff-cloud density, MK-129 chaff bombs were dropped throughout the chaff area, especially where turns for strike aircraft were being planned.[23] The Iron Hand F-105G/F-4C Weasels were reunited with F-4Es carrying cluster-bomb units (CBUs), and the Hunter-Killer teams were reinstituted for the night attacks.[24] Although poor visibility would still hamper the team, there were expected to be isolated areas where there were breaks in the cloud cover.[25] The T-8209 I-band radars were difficult to counter, and then only with the often unreliable AGM-78 missiles (of which only fifteen remained in the 388th TFW at the time).[26] The revival of the Hunter-Killer teams would at least make it possible to destroy SAM sites after they launched missiles (provided the F-4Es could find them through breaks in the cloud layers).

The 30 B-52Ds were scheduled against targets at Quang Te Airfield (6 B-52s), Bac Mai Airfield (12 B-52s) and the Van Dien supply depot (12 B-52s). Some notable changes were made to the attack plan, which included a number of the improvements recommended for Day Five. Although the bombers still flew on a southeasterly attack heading, several significant tactics had been altered. The time between cells was cut from four minutes to between 90 and 120 seconds, to compress the bombers' TOT and to reduce each wave's exposure over the target area to about 15 minutes (versus 30 to 40 minutes as in days One to Three). Altitude separation between cells was increased and base altitudes were varied from 33,500 to 38,000 feet. For the first time the bombers would exit the target area to the southeast, toward the Gulf of Tonkin, and use the overwater ("feet wet") withdrawal route back to base.[27]

The F-111s were again fragged against targets that included the five major airfields, the Bac Giang and Kep railroad yards, the Viet Tri transshipment point, and the Hanoi port. All the missions were scheduled to fly at far earlier times than the scheduled B-52 missions. This prevented the North Vietnamese forces from closely estimating the probable TOTs for the B-52 single-wave attacks. In some cases the North Vietnamese must have thought the F-111 attacks were being conducted by B-52s, since the F-111s came under heavy AAA fire and several SAM attacks.[28]

At approximately 0333 hours the first 6 B-52s attacked Quang Te Airfield. This was the only attack against that airfield during the entire offensive. Only two SAMs were observed, along with some AAA fire, and none of the 6 bombers was hit. The next 12 B-52s attacked the Ven Dien depot, and although numerous SAMs were fired by eleven sites in the target area, again no B-52s were hit. The 12 B-52s striking the storage areas at Bac Mai were not as fortunate.[29] The lead B-52, Scarlet 01, experienced a failure of its bombing radar just short of the initial point (IP). In order to have an operable navigation system on the lead position, the crew attempted to exchange positions with Scarlet 03. While doing so, the B-52 (now Scarlet 03) separated from the cell by approximately six miles, becoming an isolated clear target to alert SAM crews. Fifteen SAMs were launched, and Scarlet 03 was hit and lost at approximately sixty seconds before the bomb-release point.[30] The aircraft commander, Capt. Pete Giroux, gave this account of its final mission:

We proceeded north through Thailand and Laos, and the mission was proceeding normally. Then, as we approached the IP, the radar began to deteriorate. I asked the Radar if he wanted a position change [from lead to another cell position, since the lead bomber had to have a working radar], and he said yes. Normally the change was time consuming, but by taking advantage of the upcoming turn, we could complete it and hopefully stay in position. At that point we still had range information available and could drop off lead or 02 with some assistance. I directed [Scarlet] 02 to take lead and outlined what I was going to do. He called his turn, and 03 followed as we paralleled and began to move into the number-three position. It was going to work out, and I called for the cell to adjust altitude. All we needed now was a little help from the preceding gunners. They could give us a "bonus deal" by directing our release position with their gunnery radar and giving us the range that would put us over the same release point they used if we timed it precisely.

As we rolled out, we lost the radar completely and, at about the same time, the gunner called for the TTR maneuver which was designed to counter enemy radar, but when the gunner asked for it, it meant MIGs. Damn! It couldn't have come at a more inopportune time. I began the maneuver realizing it would back us out of the cell slightly and affect our electronic-countermeasures protective shield. Just a second or two later Louie [MSgt. Louis Le Blanc] excitedly called for flares and began firing at the attackers. This was happening too fast. I made a call like "Bandits on Scarlet 03" as that happened, but apparently the other aircraft didn't hear it. The flares were designed to lure the incoming infrared missiles away from the heat signature of those eight engines. They worked. I saw two of the missiles pass under us as I concentrated on the maneuver. Then the gunner yelled "I got one" over the interphone [the MIG kill wasn't allowed, as it was unverified]. He continued to fire short bursts, and later told me he thought he'd gotten several hits on the second aircraft. Then the attackers broke off and I continued to work the maneuver back to a bomb-run heading, as I hoped we still had a chance at the release. But directly below us were two SAMs steady in the window, which meant they were coming straight for us. These were only the ones I saw, as apparently there had been a salvo fired at us. I called the missiles to the crew, turned hard back to the right and said a short prayer. I loaded the aircraft up, hoping it might be enough of a change that the missiles wouldn't react. The EWO, Captain Pete Camerota, said he didn't have any signals, and in a couple of seconds there was a sharp bang something like a paper bag exploding. It had probably hit near centerline and toward the front of the aircraft but slightly below. Another went by the tail but failed to explode. I rolled the aircraft out on heading. I was okay; some pieces of shrapnel had hit my legs, and some smaller pieces hit both wrists. The aircraft was flying, but I could see the left wing was already on fire. My side panel was a mess, my interphone seemed to be out, and the hydraulic warning lights were just about all on, or so it seemed.

The crew checked in, each one was okay, but I couldn't hear them over the interphone. The only thing I did hear was the gunner say that engines five and six were on fire and the flames were reaching past the tail [He may have used the Call position which overrides all other interphone functions]. I looked at the copilot

[Capt. Thomas Waring Bennett], tried him again on interphone, and then shut down both five and six as the fire lights came on for engines one through seven. I still thought we might make it to the coast and "feet wet," where our chance of rescue would be improved. Then the aircraft began a bank to the right, probably due to the loss of engines on that side. I stood on the rudder, trimmed, and then tried differential power by cocking the throttles. Waring was with me on the controls, but the bank angle was increasing. I looked again at the hydraulic panel and saw that there wasn't much left to help in the form of controls. It didn't look like we were getting out of this turn. Then we experienced a complete electrical failure. I watched the copilot at once go through the emergency procedure correctly and deliberately. Nothing. Finally the emergency instrument-lighting system began to go. I looked at Waring and then reached for and turned on the Abandon light on the rear of the center console between us. I then heard an ejection seat go immediately, and two more followed it as the aircraft depressurized. I realized the oxygen wasn't giving me the pressure it should have.

The next thing I knew I was upside down in the aircraft. All I could see was the shattered window directly in front of me. I was hanging in the straps even though I had tightened them before the world had begun to come apart. I knew the seat would probably give me a compression when it hit me, but it was the least of my worries. I reached for the arming levers on the side of the seat near my knees and pulled them up and tried to squeeze the trigger to fire the seat. Nothing happened. My little finger was between the trigger and the arming lever. I squeezed again as hard as I could and the seat fired.[31]

Captain Giroux luckily escaped the aircraft and was captured soon after he touched down. The EWO, Captain Camerota, and the gunner, Master Sergeant LeBlanc, also had ejected and become POWs. The gunner had left the aircraft just as the right wing had burned through and was starting to fold over the top of the aircraft.[32] No word had ever been heard of as to the fate of the copilot, radio navigator, or the navigator, and they are still listed as MIAs.

Two cells behind Scarlet, Blue Cell was engaged by up to ten SAMs. Blue 01 was bracketed by two as bombs were dropping from its bomb bays. The crew all managed to eject and became POWs. The EWO onboard Blue 01, Lt. Col. Bill Conlee, said:

Our target was the Bac Mai storage in Hanoi, with a release time of 0347 hours local time on the twenty-second. This mission was routine until we reached the IP on the bomb run. At this time the copilot, Captain Dave Drummond, remarked: "It looks like we'll walk on SAMs tonight," as he could see numerous SAM firings ahead of us [He was seeing the SAM attacks against Scarlet cell]. This comment proved only too true.

Between IP and bomb-release point, ten SAMs were fired in the vicinity of Blue cell. At bombs away we were bracketed by two SAMs, one going off below us and to the left, the second exploding above us and to the right. Shrapnel cracked the pilot's outer window glass, started fires in the left wing, and wounded Lieutenant Colonel John Yuill, the pilot; Lieutenant Colonel Louis Bernasconi, the R.N.; Lieutenant William Mayall, the navigator; and myself. We also experienced a rapid decompression and loss of electrical power. Shortly after this, with the fire worsening, Lieutenant Colonel Yuill gave the emergency bailout signal via the alarm light and I ejected from the aircraft.[33]

Lieutenant Colonel Yuill also gave his account of the fate of Blue 01, as well as what happened during those first days of the campaign:

The first night we flew in the second wave. I remember seeing the fellows return from the first wave. I didn't have to say a word to them—just one look at them and I knew it was going to be a bad night. I remember sitting in the briefing, thinking that it must

have been like that during World War Two. I also recall
saying to myself, I wonder how many of these guys
sitting here will not come back in the morning, maybe
I will be one that won't be back. I assure you, it was
a very sobering moment. The target that night was Radio Hanoi, and the SAMs came at us from everywhere.
We made it back and had another sobering experience
when we checked the bulletin board and saw that the
schedule included my crew for the second night. The
second night was more of the same, and again we made
it back. The third night my crew did not fly but we
were on call in case someone was sick, etcetera, but
none of my crew was called out to fly.

When, on the fourth night, we again made the schedule, I had a couple of interesting conversations. Just
prior to the briefing, I went into the bomber-scheduling
office and expressed my feelings about men flying three
out of the first four nights. Major Luse [the scheduler]
listened to me, then gave me his solemn vow that the
crew would not be scheduled to fly the next night. He
was so right, we did not fly the next night because we
were shot down over Hanoi. I also spoke with the wing
commander, Colonel Donald Davis, telling him I didn't
think we could keep up the pace for too much longer.
At any rate, we took off for Hanoi again, and this time
our luck ran out, as we got hit by a SAM. When I made
the final decision to bail out the crew, our interphone
was inoperative and the left wing was on fire. I turned
on the bailout light, and when it is used, the crew
"steps" out without regard to normal bailout order. I
had what was probably one of the most senior ranking
crews at the time, with three lieutenant colonels. It was
interesting to find out later that the three (one being
myself) bailed out first, followed by the three remaining crew members, the captain, the sergeant, and the
lieutenant, in that order. The R.N., copilot, and myself
all landed in the same area, the navigator and gunner
landed together, and the E.W. (Lieutenant Colonel
Conlee) landed by himself. The E.W. was picked up
quite close to Hanoi and was inside the POW camp,
the Hanoi Hilton, within two hours from bailout. The
rest of us landed so close together that we were assem-

bled and rode in the same truck to the Hilton, arriving several hours after the E.W. I was placed in solitary for the first week. While in solitary I kept thinking about my order to bail out, thinking that it might have been the wrong decision. After the first week I was placed in a cell with seven others, two of them being my E.W. and navigator. I discussed with them my concern over the bailout. My navigator informed me that I had definitely made the right decision, because after his chute opened, he saw the airplane completely engulfed in flames, then saw it explode.[34]

The Blue 01 crew was lucky since this was the only loss over the Hanoi area where all crew members were able to eject safely after being hit by a SAM. Both of the other B-52s in Blue cell had reported definite T-8209 I-band signals just prior to the bomb-release point.[35] To make matters worse, the bomb train from Blue 01 caused damage to the Bach Mai Hospital and adjacent residential areas as the pilot lost control of the aircraft. The NVN were able to use photographs of these areas for propaganda purposes as "proof" that the U.S. was using indiscriminate carpet bombing over Hanoi.[36]

Only one MIG had been detected by MIGCAP forces, but the MIGCAP F-4s were not able to fire on the enemy aircraft even though they had established good lock-ons. This was due to the close proximity of several friendly aircraft.[37] Bucket flight continued to pursue the MIG from a position seven to eight miles behind. The MIG pilot, apparently thinking he had shaken his pursuers, headed for Yen Bai Airfield. As the MIGCAP flight closed in on the MIG orbiting over Yen Bai, the MIG pilot must have been warned of the approaching F-4s. He turned his aircraft toward the northeast. The F-4s continued the chase until fuel considerations required a termination of the engagement. However, the enemy aircraft must have also been low on fuel, since it went down approximately sixty miles from Hanoi. The F-4 aircraft crew on Bucket 01, Capt. Gary L. Sholders and his weapon system operator (WSO), First Lt. Eldon D. Binkley, received credit for the downed MIG because their continued pursuit resulted in fuel starvation for the enemy aircraft.[38] According to Captain Sholders:

Our flight dropped off the tanker at 1948Z and proceeded north toward the assigned orbit point. Upon contact with Red Crown, the flight was advised of enemy aircraft activity west of Hanoi. Red Crown began vectoring at 2003Z. We elected not to pursue the bandit immediately because his altitude was below an overcast which covered virtually all of the Hanoi area. Our flight established a left-hand orbit at approximately 2018Z, when Red Crown advised that the bandit had climbed to sixteen thousand feet.

We made a hard left turn to one hundred degrees, established immediate radar contact with a single enemy aircraft crossing right to left, range eighteen miles. Clearance to fire was obtained from Red Crown, and we rolled into a five-mile trail position on the bandit. The bandit then engaged his afterburner and began a steep climb. We obtained a lock-on using boresight mode and closed to approximately three miles when the radar broke lock at approximately 2022Z. Red Crown advised our flight shortly thereafter that the bandit was south at ten miles. We then turned to reengage. The flight remained within eight miles of the bandit in a maneuvering engagement, using intermittent radar returns and vectors from Red Crown, until approximately 2033Z. We were unable to obtain a radar lock-on during this period of time. Red Crown advised the flight at 2033Z that the bandit was south at seven miles, heading home. We then turned southeast, attempting to reacquire the bandit heading toward Hanoi; no contact was made on this heading. We then made a right turn to the northwest and immediately acquired radar contact with an enemy aircraft at twenty-five miles on the nose, apparently heading for Yen Bai Airfield.

We pursued the bandit, closing to approximately twenty miles as the bandit appeared to be orbiting Yen Bai. The bandit then turned northeast. Using radar, we were able to close to approximately seven miles. We pursued the bandit until approximately 2046Z, when the engagement was terminated for fuel considerations. At the termination of the engagement, the bandit was on the nose at seven miles. Our position at the time was approximately 010 degrees, sixty miles from Hanoi. Shortly after termination of the engagement, one of the controlling agencies called a bandit north of Hanoi. Intelligence sources confirmed that an enemy aircraft went down in the early morning hours of 22 December 1972. Ours was the only flight in the area that engaged an enemy aircraft for any length of time on 21-22 December; in addition, the only flight that pursued an enemy aircraft after he had apparently attempted a landing at Yen Bai Airfield. On the strength of the aforementioned evidence, we claim one enemy aircraft destroyed due to continued pursuit which resulted in fuel starvation for the enemy aircraft.[39]

On this night, as on others, the B-52 jamming and IFF procedures made it difficult to guide the F-4 escorts to their B-52 rendezvous points, so the rendezvous were all flown according to planned timing, since they were unable to maintain visual or radar contact with the BUFF cells.[40]

The Wild Weasels and EB-66s definitely confirmed the use of the T-8209 radar as a SAM guidance system on Day Four. The cloud cover during the strike was a solid undercast at six thousand feet. There was a full moon with unlimited visibility. With only one exception, none of the active launch sites that night radiated a recognizable track-while-scan Fan Song signal. Though numerous SAM sites were within range of the B-52 cells, the only engaging SA-2 sites appeared to be directly ahead of the bombers. There were no observed beam or stern engagements. All sites engaged with multiple missile launches. The initial launch contained two missiles, with subsequent launches using four missiles. The time interval between the SAMs was a consistent two to three seconds. The entire sequence from missile launch to impact of B-52 Scarlet 03 was observed by Suntan 01, a Wild Weasel F-4C. The Weasel was at the B-52's one to two o'clock position, 15,000 to 20,000 feet low, at an estimated range of two to three miles. The launching site was at the B-52's eleven to twelve o'clock position, approximately ten miles away. Four missiles appeared through the undercast two to three seconds apart. All missiles appeared to have an initial launch angle of 50 to 60 degrees. Suntan 01 lost missiles one and two during an attempt to turn into the site. Missiles three and four continued at a consistent angle and appeared to be on a trajectory well astern of Scarlet 03. When 5000 to 10,000 feet below the victim and slightly in front of the target, missile three pitched up to a 70- to 80-degree climb and struck beneath the aircraft's wing. Missile four followed and identical profile on a different flight path and detonated below the aircraft in the same area. These profiles tended to confirm some type of missile guidance during flight, even though Fan Song signals were not detected by the Weasel. The B-52 crews in the cell verified, via UHF communications, the presence of the T-8209 signal.[41]

As soon as this information was presented to the 388th TFW commanders, a priority message was sent to the 7th AF requesting the immediate shipment of the AGM-45A-6 and additional AGM-78 antiradiation missiles which could home on I-band frequency radiation.[42] The request was approved, and this prompted the emergency requisitioning and subsequent airlift of the missiles to Korat from the Fighter Weapons Center at Nellis AFB, Nevada. Six AGM-78s arrived almost immediately, and the additional AGM-45A-6s were scheduled to arrive on 27 December. In the meantime, the 388TH TFW director of operations directed the Wild Weasel force to be extremely selective, using their AGM-78s only against radars posing an immediate threat to the strike or support forces.[43] Other recommendations included a greater coverage of the chaff zones, since chaff dispensed by the ALE-38 was effective against I-band radar. Additionally, the Marines would begin providing up to seven EA-6As nightly, which could jam I-band radars. Da Nang Air Base was used as the staging base for the EA-6As.[44]

Another continuing effort concerning the SAM threat would significantly alter the outcome of Linebacker II. SAC planners had decided to identify, seek out, and systematically destroy North Vietnam's SAM defense capabilities. Photo reconnaissance shots revealed that although individual SAM sites seemed to have an inexhaustible supply of missiles, there did not appear to be great numbers of spare missiles at the firing sites. Therefore, the missiles obtained for reload purposes were thought to be located at centralized warehouses and depots where they were assembled, checked out, and then shipped to the SAM sites. Throughout the next several days of the offensive, USAF intelligence units started looking for the depots, and within eighteen hours of searching, began finding them. As they were discovered, they were added to the approved-target list.[45]

Day Five Attacks

DAY FIVE—TACAIR STRIKES

The Tacair force on 22 December was composed of 76 strike aircraft and 81 support aircraft. The targets were the Thai Nguyen thermal power plant (4 LGB F-4s), Lan Lau railroad bridge (4 LGB F-4s), Bac Giang TPP (4 LGB F-4s), Kep rail yards (16 F-4 LORAN), Bac Giang rail siding (16 F-4 LORAN), and Viet Tri transshipment point (24 A-7s and 4 LORAN F-4s). Weather in the area prevented strikes by the LGB aircraft. AAA and SAM reactions were light.[46] The A-7 strike flights reported no defensive reactions at all. The Viet Tri transshipment point (TSP) was a complex used to unload supplies coming from China on a water route. The 24 A-7s split into two attack waves, two minutes apart. Each wave of 12 aircraft flew with one element of the F-4 Pathfinders. The strike flight leader estimated good accuracy on the drop based upon information available from the A-7 radar-mapping systems and F-4 LORAN equipment.[47]

The Ubon F-4 strike flights all used LORAN guidance and dropped their loads. There was MIG activity, and one MIG kill was claimed by the Udorn MIGCAP. Three MIGs had positioned themselves between the MIGCAP and the target. Red Crown vectored Buick flight into a position between the MIGs and the strike force, and the F-4s obtained a good lock-on. Buick flight received clearance to fire and initiated a frontal pull-up attack on the MIGs. Buick 01 obtained a visual identification on a MIG-21 and fired all four of his AIM-7s in rapid succession. The second or third missile struck the MIG, blowing it apart. Lt. Col. James E. Brunson and Major Ralph S. Pickett received credit for the kill. Lieutenant Colonel Brunson, the flight leader, described the encounter with the MIGs:

After prestrike refueling—the ingress MIGCAP in this Linebacker mission—proceeded north toward Phu Tho en route to their assigned CAP area near Kep Airfield . . . two bandits started climbing out to the northwest of Hanoi. Red Crown was controlling the flight as they crossed into North Vietnam. Red Crown reported the MIGs as heading 290 degrees and climbing through 26,000 feet. Red Crown gave our flight a vector of 020 degrees and called the MIGs 030 degrees right, forty-six miles, at 29,000 feet, with friendlies between our flight and the MIG's.

The MIGs turned south toward us and the friendlies. Red Crown vectored us for a head-on intercept. Red Crown called the MIGs at 020 degrees and sixteen miles from us when the flight leader got a radar lock-on in that position and asked for clearance to fire. Red Crown cleared him to fire if a visual identification was made, as friendly aircraft were still in the area.

Our flight jettisoned the centerline fuel tanks and accelerated. The MIG was about 10,000 feet higher than the flight, and as aircraft 01 started his pull-up to center the radar steering dot, he saw a silver MIG-21 above him. The flight leader put the MIG in his gunsight pipper and fired four AIM-7 missiles in rapid succession with full radar lock-on, maintaining a steep climb toward the MIG. Both the aircraft commander and WSO observed one of the AIM-7 missiles detonate in the tail section and large pieces . . . to separate. The MIG went into an uncontrollable spin. No bailout was observed.

The flight was still in good formation, and turned to engage the second MIG in the flight, which was observed by aircraft 03. This MIG escaped, and the flight returned to base due to fuel.[48]

Another MIGCAP flight, Vega, engaged two other MIGs. The two MIGs had positioned themselves in trail with Buick flight about three miles back. Upon observing Vega flight, the MIGs broke off to the left and Vega began a stern chase. Vega lost the bogies in the clouds as the MIGs headed back to Hanoi.[49]

The weather in the target area was unsuitable for Hunter-Killer operations due to heavy undercast. The F-105Gs expended some shrikes preemptively, but did not expend their remaining ordnance due to a lack of suitable targets. The North Vietnamese were still withholding their SAMs for the night efforts.[50]

DAY FIVE—B-52 STRIKES

The targets for Day Five were all located in the Haiphong area. For the first time, 30 B-52s would approach the targets from a westerly heading over the Gulf of Tonkin and then exit again over the Gulf. 12 B-52Ds were scheduled to attack the Haiphong railway siding, and the remaining 18 were targeted against the nearby Haiphong PPS area (the same target attacked by the B-52s in April).[51]

The F-111s again flew airfield suppression sorties just prior to the arrival of the B-52 strike force. Throughout the night the F-111s randomly struck ten different targets in the Hanoi area, which included airfields, transshipment points, RADCOM, and port facilities.[52] During the attack on the Hanoi port facility at 2138 hours, F-111 Jackel 33, piloted by Capt. Bob Sponeybarger with his WSO, Capt. Bill Wilson, was downed by enemy AAA fire. After the F-111 crew had pickled off the twelve 500-pound bombs and scored direct hits on the port facility, the aircraft was hit by AAA. The crew had to shut down the right engine as they attempted to leave the area. At a point fifty-three miles west of Hanoi, they lost control of the aircraft and ejected. On the third day after the ejection, Captain Sponeybarger was captured by NVN Army troops searching for the crew members. The next day an intensive SAR effort attempted to recover Captain Wilson. As the HH-53 approached his position, a .50-caliber

gun position nearby raked the chopper, shot off the refueling probe, wounded the copilot, and caused numerous fuel leaks. Despite this, the helo crew continued to
hover for a pickup. Unfortunately, Captain Wilson lost
his balance while reaching for the penetrator device and
rolled down a hill. The HH-53 could not stay any longer,
since North Vietnamese soldiers were getting extremely
close to the chopper and they were all firing automatic
weapons. Extensively damaged, the HH-53 barely
reached a mountaintop in Laos and had to be abandoned
while under enemy fire. The crew was picked up by the
backup Jolly Green. For two more days Captain Wilson
successfully evaded the enemy search parties, but was
finally captured after Christmas while trying to reach food
and water dropped by orbiting A-7s. Both crew members
were released several months after their capture. A superb account of this mission and rescue effort as described by Captain Wilson can be found in Lou Drendel's
book, *F-111 in Action*.[53]

The chaff coverage for the Haiphong attacks was provided by 16 F-4 chaff bombers. Two tracks were flown
with 8 aircraft in each flight. The first flight, offset to the
left, was equipped with 8 ALE-38 pods and 48 chaff
bombs. The second flight, offset to the right, was
equipped with 10 ALE-38s and 24 chaff bombs. To permit the chaff clouds to merge, the left corridor was completed ten minutes prior to the one on the right. The chaff
area was approximately thirty miles long and twelve miles
wide, and was centered about ten miles west of Haiphong. The chaff had some holes as the result of the
crisscrossing chaff corridors.[54]

As the B-52 attack materialized, it must have put the
defensive command and control net in shock. To confuse
the defensive elements, the B-52s entered the target area
on six different tracks, none aimed at the primary target
areas. Several of the B-52 tracks were aimed toward the
coastline south of Haiphong, as if Hanoi were a possible
target. Then, as the B-52s converged about thirty miles
south of their intended release points, the cells abruptly
zeroed in on Haiphong. Between the innovative attack
plan, the ECM support provided by the EB-66 and Navy
EA-6B aircraft, and a better coverage of the chaff corri-

dors, the North Vietnamese were not able to respond effectively. Only forty three SAMs were fired, and for the second day of the operation no B-52s were downed nor did any receive even minor battle damage. All the B-52 targets in North Vietnam were successfully attacked.[55] Some enemy aircraft were observed, but the MIGCAP F-4s prevented their engaging the B-52 force. On the other hand, the escort F-4s were not able to find their B-52 cells, and the problem was compounded by a last-minute change to the B-52 routes. Meanwhile, the Iron Hand flights fired nine Shrikes (AGM-45s) and one AGM-78 against firing SAM sites and active site signals.[56]

Day Six Attacks

DAY SIX—TACAIR STRIKES

Four targets were fragged for attacks by 68 fighter-bombers and 77 support aircraft. The targets were the Hanoi RADCOM receiver, the Ha Gia and Dai Loi railroad bridges, and the Hoa Lac Airfield. Due to poor weather, the LGB strikes against the bridges were canceled prior to takeoff. The RADCOM receiver was hit by 32 F-4s loaded with MK-82 bombs and guided by LORAN-equipped F-4 Pathfinders. Hoa Lac Airfield was struck by 24 A-7s also guided by LORAN-equipped F-4s.[57] Each pathfinder escorted 12 A-7s (6 on each wing) and called the drop. The weather was solid undercast, and both cells reported good LORAN drops.

Although no SAMs were noted, several MIGs attempted attacks on the strike forces. Buick flight attempted a quartering head-on attack on a MIG-21. The crew fired three AIM-7s and two of the missiles appeared to guide. The MIG-21, which was painted an unusual light-green color, was last observed in a diving right-roll.[58] The Hunter-Killer teams were engaging a single active SAM site when two MIG-21s positioned themselves behind one of the F-105G flights. The team's F-4E flight jettisoned their CBUs to engage the MIGs, but the MIGs fled before the F-4Es could maneuver on them.[59] Pontiac, a strike-escort flight, had a close call during this period. The backseater in Pontiac 02 called a visual on a MIG, and the aircraft commander looked away from his leader to attempt visual acquisition of the MIG. He saw nothing, and looked back toward Pontiac 01 at the instant two Atoll missiles detonated approximately fifteen hundred feet behind Pontiac 01. The MIG that had attacked the flight then departed the area successfully.[60]

DAY SIX—B-52 STRIKES

Day Six for the B-52 crews presented a different kind of scenario from what they had been facing. The targets were not even close to the Hanoi-Haiphong complexes hit previously. 30 B-52s were scheduled to attack four targets beginning at 1910 hours Hanoi time. The B-52s from Guam rejoined the attacks over North Vietnam with 12 B-52Ds from Anderson and 18 B-52Ds from Utapao.[61] The targets were the Lang Dang rail yards, only eighteen miles from the Chinese border, and three nearby SAM sites (VN 660, VN 537, and VN 900). Although the crews did not understand why those particular SAM sites had been selected for destruction, the reasons would become evident during subsequent strikes later that week.[62] Due to the proximity of the Chinese border, the 30 B-52s would follow a common route northwest through the Gulf of Tonkin until they turned northwesterly and inland toward their targets. Coming off the targets, they would then turn back on a southeasterly heading to withdraw over the Gulf. To complicate the enemy's targeting problem, each aircraft would descend two thousand feet just 180 seconds prior to bomb release. After release, they would change altitudes again. For those cells hitting the SAM sites, the post-target turn was delayed, accomplished so that all aircraft would not be in a high angle of bank simultaneously, to avoid causing the associated degradation of their ECM patterns.[63]

Because of poor weather over Thailand, late receipt of the B-52 frag, and problems with control-agency communications for tanker rendezvous, most of the Tacair forces were not able to join up with the B-52 force in time to cover their approaches,[64] but SAC commanders made the decision to press on with the attack regardless.[65] The F-111s performed their missions on time, providing airfield suppression against the bases at Yen Bai, Kep, and Phuc Yen. They also hit other targets randomly through the night, including the Duc Noi and Trung Quan rail yards, the Cao Nung railroad bridge, transshipment points, and RADCOM facilities.[66]

The B-52s hit the Lang Dang rail yards within a sixteen minute period. Only four or five SAMs were fired at the force, but MIGs reacted strongly to the northeast attacks. Apparently, the North Vietnamese were caught off guard, because the target area had not been "prepared" by the Tacair support forces. However, four MIGs did engage two of the cells and fired four Atoll missiles which all passed above the bombers. None of the B-52s were lost or damaged that night.[67]

Day Seven Attacks

DAY SEVEN—TACAIR STRIKES

The planned Tacair strikes were kept at a minimum on 24 December in anticipation of a thirty-six-hour bombing stand-down over the Christmas holidays. The only daytime missions conducted against North Vietnam were by thirty-two LORAN-guided F-4s. The targets were the Thai Nguyen and Bac Giang thermal power plants (TPPs). The attacks took place at noontime, and no defensive reactions were observed at all.[68] A significant discovery was made on Day Seven concerning the communications problems on the MIGCAP frequency (322.2 MHz). Technicians at Korat discovered that the problem occurred whenever EB-66 aircraft were voice-jamming North Vietnamese networks at 160–170 MHz. The second harmonic of those frequencies overlapped the MIGCAP frequency, jamming our own communications. The problem was fixed by changing EB-66 jamming procedures and establishing alternate MIGCAP channels.[69]

The only other missions scheduled for the day were in support of the search-and-rescue efforts for the crew of Jackel 33. This rescue attempt resulted in the loss of

Korat's second A-7D of the year. On this day Capt. Charles "Chuck" F. Riess was flying with a call sign of Slam 04. He was returning to base after another unsuccessful effort to retrieve the downed F-111 crew up north when his flight was directed to rendezvous with a forward air controller over the Plain of Jars in Laos. The target was a known enemy gun position. The FAC first briefed all four aircraft on the target and then cleared them to attack the target using random roll-in headings. As Captain Riess started his dive on the target, he saw that the FAC was beginning a hard climbing-turn directly into his attack heading. Captain Riess attempted to dive underneath the FAC, but the A-7's canopy did not clear the 0-2 (Raven 21), and the next thing Captain Riess saw was flames on the right side of his aircraft. The 0-2 pilot was apparently killed, and his aircraft plummeted to the ground (his body was never recovered). Meanwhile, the A-7 was out of control and the g forces caused by the diving aircraft prevented Captain Riess from reaching his ejection handles until he was approximately three thousand feet from the ground.

Captain Riess landed in the middle of a large concentration of enemy troops near the aircraft crash site. He took a few steps and then realized that his right foot was injured. He then heard automatic weapons being fired at him from the west, so he immediately dove into the high grass in which he had landed. He crawled about a hundred feet to get clear of his parachute, then used his survival radio to notify the flight of his location, his injury, and the hostile fire nearby. A wave of Pathet Lao or North Vietnamese was quartering the area around him, and one of the troops stepped on Captain Riess's foot. As the enemy soldier raised his rifle at Captain Riess, he slowly raised his hands over his head. The soldiers then knocked Captain Riess to the ground and stripped him of everything except his flight suit. His hands were bound behind his back and he was led off to a nearby gully. He could see his A-7 flight, along with other aircraft, in the area, still looking for him.

In an underground bunker in the gully he was searched by another soldier. When the soldier found nothing of value remaining, he became irritated and slapped Captain Riess several times, then placed a bayonet at his throat, but an officer entered and proceeded to chew out the troop. That night Captain Riess was taken to a small compound near the Laos/North Vietnam border. During the march he met several groups of Pathet Lao and NVA soldiers on the trail. Once a soldier placed a small submachine gun to his head, but a senior NCO or officer immediately reprimanded the threatening soldier. After a march of several days, Captain Riess was placed on a truck and sent to Hanoi. His truck convoy was attacked twice by American aircraft. During the first attack, the truck in front and the one behind his truck was destroyed. During the second attack, bombs exploded near Captain Riess but he was not injured. The convoy continued without further incident to his final destination in a POW camp. Having spent ninety-four days in captivity, Captain Riess was released after the eventual ceasefire on 28 March 1973.[70]

DAY SEVEN—B-52 STRIKES

All 30 B-52s scheduled on Day Seven were provided by Utapao, with 12 aircraft targeted against the Kep rail yards and 18 against the Thai Nguyen rail yards. Both targets were about forty miles north of Hanoi, and again the bomber formations would split up their forces at varied altitudes as they attacked the targets. These tactics again apparently surprised the enemy defense forces. Even though the force was engaged by nineteen SAMs, some MIGs, and intense AAA fire, only one B-52 was damaged. Purple 02 was hit over Thai Nguyen by AAA at a point between the initial point and bomb release, causing minor damage. One of the MIGs that engaged two of the B-52 cells was shot down by Airman First Class Albert Moore, a gunner on Ruby 03. Airman Moore acquired the MIG on his radar scope and at two thousand yards he opened fire. The MIG exploded into a fireball and fell away into the undercast. Moore described his feelings that night:

On the way home I wasn't sure whether I should be happy or sad. You know, there was a guy in that MIG.

I'm sure he would have wanted to fly home too. But it was a case of him or my crew. I'm glad it turned out the way it did. Yes, I'd go again. Do I want another MIG? No, but given the same set of circumstances, yes, I'd go for another one.[71]

For the third day in a row the bomber forces returned to base without suffering any losses. The damage caused to Purple 02 was the only confirmed AAA hit on a B-52 during the entire offensive.[72]

Only three F-111s had been scheduled to strike that night against the airfields at Yen Bai, Kep, and Phuc Yen prior to the B-52 strikes. All three F-111s came under intense AAA fire but were not hit, but the North Vietnamese were beginning to develop tactics to counter the low-flying F-111s. Over certain areas near Hanoi the NVN had apparently set up jamming systems designed to upset the F-111's terrain-following radar (TFR) system. The first incident had occurred on 22 December as an F-111 descended out of the mountains into the delta area around Hanoi. A large blip was observed on the RHAW scope along with audio indicating that radar was painting the aircraft. About fifteen seconds later steady conical audio was noted, indicating a tracking lock-on which remained present the entire period the aircraft was in the delta area. Shortly after the tone had begun, the TFR channels failed and the aircraft started a fly-up maneuver. The pilot had to fly the aircraft manually to remain at low level while the WSO attempted unsuccessfully to reset the TFR. After the F-111 descended behind Thud Ridge, the TFR reset and functioned normally. Such events began to occur frequently during missions within twenty miles of Hanoi. A source radiating near Hanoi seemed to be using a line-of-sight acquisition to jam the TFR systems, trying to force the aircraft to climb to altitude (a characteristic built into the TFR for safety in case of system failure), making the F-111s more vulnerable to ground fire.[73] Concerns over the new North Vietnamese techniques were noted in a message from CINCPACAF to 7th AF:

The necessary similarity of daily F-111 operations in NVN give rise to the question whether the F-111s will be able to survive nightly low-level attacks on the same few airbases. I realize timing, approach headings, and altitudes for attack are difficult to vary to any degree and are driven by the main striking force, escape routes, and aircraft capabilities.

Hopefully, however, we could do something to increase their flexibility and survivability. It might be appropriate to pick some entirely new targets for variety or diversion, and even stand-down for a night or two to break the trend. I can't add much in the way of solid recommendations other than to express concern and suggest we all be alert for ways to counter the repetitive tactics of the F-111s.[74]

THE CHRISTMAS STAND-DOWN

A thirty-six-hour stand-down against targets in North Vietnam began as scheduled at midnight on 24 December. President Nixon had ordered the stand-down as a gesture of goodwill and in observance of Christmas Day. All B-52 missions over South Vietnam were also canceled in anticipation of a maximum effort against the north on 26 December. The time was well spent by the USAF personnel assigned to the bases involved in the offensive. The aircrews got some well-deserved rest, the planners continued to plan the maximum effort, and maintenance men throughout Southeast Asia performed needed maintenance on the aircraft.[75] Through the supreme efforts of the maintenance force, some of the more serious deficiencies on the degraded aircraft systems were repaired, and the aircraft were again brought up to some measure of their full capabilities.[76] Although the North Vietnamese were also rebuilding their defenses, the break was probably more beneficial to the U.S. forces, since their effectiveness and ability to restrike the north was largely restored.[77]

Chapter Six

PHASE THREE: THE FINAL EFFORT

SAC Revision of the Attack Plan

The 26 December B-52 strikes incorporated many of the aircrews' suggestions based on their firsthand knowledge of the mission. SAC headquarters delegated almost total control to the wing staffs to adopt their own concepts and tactics to best fit the specific mission requirements.

The revised plan for Phase Three of the offensive was to have a single mass assault of 120 aircraft striking ten different target complexes at the same time-on-target within fifteen minutes. The first cells in each attacking group were to release their bombs at exactly the same time. The intent was to oversaturate the NVN command and control system. To avoid stereotyped attack patterns, spacings and altitudes for cells were different, so SAM crews could not rely on the first cell over the target to provide track information for the follow-on cells. Also, the unmodified B-52Gs with weaker ECM equipment were no longer to be scheduled for attacking targets over the Hanoi area; they would only attack targets in lower-threat zones.[1]

Day Eight Attacks

DAY EIGHT—TACAIR STRIKES

The Tacair force planned for resuming strikes against the north on 26 December was composed of 48 strike aircraft (32 A-7s and 16 LORAN-equipped F-4s) and 53 support aircraft. The entire force was assigned to strike a single target: the Hanoi transformer station, the largest in North Vietnam and the main junction point for the Hanoi area. Destruction of the transformer station would greatly reduce the electrical power available to the Hanoi area. The enemy defensive effort consisted of only six unsuccessful SAM firings, and no reactions from either AAA or MIGs. The transformer station was successfully struck, causing moderate damage to buildings and power-line poles, and presumably did result in a temporary interruption of power to the Hanoi grid network.[2]

DAY EIGHT—B-52 STRIKES

Day Eight saw the largest formation of B-52s ever massed into a single wave. Of 120 B-52s, Anderson provided 78 of the aircraft (45 Gs and 33Ds) and Utapao provided the remaining 42 Ds. A force of 72 B-52Ds was assigned to targets in Hanoi, including the Kinh No complex (9 B-52s attacking from the N.W.), Duc Noi rail yards (9 B-52s from the N.W.), Hanoi rail yards (9 B-52s from the N.E.), Hanoi petroleum-products storage areas (9 B-52s from the N.E.), Giap Nhi rail yards (18 B-52s from the S.W.) VN 549 SAM site (3 B-52s from the S.E.), and the Van Dien vehicle repair depot (15 B-52s from the S.E.). The more vulnerable B-52Gs were assigned to hit the Thai Nguyen rail yards (15 B-52Gs and 3 B-52Ds from the N.W.), Haiphong rail yards (15 B-52Gs from the S.E.), and the Haiphong transformer station (15 B-52Gs from the N.E.).[3]

The support consisted of 114 Tacair craft from both the USAF and the Navy. The chaff flight was composed of 24 F-4 chaff bombers, which created a large, dense chaff blanket centered over the target areas. The escorts protected the chaff flights. The ECM support was covered

by 6 EB-66 and 4 EA-6 aircraft. Protection against the
MIGs was provided by 18 USAF and 4 Navy F-4s, and
the bombers were escorted by 20 F-4s. The SAM suppression forces consisted of 10 USAF and 8 Navy Iron
Hand aircraft, along with 10 F-4Es for Hunter-Killer support. Again, the F-111s attacked the major MIG airfields
prior to the B-52 attacks, along with targets that included
transshipment points rail yards, bridges, and RADCOM
facilities.[4]

The new tactics were very effective. The defenses were
saturated, confused, and degraded. The North Vietnamese SAM forces had to alter their firing techniques, and
the majority of the firings were associated with the less
effective, passive track-on-jam technique.[5] The enhanced
chaff blankets over the targets, supplemented by ECM
jamming of the T-8209 range trackers, probably aided
this. As planned, two bomber streams approached from
the northwest and southwest via Laos, departing by way
of the Gulf of Tonkin. Two other streams flew a reverse
course, coming from the northeast and southeast over the
Gulf and exiting through Laos. The approach from the
northeast was the reason why the three SAM sites had
been attacked on Day Seven. Planes attacking Haiphong
came in from the northeast and southeast (Figure 13).[6]
  The 9 B-52s striking the Hanoi rail yards received ten
SAMs and heavy AAA in return. The 9 B-52s that struck
the Hanoi PPS received six SAM firings. The 18 bombers
hitting the Thai Nguyen rail yards had 16 SAMs fired at
them unsuccessfully. Certain cells were dropping chaff,
and the aircrews reported that some of the SAMs detonated upon entering the chaff clouds that had been dispensed behind the aircraft. The 15 aircraft bombing the
Van Dien depot received heavy AAA fire, and at least 12
SAMs were launched against them without effect.[7] Of the
18 B-52s scheduled to strike the Giap Nhi rail yards, only
17 actually attacked, due to a ground-abort of a B-52 in
Utapao. Because of the abort, Ebony cell only contained
two aircraft. The bomber stream was attacked by 27 to
30 SAMs, four of which were fired at Ebony 02. The
aircraft was hit forward and to the left during its PTT,
mortally wounding the pilot. Soon after a second SAM

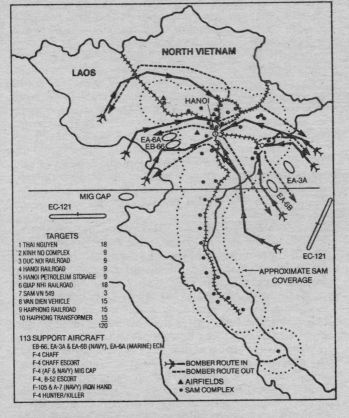

Figure 13. Day Eight B-52 Attack Plan

struck the tail section, the copilot lost control of the air-craft and ordered the crew to bail out. The crew ejected, and of the six crew members, the pilot was KIA, one became MIA, and four were captured. The cause for the loss was attributed to insufficient mutual ECM support caused by the two-ship cell formation.[8]

Col. James R. McCarthy, the Mission Airborne Commander in the lead aircraft (Snow 01) over Hanoi, recalled the action that night:

When we crossed the seventeenth parallel, we were committed. That was the last point at which I or higher headquarters could recall the forces. From here until the target area we would be using radio-silence procedures. The only radio call allowed would be if you got jumped by a MIG and you needed MIGCAP support. As Haiphong passed off our left wing, we could see that the Navy support forces were really working over the SAM and AAA sites. The whole area was lit up like a Christmas tree. We could hear Red Crown issuing SAM and MIG warnings to the friendly aircraft over Haiphong. We hoped that this activity would divert their attention from our G-model bombers, who would soon be arriving. Even though they weren't going to downtown Hanoi anymore, they were headed for the port city. As we all knew, that was plenty tough duty.

We coasted in northeast of Haiphong and headed for our IP, where we would turn southwest toward Hanoi. The IP turned out to be in the same area that had led BUFFS on the twenty-third against the SAM sites that had the reputation of being such lousy shots. The flak started coming up when we made our first landfall. Once again, we were most vividly aware of the heavy, black, ugly explosions which characterized the one hundred mm. Even at night the black smoke from these explosions is visible. Since we were at a lower altitude than we had flown before, our wave would be more vulnerable to this AAA than on most previous missions. Close to the IP the flak became more intense and the explosions were closer to the aircraft. As we turned over the IP we picked up the first SAM signals.

We could see them lift off, but their guidance seemed
erratic. The SAMs exploded far above us and at considerable distance from the formation. It appeared that
F Troop [the name given to these SAM-site crews by
the aircrews] was still in business and their aim was as
bad as it had always been.

However, inbound to the target, the SAM signals became stronger. Captain Don Redman, the E.W., reported three very strong signals tracking the aircraft.
Major Bill Stocker [pilot] ordered the cell to start their
SAM threat maneuver. The navigator, Major Bill Francis, reported that we had picked up the predicted
hundred-knot head winds. Then the SAMs really
started coming. It was apparent this was no F Troop
doing the aiming. The missiles lifted off and headed
for the aircraft. As we had long ago learned to do, we
fixed our attention on those that maintained their same
relative position even as we maneuvered. All of the
first six missiles fired appeared to maintain their same
relative position in the windshield. Then A1C Ken
Schell [gunner] reported from the tail that he had three
more SAMs at six o'clock heading for us. The next
few minutes were going to be interesting.

Now that the whole force was committed and we
were on the bomb run, I had nothing to do until after
bombs away, so I decided to count the SAMs launched
against us. Out the copilot's window, First Lieutenant
Ron Thomas reported four more coming up on the right
side and two at his one o'clock position. Bill reported
three more on the left side as the first six started exploding. Some were close—too close for comfort. Listening to the navigation team on interphone downstairs,
you would have thought they were making a practice
bomb run back in the States. The checklist was unhurried. Captain Joe Gangwish, the R.N., calmly discussed the identification of the aiming point that they
were using for this bomb run with his teammate, Major
Francis.

About a hundred seconds prior to bombs away, the
cockpit lit up like it was daylight. The light came from
the rocket exhaust of a SAM that had come up right
under the nose. The E.W. had reported an extremely

strong signal, and he was right. It's hard to judge miss-distance at night, but that one looked like it missed us by less than fifty feet. The proximity fuse should have detonated the warhead, but it didn't. Somebody up-stairs was looking after us that night. After twenty-six SAMs, I quit counting. They were coming up too fast to count. It appeared in the cockpit as if they were now barraging SAMs in order to make the lead element of the wave turn from its intended course.

Just prior to bombs away, the formation stopped ma-neuvering, to provide the required gyro stabilization to the bombing computers. Regardless of how close the SAMs appeared, the bomber had to remain straight and level. One crew during the raids actually saw a SAM that was going to hit them when they were only sec-onds away from bomb release. The copilot calmly an-nounced the impending impact to the crew over interphone. The aircraft dropped its bombs on target and was hit moments later. That's what I call "guts football."

At bombs away it looked like we were right in the middle of a fireworks factory that was in the process of blowing up. The radio was completely saturated with SAM calls and MIG warnings. As the bomb doors closed, several SAMs exploded nearby. Others could be seen arcing over and starting a descent, then deto-nating. If the proximity fuse didn't find a target, SA-2s were set to self-destruct at the end of a pre-determined time interval. Our computer's bombs-away signal went to the bomb bay right on the time hack. Despite the SAMs and the hundred-knot head winds, the nav team had dropped their bombs on target at the exact second called for in the frag order.

Some minutes afterward, as we were departing the immediate Hanoi area, there was a brilliant explosion off to our left rear that lit up the whole sky for miles around. A B-52D (Ebony 2) had been hit and had ex-ploded in midair. Momentarily, the radios went silent. Everyone was listening for the emergency beepers that are automatically activated when a parachute opens. We could make out two or possibly three different beepers going off. Miraculously, four of the Kincheloe

Air Force Base, Michigan, crew escaped the aircraft, becoming POWs. Then there was a call from another aircraft, Ash 01, stating that he had been hit and was heading for the water. The pilot reported that he was losing altitude and he was having difficulty controlling the aircraft. Red Crown started vectoring F-4s to escort the crippled bomber to safety.

As we withdrew farther from the target area, the gunner reported an additional barrage of SAMs headed our way. Bill gave the order to the formation to again start their maneuvers. It seemed like an eternity before the gunner reported that they had gone over the top of the aircraft and had exploded. That was our last encounter with SAMs that night. Now came an equally hard part—sweating out the time until the entire bomber stream had dropped their bombs and the cell leaders reported their losses. From the congestion on the radios it was apparent that the NVN had loaded up plenty of missiles and were using them.

Suddenly, one of the cells in our wave reported MIGs closing in and requested fighter support. Red Crown, who had been working with Ash 01, started vectoring other F-4s to the BUFF under possible attack. I gave the command for all upper rotating beacons and all taillights to be turned off. As the F-4s approached, the MIG apparently broke off his attack, because the fighters couldn't locate him and the target disappeared from the gunner's radars. This appeared to be another one of those cases where the MIGs were pacing the B-52s for the SAM gunners. It was speculated that if, while doing this, they thought they saw a chance for a one-pass quick kill, they would try to sneak within range and fire off a missile. Either that or make one screaming pass through the formation and then disappear. It was apparent that they didn't want to mix it up with our F-4 escort.

Finally, the last cell had exited the threat zones and reported in. The customary expression of this was, "So and so cell, out with three." A more picturesque expression which sort of captured what was happening, was when a formation reported themselves "over the fence with three." Except for the violent loss of Ebony

02 and the problems Ash 01 was having, the rest of the force was intact.[9]

Meanwhile, the 17 B-52s that bombed the Duc Noi rail yard were fired upon by 23 SAMs, but no aircraft were hit. The 3 B-52s striking VN-549 were not hit, but their bombs hit an empty SAM site location. VN-549 had moved since the last intelligence sighting.[10] Nine aircraft had been scheduled against the Kinh No complex, but due to two ground aborts, only seven aircraft were in the attack. At least 29 SAMs were fired at the B-52s, two cells of which were composed of only 2 B-52s. Again, a B-52 in a two-ship cell was struck by a SAM. Ash 01 was hit by 2 SAMs on the right side of the aircraft. The number-eight engine was shut down, number seven remained idle, and fuel was leaking from the right wing. The crew attempted to return to Utapao, and their aircraft was escorted by F-4s out of the threat zones.[11] Colonel McCarthy continues with his narrative of the outcome of the crew's fight for survival:

As we turned south, we could overhear Ash 01's conversations. He had made it to the water okay and was now heading south. Red Crown was giving him the positions of friendly ships in the area. However, Captain Jim Turner [the pilot in Ash 01] reported the aircraft seemed to be flyable and he was going to try to make it to Utapao. There were probably a couple of thousand guys who were listening that were praying he would make it. He almost did. He crashed just beyond the runway at Utapao, a tragic loss after so heroic an effort. Only the gunner and copilot survived the crash, and the copilot would not have made it without the bravery of Captain Brent Diefenbach, who had landed only a few minutes earlier. His quick thinking and ingenuity enabled him to reach the crash site, where he pulled First Lieutenant Bob Hymel from the wreckage. Technical Sergeant Spencer Grippin escaped the burning wreck when the tail section broke free on impact.[12]

The Utapao wing scheduler, Major Charles Luse, was walking outside Wing Headquarters to watch the returning aircraft land and was there when Ash 01 made its approach to land. He vividly recalled the events:

The night was rather dark as the aircraft continued its approach, then I heard the engines roar and come into life as the pilot obviously decided he could not land and was attempting to go around for another approach. I could see the aircraft was not accelerating and climbing as in a normal go-around, and then the aircraft disappeared, too low to see. Within seconds I heard a tremendous explosion as the aircraft hit the ground approximately one mile beyond the end of the runway. Intense flames immediately flared a hundred to two hundred feet in the air, and the entire sky was lit up by the fire. As I watched, I was sure no one could have possibly survived the crash. Deeply saddened, I returned to my office.[13]

But a dramatic rescue effort was being made. Captain Diefenbach later provided his recollections of that night:

We took off from Utapao in aircraft 074 for a 3.8-hour mission. The mission was over and we (the crew) were on our way to maintenance debriefing on a bus. Our aircraft parking spot had been on the opposite side of the runway from the main base, so the vehicle had to wait for aircraft taking off or landing before driving around the end of the runway. This is the position I was in while the battle-damaged aircraft was making its approach. It was quite dark, but we could see the aircraft bathed in the ground lights. Things didn't look nor sound right as I watched—then I heard the engines roar as power was added for a go-around. I watched sadly as the huge and awesome machine was unable to catch the sky and plunged like a wounded eagle back to earth. I then saw what I had only seen previously on the movie screen—a fireball and explosion almost too spectacular to have happened in front of my eyes instead of on the screen.

For some reason I became angry—angry at the whole lot—so I got off the bus for a walk, to settle down. Before I knew it, I was at an entrance gate where a guard was posted. Only a few words were exchanged as I told him I was going off the base, and I did. It was running through my mind that I had to get to the site of the crash—I didn't know why, but I just had to. It appeared obvious to me that no one was alive, but something kept drawing me to go. I knew I had to get there fast, so I scrambled in the back of a Baht bus (Baht is the name of the Thai currency, and short rides would often be only a few Baht, so Americans coined the name Baht bus). The ride was short and the driver refused to go any farther—I had no Baht on me anyway, so I bid him adieu and started jogging down the road toward my goal. I spotted a white sedan parked alongside the road and attempted to get in—the doors were locked, so I went back to jogging. Arriving at a spot adjacent to the crash site, I spotted a worn path in the tall grass that seemed to lead to the aircraft. For a second I thought, Why go, no one is alive in that inferno? But I went on. I stopped short of the blaze, and for some reason or another I called out to see if anyone was still inside. To my complete shock, I heard a voice calling for help. What a surprise! I heard a rescue chopper, so I called out that help was on the way. The chopper must have swung around, so that I could no longer hear or see it. However, I could still hear the call for help, and all I could see was my own life and a glimpse of my family as I rolled down my flight-suit sleeves, tightened up the zipper around my neck, and started for the aircraft. How I wished I had my fireproof flying gloves, but they were in my helmet bag. The individual was still crying for help, so I called out to him—I told him that the fire trucks were coming, that the helicopter was behind me, and that we were all going to get him out. But in reality, there was no one—no one at all, except me.

As I entered the burning aircraft, I called for him to keep on hollering so I could find him. There was total silence from the other crew members. However, he kept yelling, and I finally made my way to the copilot's seat. He flipped off his helmet, we exchanged some words, and I found out that not only was he badly injured, he was also stuck in the seat by the smashed angle of the wreckage. In addition, he still had his seat belt, shoulder straps, and leg straps on. The time seemed to drift by, almost as if suspended in animation. It was getting warmer and warmer, and more items started exploding, and with each explosion, I'd jump a little bit higher. I had no way of knowing if there were still any bombs aboard which could explode, but the copilot seemed to be dying on the spot, so I had to hurry. In my attempt to loosen him, I recall that I accused him of not helping, and of falling asleep—anything to keep him conscious. He helped me pull on his leg and we finally pulled it loose. By that time the explosions, the heat, and the smoke were nearer than I care to think about.

At last I pulled him clear of the wreckage and picked him up in the fireman's carry to get away from the exploding aircraft. Not only did I fall down once, but twice. I saw a fire truck then, and also a helicopter had landed. One of the helicopter rescue men tried to approach the aircraft but was unable, due to the fire and explosions. Before I knew it, we were aboard the helicopter and on our way to the hospital.

A short time later I had worked my way back to the headquarters building, where I was taken to the command post by one of the scheduling officers [Major Luse]. I told my story, then went to the hospital myself for some minor repairs and bandages. I later found out that there was a lot of thank-yous in order for the chief pilot in the sky, since the ejection sequence had been initiated and the copilot's seat was armed for firing.[14]

In his article for a military magazine, Capt. Dana Drenkowski, a F-4 pilot, noted an additional twist to Captain Diefenbach's heroic actions. Apparently, the base's fire and rescue trucks were held up at the front gate of the base while Captain Diefenbach was awaiting assistance. The gate guards were under orders not to allow their passage, because the fire equipment might be required to support other returning bombers. Apparently, Captain Diefenbach was also pending a court-martial for his rescue effort because he violated several SAC regulations when he left the base without permission.[15] However, in the face of rising protests of his fellow crew members, the court-martial charges were dismissed, and instead, Captain Diefenbach was later presented with the Airman's Medal for heroism by the SAC commander. [16]

The copilot rescued by Captain Diefenbach, Lieutenant Hymel, was hospitalized for twenty-nine days at Clark AFB hospital in the Philippines. His injuries included a broken left arm, broken right leg, both hands broken, numerous cuts, and facial injuries. In December of 1976 Lieutenant Hymel recalled the events of that day:

The evening before the flight, I recall that it was extremely tense for everyone. We were concerned about the Christmas bombing halt; afraid that the North Vietnamese had used the halt to restock and repair their SAM facilities. That evening I had a very strange feeling; hard to explain, but I had a feeling that something was going to happen. The thought crossed my mind that I could go DNIF [duty not involving flying] for a cold, but I suppose I was just conditioned to the fact that I had a job to do and that was it. I wasn't really excited about going. There were those who really wanted to go that night, as they felt they were doing some good. I really don't know whether I believed that or not.

Later that afternoon I went to church. I remembered the church being overly crowded; possibly the holiday season, possibly for other reasons. Later, I tried to call my wife—I really wanted to talk to her. As I recall, the phone lines were bad, so I walked over to the MARS [Military Affiliate Radio Station] station. I remember going through Alaska and the phone patch was really bad. We were only able to talk for a few minutes. I wanted to know how my daughter was, for I had not seen her since her birth in October. I really didn't have much to say. I just had to talk to someone.

I returned to my trailer, changed into my flying clothes, and the time came to proceed to the briefing. I believe the target was northwest of Hanoi [Kinh No complex], but I don't remember exactly. As we approached the target area, things really got moving. We could hear other aircraft calling visual SAMs, and our anticipation of encountering extremely large numbers of SAMs was correct. The aircraft ahead of us were really getting "hosed down." As we approached Hanoi, we also picked up visual SAMs. The pilot had his hands full flying the airplane, constantly turning, descending, or climbing. We rolled the wings level just prior to bomb release, and after release, immediately rolled into our post-target turn. As we rolled off target heading, the gunner said, "Copilot, we have too many SAMs coming up from the left rear." As I turned my head, I could see two SAMs coming up side by side, the one on the inside slightly ahead of the other. As the SAMs approached, they seemed to be turning directly for us. The pilot put the aircraft in a descending turn, and the SAMs went off alongside the right side of the aircraft. It felt as though we had been kicked in the pants. We checked to see if everyone was all right. All of us up front were okay, but the gunner had received some shrapnel in his legs. The airplane had been hit bad. I didn't know if we could keep it in the air.

We headed out over water and turned for Da Nang in South Vietnam. We had the number-eight engine shut down, number seven in idle, and were losing fuel from the right side. We asked for some tankers and refueled several times. We had excellent support. When we reached Da Nang, we decided to continue on to Utapao, where the gunner might get better medical aid. We set up the aircraft for a straight-in approach, lowered the gear, and the aircraft vibrated for a moment. As the aircraft approached the runway it veered to the left. The pilot got on the radio to the ground control and told him the airplane wouldn't turn to the right. Then it seemed like it came back that way, to the right. We were using the outboard engines to create some asymmetrical thrust. The pilot then pulled the throttles off, trying to set it down where it was, still short of the runway, but the plane wasn't responding. Then he added power, trying to get some altitude for ejection (especially since the navigators needed about four hundred feet of altitude to eject successfully from their downward ejection seats) or go around for another try. The nose pitched up and control seemed to be lost. It seemed like the airplane was pointed straight up in the air, with the altimeter winding up and the airspeed going in reverse. I decided it was time to jump out of the airplane, and I came out over the intercom and said, "Bail out! Bail out!"

The next thing I knew, the aircraft had come to rest and I tried to unstrap myself. I was hunched over, cramped against the seat, and couldn't seem to unbuckle my seat straps. I then began yelling for help, hoping that someone may be outside. Brent [Captain Diefenbach] heard me yelling and came to help. I remember talking with him, and that he couldn't get me out because my leg was caught. I knew my leg was broken, so I told him to pull it off if he had to. It finally came loose.

Once outside, Brent said we must get away from the aircraft, so he began to carry me away. He fell, got back up, and fell again. He then said the fire truck was heading for us, and got up to keep it from running over us. I remember being loaded in the helicopter, but nothing else until I woke up in the emergency room.

Prior to the aircraft hitting the ground, I had attempted to eject myself. I remember raising the arming levers but don't recall that I ever squeezed the trigger. It must have been a miracle that the seat did not get fired while Brent was wrestling to get me free.[17]

For his part, Lieutenant Hymel was awarded the Distinguished Flying Cross, the Air Medal, and the Purple Heart. The gunner, Technical Sergeant Grippin, had managed to escape from the gun turret position, and hobbled off to safety on his wounded legs. The remaining crew members (pilot, EWO, R.N., and Nav) all perished in the crash.

The Day Eight attacks finished up with 15 B-52Gs striking the Haiphong rail yards. A total of 36 SAMs were fired at the aircraft, but none hit. 15 other B-52Gs simultaneously attacked the Haiphong transformer station, experiencing only light defensive reaction. Of the 120 B-52s scheduled in the strike, 113 effectively completed their missions. Seven had ground-aborted, and the use of two ship cells due to the shortages had contributed to the two losses due to the insufficient ECM cell coverage. In the Day Eight attack the B-52s had dropped 9932 bombs totaling over 2100 tons in less than twenty-two minutes.[18] Up to 68 SAMs had been fired at the B-52s, but the new tactics combined with vast numbers of Tacair support had limited the effectiveness of the missiles. Some MIGs had attempted intercepts but were driven off by the F-4 MIGCAPs and escorts. The outcome of Day Eight was a tactical masterpiece, demonstrating how well the lessons of the previous raids had been learned. Certainly the tremendous shock of the huge raid rocked the communists severely. Airpower was being applied with surgical accuracy and at a level sufficient to force some "behavioral changes" on the North Vietnamese.

The POWs in Hanoi were able to view firsthand the impact the raids were having on the Vietnamese. Major Pete Giroux, who had been a POW since 21 December when his B-52 was shot down (Scarlet 03), noted:

There had been a break in the bombing on the twenty-fifth. I wondered whether the North Vietnamese would take advantage of it to make overtures to reopen the negotiations. They certainly weren't going on with the bombing in progress. But the night of the twenty-sixth the bombing resumed with a great deal of intensity. It was strangely exciting, and some of us were yelling encouragement up to our friends. There appeared to be SAM sites quite close to us as the "whoosh" of the launch was accompanied by the bright light of the engine. There was also some anti-aircraft artillery in the area. I knew how intensively the nav team had been briefed on the location of the several camps, and knew this was the safest place to be [there was a tall radio tower near the Hanoi Hilton which served nicely as a radar return to ensure that no bombs would be released in that area]. Then the bombs all began to hit. They weren't far away, as the closer ones exploded with sharp cracks and knocked some plaster on me. I couldn't yet walk, and I was sitting on the end of the bed looking up and out of a window on the opposite wall. Despite the closeness of the bombs, there were several people still standing near the windows looking up when we saw a B-52 disintegrate and spread its fuel across the sky in a fiery swath [Ebony 02]. Then it was over rather quickly, which surprised me. The tactics had to have changed, and they had. It was an impressive show, although we were concerned for the crew that had been shot down. The guards who were normally harassing us were nowhere to be seen, and looked badly shaken the next morning. Moving around the camp later, we could see the hastily dug shelters.[19]

A similar story was provided by Lt. Col. Bill Conlee, who had been shot down in his B-52 (Blue 01) as well on 21 December:

On the evening of 26 December the walls of the Hilton shook with the proximity of the B-52 bombing, which was a great encouragement to me. It was immediately obvious that SAMs were being fired from several sites located right outside the prison walls. I could also hear AAA fire coming from the roof of the Hilton, using the prison as a sanctuary from attack. The next morning a large group of ashen-faced Vietnamese came into my room and asked how close the bombs were and what airplanes were dropping them. I said, "Very close, and you know already," and smiled. This proved to be a mistake, as I was quickly subjected to a rough briefing, the worst I received during captivity. From this experience I concluded that the North Vietnamese were genuinely terrified about the B-52 bombing and were striking out in fear and frustration at an available target—me.[20]

Several of the older POWs related the same basic observations. One of them gave this account:

During earlier air strikes the guards would fire at passing aircraft with their AK-47s. After the air strikes, the patriotic guards would shake their fists in our faces as a sign of defiance and would be laughing and joking.

During the B-52 raids, you could see a different effect in the guard's faces. There was no joking, no laughing, no acts of defiance or reprisal. The guards, some openly weeping, simply headed for their shelters— individual manholes—and pulled concrete lids over their heads.[21]

Another POW described the changing reactions of the guards. The guards would try to smash the fingers of POWs with their rifle butts when the prisoners watched earlier raids. But when the long strings of B-52 bombs started going off, there was no such reaction. The POW saw one guard "trembling like a leaf, drop his rifle, and wet his pants." The best summation of the impact of the bombing was probably put forth by Col. John P. Flynn, the senior POW officer: "When I heard the B-52 bombs go off, I sent a message to our people. It said, 'Pack your bags—I don't know when we're going home, but we're going home.' "[22]

Tanker support for the raids of 26 December was noteworthy. Although only 194 KC-135 tankers were available in the theater, they supported a total of 763 refuelings within a twenty-four-hour period. The Tacair force alone required 607 of these refuelings.[23] The aircrew and maintenance activities to support such a Herculean task were some of the more notable achievements in the Linebacker offensive. The job could just not have been possible without these important assets.

Day Nine Attacks

DAY NINE—TACAIR STRIKES

The Tacair force on 27 December consisted of 52 strike and 65 support aircraft fragged against three targets. The targets were the Hanoi AM transmitter (Radio Hanoi), Hanoi International RADCOM transmitter site, and Hanoi RADCOM transmitter number two. 12 F-4s loaded with laser-guided bombs were assigned to strike all three targets (4 F-4s per target). 32 A-7s were scheduled to attack both of the RADCOM transmitters (16 A-7s per target). Bombing by the A-7s was to be done visually if possible, but 8 F-4 LORAN Pathfinders accompanied the force if the weather turned out to be poor. All attacks were planned to occur at 1300 hours, local Hanoi time.[24]

The morning started out badly, when a runway closure during the launch at Korat affected the entire strike package. At the beginning of the launch sequence, one of the F-105Gs (Eagle 02) experienced a failure of its water-injection system during liftoff and the aircrew jettisoned its 650-gallon centerline fuel tank along with the Shrike missiles. The F-105G continued to climb to altitude and joined up with Eagle 01. Directly behind Eagle 02 one of the F-4Es loaded with cluster-bomb units Eagle 03, had already begun a takeoff roll, and the aircraft flew directly through the exploding fireball on the runway and miraculously suffered no damage. The wingman in Eagle 04 intelligently decided to abort his takeoff roll, and taxied off the first taxiway. The entire A-7 strike force along with the EB-66s and additional Hunter-Killer teams was lined up on the taxiways awaiting takeoff. All TOTs were slipped while the runway was cleaned up.[25]

Within a short time the Korat runway was cleared and the strike and support forces were able to proceed to target. Weather over Hanoi was clear and the A-7s were able to attack using visual means. The LGB bombers were especially effective against the Radio Hanoi transmitter. All targets received extensive damage from the Tacair strikes. The Hanoi International RADCOM transmitter received several hits, resulting in one transmitter and control building along with two medium-size support buildings being destroyed. Four other buildings received medium to heavy damage. The target was reported to be one of the largest and best-equipped radio transmission facilities in North Vietnam. The damage caused to this facility would cause overloading of the other transmitting facilities in the Hanoi area. The bomb damage assessment reported that the strikes on the RADCOM transmitter number-two site showed similar results. The target took several direct hits, resulting in the destruction of four support buildings, heavy damage to the control building, and moderate damage to the remaining structures. This facility was linked to the Hanoi Defense Communication Network and supplemented early-warning electronic sites. The destruction of this target undoubtedly hampered the air-defense effort around Hanoi and resulted in the loss of valuable communication systems.[26]

The Radio Hanoi transmitter housed the main North Vietnamese propaganda network and communications net for the army. The facility had already been attacked previously by 36 B-52s, which dropped 2016 bombs around it.[27] Although the B-52 attacks had damaged the barracks areas, outbuildings, and main power supply, the tiny building housing the actual transmitter and antennae was surrounded by a thick, twenty-foot-high revetment wall, and it had not suffered any damage. It would require a direct hit on the building to destroy it, and 4 F-4 LGB bombers accomplished just that on Day Nine by dropping their ordnance directly into the revetment. The building's walls contained and reflected the shock waves and virtually pounded the transmitter into dust.[28]

The enemy's defense was intense on Day Nine, with SAM firings, MIG attacks, and heavy AAA fire. To counter the enemy SAMs, the Hunter-Killer teams attacked a number of sites. Condor flight was one of these teams:

Condor flight hoped to establish visual contact with a SAM site that had been responsible for the downing of one B-52 and the damaging of several others. While making a surveillance run in search of the site [VN-271], the flight came under intense accurate AAA from two gun batteries. One of them, an eighty-five mm battery, had radar tracking [Fire Can]. Condor 01 was able to attack with one of his Shrike missiles, and the radar was silenced at the computed missile-impact time (which indicated a direct hit and subsequent destruction of the site).

Condor 03 [an F-4E] was able to locate the site visually from the smoke caused from the destroyed radar, and positioned the flight for an attack. The first attack was broken up by a SAM launch from a nearby site. After recovering from the SAM breaks, Condor

03 and 04 repositioned for the attack. Condor 03 dropped half its ordnance [CBUs] and destroyed 3 SA-2 missiles on their launchers. Also destroyed were 2 AAA guns. Condor 04, using the wind-drift information from the Condor 03 drop, was able to destroy all of the remaining radar facilities as well as 2 more SA-2 SAM missiles.

Meanwhile, the Condor F-105Gs were providing SAM protection for the F-4Es. Condor 02 launched his remaining Shrike at a Fan Song, and it went off the air. Since they were now out of ARM [antiradiation missiles] missiles, they continued to make mock attacks to force new threat signals off the air.[29]

Crow flight, another Hunter-Killer team, expended one of the newly arrived AGM-45A-6 missiles on a T-8209 I-band tracker with a possible kill on VN-004. F-4E Crow 03 then dropped two CBUs on the site and reported hundred-percent coverage (meaning that the entire site was peppered with CBUs).[30] One of the F-4E Killers, however, could not expend any ordnance. It was originally Eagle 04, which had aborted takeoff on the Korat runway. After the aircraft had taxied off the runway and parked to await another takeoff, the pilot was unaware that the munitions end-of-runway crews had repinned his missiles, CBUs, and fuel tanks for safety purposes. The pilot took off thinking the aircraft was still armed. The F-4 maintenance officer (this author) had been notified of the mistake by the end-of-runway crews and he immediately informed the command post. The F-4E had already joined up with a Hunter-Killer flight by then, and the flight leader ordered the F-4E aircrew to remain on-station to preserve the flight integrity. It would also fool and deter the North Vietnamese SAM-site personnel, since they had no way of knowing that the F-4E could not drop its CBUs.[31]

The MIGCAP flights were actively engaged with MIGs throughout the strike. Red Crown reported two MIGs airborne out of Phuc Yen and vectored Vega flight toward the enemy aircraft. Vega 01 acquired radar contact at fifteen miles range and was cleared to fire. The flight closed to five miles and a MIG-21 was acquired visually.

At two miles Vega 01 unsuccessfully attempted to fire an AIM-7. A second AIM-7 was fired, but exploded low inside the MIG's turn at approximately fifty meters. The MIG then went into the clouds, followed by Vega 01 and 02. At this time Vega 03 and 04 lost the first element and were directed to leave by Vega 01. Vega 01 then began to experience pitch-control problems. Before disengaging, Vega 01 launched an AIM-9 as the MIG went into a low cloud deck, and no results were observed. Vega 02 lost sight of Vega 01 and was directed to depart the area. Vega 01 then lost his left engine and had to join up with Vega 03 for escort out of the area and a return to base. Vega 04 had already left because it was low on fuel.[32] Vega 02 could not be reached again, and it was discovered later that a MIG had shot the F-4 down with an Atoll missile. The aircrew successfully ejected but was captured.

Problems with MIGs were also faced by Desoto flight escorting the A-7 strike flights. On leaving the target area, Desoto 03 visually sighted a MIG-21 but did not receive clearance to fire. The visual on the MIG was lost, and Desoto 03 and 04 disengaged. As they climbed to rejoin the force, an Atoll missile struck Desoto 03 and it caught fire. The crew ejected and was captured by the North Vietnamese. The bomb-damage assessment for the strike force was excellent on Day Nine, but the price included the only two USAF Tacair F-4 losses of the entire offensive.[33]

DAY NINE—B-52 STRIKES

The B-52 raids on Day Nine were a replay of the ones on Day Eight, on a smaller scale. The strike force consisted of 57 bombers (21 B-52Gs and 36 B-52Ds), 30 of which came from Utapao. The 21 B-52s were scheduled to attack the Lang Dang rail yards. The B-52Ds attacked the Duc Noi rail yards (9 B-52s), Trung Quan rail yards (12 B-52s), Van Dien depot (6 B-52s) and three SAM sites (VN-234, VN-243, and VN-549; 3 B-52s each). THe F-111s flew the usual prestrike airfield suppression missions. They also randomly attacked RADCOM transmitters, rail yards, transshipment points, two railroad bridges, and for the first time, a SAM site (VN-549). The Tacair support package included 101 aircraft, and as with all other days, F-4s laid a chaff blanket over the target area.[34]

The 21 B-52Gs successfully attacked the Lang Dang rail yards and were fired upon by 6 SAMs, but no aircraft were damaged. Ruby cell attacked SAM site VN-234 to cover the attack route of the following three cells assigned to attack the Duc Noi rail yards. Four SAMs were fired at Ruby and 15 SAMs were visually sighted by the following cells. Black 03 received minor damage from a SAM that detonated two hundred feet away, but returned to Utapao without difficulty. As the 12 aircraft assigned to strike the Trung Quan rail yards released their bombs, Cobalt 01 experienced a near-direct hit by one of 45 SAMs fired at the cells.[35] Every crew member on board received injuries from the impacting SAM fragments, and the navigator was mortally injured. The pilot, Capt. Frank D. Lewis, attempted to maintain control of the aircraft as it headed west. The wings were on fire and the ruptured fuel tanks fed the rapidly spreading fire. All electrical systems were out, as well as the crew interphone system. The pilot verbally gave the order to bail out only forty seconds after the SAM impact, and the crew began ejecting the aircraft. The gunner, MSgt. James A. Gough, could not hear the ejection order, but he knew that he would have to leave the aircraft soon. The flames from the burning aircraft extended back on both sides of the B-52 to the gunner's turret, and he decided to wait for a better chance as long as the aircraft was still in level flight. By then the other crew members who were able to eject had already departed the plane. When the gunner saw that the aircraft was descending into the low undercast, he knew he had to leave right then, or he might not have any chance at all. When he jumped, he went through the burning debris of the disintegrating engines and wings and had numerous pieces of wiring and metal fragments embedded in his body. Luckily, he was able to deploy his chute and was captured after he landed on the ground.

Meanwhile, the other crew members had also landed and were being captured by NVN troops. All had successfully ejected except for the navigator, First Lt. Ben L. Fryer, who was apparently killed by the SAM explosion. No one knows why Major Allen L. Johnson, the EWO, was not accounted for after the bailout, but he remained in a MIA status until his body was returned by the North Vietnamese in 1986. The pilot, Captain Lewis, was lucky to be captured alive after he landed in a rice paddy. Because he was leery of carrying a loaded .38 pistol, he normally carried his ammunition in a small plastic bag in his flightsuit. During a brief struggle with his North Vietnamese captors, he realized that a North Vietnamese peasant was squeezing off his own pistol at a point-blank distance, and all he could hear was the click, click, click of the empty pistol's trigger being pulled. Almost immediately, NVA troops arrived and grabbed the pistol away from the peasant and then took Captain Lewis captive.[36] These were the last B-52 crew members to go down over North Vietnamese territory during Linebacker II.*

The 9 B-52s striking the Van Dien Depot had 8 SAMs fired against them, inflicting minor damage on one aircraft. Three B-52s attacked VN-549, but again missed the site, since the NVN crews had already deployed to another location. The 3 other B-52s attacking SAM site VN-243 were fired upon by VN-549 (from its new location site), and Ash 02 was hit by a SAM.[37] Capt. John D. Mize, the pilot, was on his fourth mission of the campaign. His aircraft had been damaged twice before in the previous missions, once by a SAM and once by AAA.[38] As his aircraft released its bomb load, a barrage of 15 SAMs was launched against it. One of the SAMs struck the left wing, between the inboard engine and the fuselage, as Captain Mize executed a steep turn away from the target.[39] Shrapnel hit Captain Mize in the lower left leg, the left thigh, and his left hand. The gunner, TSgt. Peter E. Whalen, was hit in the right leg and thigh, and the radar navigator, Capt. Bill E. North, was also hit in the legs.[40] Captain Mize described the situation:

*For Captain Lewis's own account of Cobalt 01's shootdown and the survivors' subsequent captivity, see Appendix 2.

There was a tremendous concussion—it took out four engines and all associated equipment. The whole left side of the plane was dead for all practical purposes. One engine was on fire for the first five or ten minutes, then it burned out. We started getting all kinds of indications the plane was dying. Red warning lights started flashing on and we were falling.

The bomber fell several thousand feet before Captain Mize was able to get it leveled off. This was a superhuman effort alone, since the giant aircraft had lost most of the power boost on the flight controls, and the pilot was in an injured condition. Nearly every system on the aircraft was inoperative. There was no radar, ECM, or computers. Only one alternator, a radio, and the cockpit lights remained in operation. All instruments were out except the altimeter and airspeed indicator. To prevent overloading of the remaining electrical system and to cut down the chance of fire, the crew moved quickly to shut down equipment that had not been damaged and was not needed for the moment. The B-52 was almost helpless because it no longer had the overlapping protection of the other aircraft in the cell, and it had lost its self-protection equipment. The crew saw two more SAMs, but they missed. Fortunately, no MIGs spotted the crippled aircraft.[41] The navigator, First Lt. William L. Robinson, gave Captain Mize a heading to leave the target area. With no equipment, he had to estimate the heading by working straight time and distance from the last-known position.[42]

After the flaming engine had burned itself out, the crew set about trying to nurse the aircraft back to friendly territory. As Captain Mize noted:

It was not a question of making it back to the base, but one of how far we could get before we had to abandon the aircraft. We just took it as it came and did what had to be done at the moment. The book says it will fly on four engines, and it does [but this is an extremely difficult thing to do when all four engines are out on the same side of the aircraft]. I'm not the first man to fly on four engines. I had never done any real needle, ball, and airspeed flying, or what is referred to as "flying by the seat of your pants," but the B-52 can be flown that way. I did a series of climbs and descents. It was the only thing to do. I would descend to pick up airspeed and then climb—I'd descend fifteen hundred feet and climb a thousand. I did what had to be done with what I had. I knew we would make it—provided that wing didn't come off. We knew where we wanted to go—a place that would be close to rescue helicopters [the pre-deployed rescue forces and an HC-130 were near the border of Laos and NVN]. We headed for it.[43]

The navigators calculated that if the left wing held together, they could get to the Thailand border with only a small compromise of the 10,000 feet recommended bail-out altitude. The navigator, Lieutenant Robinson, stated: "We had help. One aircraft gave us an initial heading from our basic position to the nearest friendly territory, and later a rescue ship [the HC-130] picked us up near the border of North Vietnam and Laos, gave us a heading, and flew about two miles just off our right wing tip, giving us a cross-check."[44]

As they drew closer to the safety of Nakhon Phanom, Thailand, the situation rapidly deteriorated. The bomb-bay doors fell open, one landing gear started cycling up and down, other electrical systems went awry, and the wing was still burning. In spite of the crew's efforts, it soon became obvious they would not be able to coax the rapidly descending bomber to a safe landing. It looked like time to get out.[45] But Lieutenant Robinson cautioned Captain Mize that they were over jagged mountain ranges, and if they could stay airborne for another thirty miles, they would have flat rice-paddy fields to parachute over. So Captain Mize continued his struggle with the aircraft. Finally, when the aircraft was only eight miles from NKP, Captain Mize felt a kind of death throe run through the B-52, and he ordered the crew to begin bailing out.[46] Captain Mize recalls: "I called to each crew member, giving him the order to bail out. When I called the gunner, he asked me if we really had to bail out. I told him we did."[47] So four men ejected immediately, including copilot Capt. Terrence J. Gruters, and the EWO, Capt. Dennis W. Anderson.

However, Lieutenant Robinson did not eject—he had pulled the ejection handles but nothing had happened. He explained his situation to Captain Mize. Captain Mize described what happened next:

> The others ejected, except the navigator. The seat he was on was supposed to blow downward. But it didn't. He told me he was going out the hole where the radar nav [Captain North] had ejected. After he left his seat I wouldn't be able to communicate with him, so I told him I'd give him three minutes to be sure he had time to escape. At the end I called again, there was no response, so I ejected [at this point all the electrical systems on board failed, and Mize had no choice but to leave]. They had helicopters and rescue birds on the scene as we were bailing out. They picked us all up within minutes after the last man had bailed out. All six of us had made it. From my viewpoint, there was a seventh man on board.[48]

For his heroic efforts, and especially his effort to save crew-mate Lieutenant Robinson, Captain Mize was awarded the Air Force Cross, the second-highest American decoration for valor. The other crew members received the Distinguished Flying Cross, and they all received the Purple Heart. Ash 02 was the last B-52 to be lost during the Linebacker offensive.

By the end of Day Nine, the bombing of North Vietnam had taken an enormous toll. The planners were running out of suitable targets since the damage inflicted on most targets was higher than initially predicted. It became questionable whether those few targets remaining in the high-threat areas were even of sufficient worth to continue attacks in these areas. The PACAF commander even suggested that it was time to look for targets in less dangerous areas.[49]

As on previous days, the Tacair support effectively countered the enemy defenses. The few MIGs that had managed to get airborne were driven away by the MIGCAP flights. Although up to seventy SAMs had been fired at the B-52s, their accuracy was poor. The last desperate attempts to defend Hanoi were being made.

Day Ten Attacks

DAY TEN—TACAIR STRIKES

The package for the 29 December day missions consisted of 48 strike and 61 support aircraft. The fighter bombers were fragged against two targets: the Hanoi railroad/highway bridge (8 LGB F-4s) and the Quinh Loi storage area in Hanoi (32 A-7s led by 8 F-4 Pathfinders). Again, bombing was to be visual if the weather permitted. The weather was clear enough to allow one of the Ubon laser-guided bomb flights to attack the bridge. The flight was fired at by fifty-seven mm and eighty-five mm AAA as it maneuvered over the target. The surface winds were high, and the one-foot-per-knot offset required for laser illumination placed the illumination point in the river. As a result, most of the laser energy was reflected by the water and degraded bomb guidance. However, a sufficient number of LGBs struck the bridge to drop one of the spans into the water. The damage disrupted all rail traffic on the northeast and northwest rail lines.[50]

The first wave of 16 A-7s, led by 4 F-4 Pathfinders, was able to make visual drops against the Quinh Loi storage areas. Good target coverage was reported by all the flights. Several minutes behind the second wave of A-7s had to utilize the LORAN drop technique because clouds had moved into the area. Both waves had reported medium AAA fire over the target area.

Although no MIGs were reported airborne, one of the Udorn MIGCAP flights observed 2 MIG-21s being towed on the ground at Phuc Yen, along with 4 additional MIG-21s in revetments. The Korat Hunter-Killer teams had searched for several SAM sites which had been particularly active against the B-52 forces. The F-105Gs expended 13 Shrikes (AGM-45s) and 1 AGM-78 against SAM radar signals. The F-4Es dropped 24 CBUs on SAM sites VN-159, VN-266, and VN-549, with hundred-percent target coverage. VN-549 had been responsible for downing or damaging at least five B-52s.[51] The attack and demise of VN-549 was finally accomplished in an innovative way by an F-105G:

Turning over Hanoi, the F-105Gs found the occupied SAM site and cleared the F-4Es in for a bombing pass. Due to the cloud deck, the F-4Es were unable to acquire the site. Unable to mark it by any other means, Condor 01 and Condor 02 pushed over into a steep dive through AAA and descended to four thousand feet in a rocket attack profile. Condor 01 fired one of his AGM-45 Shrike missiles [in this case, however, unguided like a forward air controller's 2.75-inch rockets] directly into the SAM site. Although the F-105G nor the Shrike are normally employed in this manner, the exploding Shrike effectively marked the site for the F-4Es. They dropped their CBUs, and the radar van, associated support equipment, three SAMs on launchers, and three SAMs in storage were all destroyed. [Presumably, the experienced SAM crew that had shot down so many U.S. aircraft during this offensive was killed as well.][52]

One of the ironies of Day Ten concerned the problems faced by the Ubon chaff flights. Due to changing upper-level winds between the chaff and strike TOTs, the chaff corridors blew away in the high winds. There was no chaff coverage for the Tacair forces on the planned strike approach or over the target areas. It was a virtual repeat of the problems faced by the chaff bombers when they supported the B-52 wave attacks during days One to Three. Because the Hunter-Killer teams were effectively suppressing the SAMs, and the North Vietnamese were probably saving them for B-52s anyway, the SAM sites did not take advantage of the strike flight's ECM vulnerabilities.[53]

DAY TEN—B-52 ATTACKS

Day Ten called for 60 B-52s, with 30 B-52Ds from Utapao and 30 from Guam (15 Gs and 15 Ds). The 60 aircraft were deployed in six bomber streams against the Lang Dang rail yards (24 B-52s), Phuc Yen SAM support facility (18 B-52s), Duc Noi storage area (12 B-52s), and two SAM sites (VN-266 and VN-158, each attacked by 3 B-52s).

A total of 16 F-111s struck airfields, rail yards, power plants, six SAM sites, and a RADCOM station prior to the B-52 ingress. The support package consisted of 99 aircraft.[54] The 22 F-4 chaff bombers using 22 ALE-38s and 131 chaff bombs flew two-mile offset tracks and dispensed their chaff west of the target area over Hanoi, creating a dense chaff blanket.[55] Several MIGs were airborne and some of the MIGCAP pilots even turned on their landing lights to lure the MIGs into their areas. A Udorn aircrew flying an F-4D, List 01, locked-on to a MIG-21 ninety-two miles from Hanoi. The wingman in List 02 also locked-on shortly afterward as the element closed in at ten miles. Both aircraft fired at the verbal command of the List 01 aircraft commander. The aircrew on List 01 fired two AIM-7s, and the wingman fired one AIM-7. All three missiles guided, and the MIG-21 was struck by one missile from each aircraft. The MIG was observed as a fireball on the ground. Although the MIG was submitted as a joint kill, the final credit for the kill was given to the List 01 crew. Major Harry L. McKee and his WSO, Capt. John E. Dubler, had downed the last enemy aircraft of Linebacker II.[56]

Every target was successfully attacked by the B-52s without any damage to the aircraft. Although approximately twenty SAMs had been fired that night, many had erratic guidance, and most of those with a steady flight profile exploded harmlessly away from the B-52s. Even the AAA was lighter and far off the mark. It was apparent that the enemy command and control network was breaking down and that they were running out of missiles.[57]

Day Eleven Attacks

DAY ELEVEN—TACAIR STRIKES

The final Tacair strikes of Linebacker II were flown on 29 December. The force consisted of 40 strike and 53 support aircraft fragged against a single target: the Trai Ca SAM support facility near Thai Nguyen. Due to poor weather, with multilayered clouds up to eleven thousand feet over the target area, the 32 A-7s were guided by 8 LORAN-equipped F-4s. No bomb-damage assessment was made due to weather, and only light AAA was encountered. Two MIGs were reported airborne, but were not engaged by the MIGCAP. The Korat Iron Hand forces reported an almost complete absence of radar signals, and no AGMs were fired. One F-105G crew had an excellent lock-on on a T-8209 radar, but its AGM-78 would not fire.[58] These were to be the last Tacair daylight operations over Route Pack Six during Linebacker II.

DAY ELEVEN—B-52 STRIKES

On the final day for the B-52s, 60 bombers were assigned to strike three targets. Utapao provided 30 B-52Ds, and Guam provided the other 30 (12 B-52Gs and 18 B-52Ds). The targets were the Lang Dang rail yards (18 B-52s), Phuc Yen SAM support facility (27 B-52s), and Trai Ca SAM storage site (15 B-52s).

Ten F-111s struck the major airfields and six SAM sites (VN-119, VN-266, VN-159, VN-563, VN-186, and VN-004). The 102 support aircraft provided the usual protective cover of the B-52 forces. The entire SAM support facility at Phuc Yen disappeared under the accurate rain of B-52 bombs. The loss of this important facility eliminated the North Vietnamese ability to provide SAM replacements to the outlying sites around the Hanoi complex. Only 23 SAM firings were noted during the final night, and all were ineffective.[59] The bomb train from Gray cell, the last cell in the Day Eleven B-52 attacks, hit the Trai Ca SAM storage area at seventeen minutes before midnight. It seemed a fitting way to end the offensive. The last B-52 bomb had fallen north of the 20th Parallel. Shortly after noon on 30 December the last B-52G touched down at Guam.[60]

CINCPAC received instructions from the Joint Chiefs of Staff that all military operations in North Vietnam north of the 20th Parallel would stop as of 0659 hours Hanoi time on 30 December. The North Vietnamese had decided it was time to return to the peace table once

again—Linebacker II was over. As the Linebacker II
campaign ended, President Nixon cabled:

> I would like to commend those who have so skillfully
> executed the air campaign against North Vietnam . . .
> the courage, dedication, and professionalism demon-
> strated by our men is a source of enormous satisfaction
> to me as their Commander-in-Chief.[61]

Chapter Seven

SUMMARY AND CONCLUSIONS

Bombing Results

Linebacker II provided the USAF with an excellent opportunity to demonstrate the totality of its strike capability. Linebacker I, which had lasted for six months, was an interdiction campaign directed primarily against the North Vietnamese supply system. Linebacker II was aimed at sustaining maximum pressure through the destruction of major target complexes in the vicinity of Hanoi and Haiphong.[1]

The Linebacker II strike effort was executed in three distinct phases (Figure 14).In the first phase, 18 to 20 December, a maximum effort was directed against the Hanoi area using three B-52 waves per night. After the severe losses experienced by the B-52s on 20 December, the SAC bombers continued to maintain pressure during the second phase but at a reduced sortie level of only thirty B-52s per night. Until new tactics could be developed to successfully penetrate the Hanoi/Haiphong complexes with a greater probability of survival for the B-52 forces, the bombers concentrated on striking targets in lower-threat zones. Between 21 and 24 December, single-wave B-52 attacks hit targets along the northeast rail line, most of which were outside the general Hanoi complex. During Phase Two, Tacair sorties outnumbered B-52 sorties and maintained the daily pressure on NVN close to the Hanoi area. In the last phase, between 26 and 29

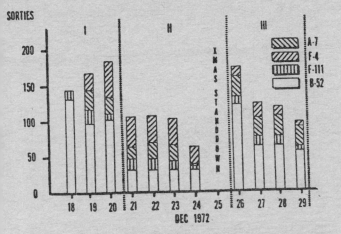

Figure 14. The three phases of Linebacker II

December, the single-wave tactic was continued by B-52s, but at a higher sortie level. During Phase Three the weight of the effort was again directed against the Hanoi/Haiphong complexes.[2]

The major target complexes struck by the B-52s and Tacair during the campaign included railroad yards, radio-communication facilities, power facilities, airfields, SAM sites, and bridges. In all, 59 designated targets were struck by 1364 USAF strike sorties, with the sortie weight of the effort ranging from a high of thirty-six percent against railroad yards to somewhat less than one percent against bridges (Figure 15).[3] The following discussion describes the results achieved and the lessons learned from strikes against each target category.

Railroad Yards

The target category that received the largest USAF strike effort was railroad yards and complexes. Thirteen targets in this category were struck by over 18,000 bombs delivered by 484 strike sorties by B-52s and Tacair. Not surprisingly, the highest overall damage achieved against

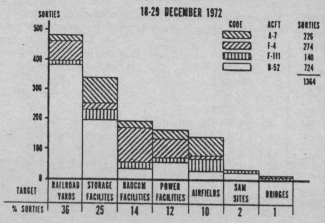

Figure 15. Linebacker II target/sortie breakout

any target category during Linebacker II proved to be against railroad yards. A damage level of sixty percent or better was achieved against two-thirds of the most important rail facilities in North Vietnam. In addition to significant facility and rail damage, a large quantity of rolling stock was destroyed or damaged, which seriously hampered movement of supplies by rail. The covered storage complexes associated with key rail yards were also destroyed by the heavy attacks.

Specifically, the bomb damage assessment (BDA) on the railroad system was as follows: 383 rail cars, 14 steam locomotives, 191 warehouse buildings, 29 vehicles, 5 POL tanks, and a large number of supplies. The Hanoi railroad yard, which was located in downtown Hanoi and had been used for years as a sanctuary due to its location, sustained heavy damage when struck by LGBs from only four F-4s. The Gia Lam yard across the river from Hanoi, jammed with rolling stock, looked like a H.O. train set that had been trampled by a herd of cattle. The Kinh No complex, North Vietnam's largest, was where they assembled and redistributed supplies. It was located where the railroad from Thai Nguyen and the northwest railroad came together, and where most of the supplies from China were offloaded. Over seventy-five percent of the yard was pulverized along with a large number of warehouses and mountains of supplies. The marshaling yard at Yen Vien, which was the intersection of the northwest and northeast tracks, sustained massive damage that effectively closed down the tracks south.[4] The same story applied to just about every rail target that was bombed by the B-52s.

B-52s proved very successful against the larger rail targets at Yen Vien, Thai Nguyen, Haiphong, and the large Kinh No complex. They also achieved significant contributions to the overall damage levels achieved at the smaller rail yards at Giap Nhi, Kep, Duc Noi, and Trung Quan. F-4s and A-7s using visual bombing techniques were also very effective in attacks on smaller rail yards. F-4 laser strikes against the Hanoi rail and classification yard were clear demonstrations of the effectiveness of terminally-guided ordnance against area targets with critical strike restrictions, such as those in the downtown Hanoi area.[5] The F-111 strikes against rail targets were light, but the damage inflicted was significant.

The destruction of rail-related targets was probably the most significant achievement of Linebacker II. It caused a complete disruption of rail traffic on the northeast rail line and the internal loop. Additionally, the massive destruction resulting from the large amount of ordnance expended against the targets near Hanoi must have had a very serious psychological impact on Hanoi's population.[6]

Storage Facilities

The target category that received the second-largest weight of effort was storage facilities. Twenty-five percent of the strike effort was devoted to fourteen targets, varying from permanent warehouse complexes to open transshipment points. Over 12,000 bombs were delivered by 339 strike sorties against these targets. The seven major storage areas in Hanoi, along with the two large complexes in Haiphong, took considerable damage; huge warehouse buildings and the associated adjacent open storage areas simply ceased to exist under the heavy weight of thousands of bombs; the NVN repair shops for trucks were incapacitated by the strikes; the port facilities in Hanoi and Haiphong were racked by over 180 secondary explosions, as huge amounts of ammunition stocks burned beyond control during the strikes.[7] Assessments indicated that the B-52s caused the most damage to these targets. It was apparent that either large numbers of Tacair, or use of B-52s, was required to achieve satisfactory damage levels against large storage areas. A notable exception was the destruction credited to F-111 aircraft at the Hanoi/Bac Mai Airfield storage area, where ten F-111 sorties achieved a damage level of sixty percent. F-111s were also successful in keeping pressure on the enemy in areas where significant damage had already been attained by the B-52s or daylight Tacair strikes. The F-4s and A-7s achieved satisfactory damage levels when delivering ordnance visually; the LORAN Pathfinder results were disappointing. The strikes against transshipment points with little or no fixed facilities yielded the lowest damage levels. In future efforts, the large strike forces could be better employed against targets with fixed facilities, such as railroad yards, permanent storage areas, or TSPs with verified large amounts of open storage. Temporary open-storage TSPs with unknown quantities of supplies should be attacked by single aircraft such as F-111s for harassment purposes and to minimize the enemy's activities.[8]

One point of interest concerning storage facilities was the almost complete destruction of the Phuc Yen SAM support facility on the last day of Linebacker II.[9] Had this central SAM assembly and checkout complex been hit at the beginning of the offensive, the SAM defenses could have been drastically reduced from the very outset. In fact, had Linebacker II continued for several more days after the destruction of the SAM facility, U.S. aircraft could have flown over the country virtually at will.

RADCOM Facilities

Fourteen percent of the sorties were devoted to striking five RADCOM facilities. Approximately 3600 bombs were dropped on these facilities by 196 strike sorties.

B-52 and F-111 bombs generally hit close to the target areas, but due to the nature of the targets, only limited damage was attained. For example, the B-52s attacking the Radio Hanoi facility at Me Tri dropped 2016 bombs, and not a single one hit the transmitter building. RADCOM facilities generally consist of a single element, the transmitter and receiver-control building. Such "point targets" are generally protected by a thick concrete blast wall, requiring a direct hit on the building to destroy it. The most effective ordnance against these targets proved to be MK-84 LGBs, as proved when only eight F-4s dropping a mere sixteen LGBs totally wiped out Radio Hanoi in a single mission.

With the exception of the virtual destruction of the Hanoi International RADCOM transmitter number two, by visual A-7 attacks, the strikes only caused a few brief periods of interrupted operations. There was also some frequency drifting and unscheduled changes, and a reduction in both domestic and international broadcasting and in long-distance military and civil radio communications. However, the redundancy in RADCOM facilities allowed the North Vietnamese to maintain all necessary operations. The five transmitter and receiver stations targeted during the offensive were primary facilities, but without complete destruction of all five as well as a number of alternate sites, the impact was minimal. This is a historic fact that current war planners should pay very close attention to. Although it appears that the impact of attacks against RADCOM targets was minimal, the timing of the periods they were down may have benefited our strike forces by degrading North Vietnamese MIG command and control capabilities.[10]

Power Facilities

This category consisted of electric power facilities, including thermal power plants and transformer stations. The power facilities received twelve percent of the sortie effort (166 sorties), delivering some 4000 bombs. The most significant damage to the electric power system was accomplished by four F-4s using MK-84 LGBs against the Hanoi thermal power plant. It was heavily damaged, resulting in disruption of power to Hanoi.

Although there were indications of some damage to the Haiphong and Hanoi transformer stations using radar and LORAN bomb-delivery techniques, the LGB proved to be the most effective munition against power facilities. Based on the Linebacker II operations, unguided ordnance provides too small a probability of damage against the critical elements of power facilities; unguided munitions are better used against area targets.

The military impact of the strikes against power facilities was significant since Hanoi's major sources of power were, for the first time, inoperable. At the start of Linebacker II, Hanoi had about 230,000 kilowatts of power capacity; by the end of the offensive, the power grid had been reduced to approximately 29,000 kilowatts. The limited amount of available power was probably supplied only to priority users, such as the more important industrial installations, foreign embassies, and selected government buildings in Hanoi.[11]

Airfields

Enemy airfields received ten percent of the sortie effort, accounting for 141 sorties which dropped approximately 2200 bombs. Five airfields were targeted, and an additional airfield, Gia Lam, was accidently damaged by nearby strikes on a rail yard facility. Four of the airfields (Hoa Lac, Kep, Phuc Yen, and Quang Te) experienced ten percent damage, and one (Yen Bai), five percent.

The most effective delivery system used against the airfields in Linebacker II was the B-52. B-52 strikes were primarily made to suppress MIG activity, and in all cases were successful in cratering the runways. F-4 and A-7 all-weather success was probably best measured at Yen Bai Airfield, where the fighter bombers constituted the major strike force; the airfield was not seriously damaged by the Tacair strikes that involved LORAN delivery techniques. The only time Yen Bai was reported nonoperational was after a successful F-111 sortie. Strikes against the airfields were of only a limited success since the already damaged bases offered few lucrative targets, and little long-term damage was added. The MIGs assigned to the bases were scattered in revetments hidden for miles around. Many of the long taxiways leading to the distant parking areas served as alternate runways when bombers cratered the primary runways. However, the runway cratering probably succeeded in hindering MIG flight operations and may have contributed to the low number of MIG engagements during Linebacker II. F-111 strikes during nighttime hours contributed an immeasurable psychological effect by harassing nighttime repair efforts, which probably affected the ready-rates for fighters during daytime operations.[12]

SAM Sites

Thirteen SAM sites were struck by two percent of the sorties. Approximately 1300 bombs were delivered by 29 strike sorties, mostly prestrike suppression. All bomb strikes against SAM sites were conducted by B-52 and F-111 aircraft using radar delivery. Two sites (VN-158 and VN-004) received fifty percent damage, one resulting from B-52 strikes and the other from F-111 strikes. On eight sites no damage was noted, and on three other sites, the damage was unknown.

North Vietnamese SAM sites could be relocated in approximately four hours. Two of the sites attacked were reported to be unoccupied. Target selection against easily movable targets is critical and should be accomplished only after an exhaustive examination of all-source intelligence. Unless the time interval between confirmation of occupied status and the strike was less than four hours, there could be no assurance that the sites would still be in the targeted area.

In considering strikes against SAM sites, two facts became apparent. The first was that the most vulnerable component was the revetted or unrevetted guidance radar. Second, if the objective of the attack is to suppress rather than destroy a site, then only Wild Weasel aircraft should be employed. In Linebacker II, all strike missions against SAM sites released iron bombs which required a direct hit to damage a site. Unless large numbers of aircraft are used to deliver iron bombs, only minimum damage should be expected. Significantly higher damage levels could have been attained if CBU munitions had been dropped by the B-52s and F-111s.[13] This was proved by the fact that at least fifteen SAM sites were destroyed by the Hunter-Killer technique employed by the Wild Weasels and F-4Es using CBU munitions.[14]

Bridges

Bridges received less than one percent of the sortie effort, illustrating the change in objectives away from interdiction. Only three bridges were struck with nine F-111 and F-4 sorties delivering sixty-eight bombs. Of the three bridges struck, one was completely destroyed and the other two received no significant damage. All damage resulted from F-4s delivering laser-guided bombs on the Hanoi railroad and highway bridge. The F-111s were generally ineffective when used against bridges, although at the Lang Lau railroad bridge new craters were observed on both sides of the river. LGBs provided the best results against bridges, but required good weather.[15]

The Linebacker offensives provided a chance to revisit several old lessons of the interdiction business pertaining to targeting bridges. In order to disrupt rail traffic in a long-term campaign, a few key bridges should be struck to isolate the traffic, followed by a large-scale effort on the major rail yards and sidings in an attempt to destroy available rolling stock and locomotives. Following these initial strikes, a balanced effort between bridges and rail yards provides the best means of disrupting the rail traffic.[16]

Operations and Loss Summary

In eleven days of operations, the USAF flew 724 B-52 sorties, 640 Tacair strike sorties, and 2066 Tacair support sorties.[17] Over 42,000 bombs had been dropped, 15,287 tons against fifty-nine targets. According to North Vietnamese reports, 1318 civilians were killed during Linebacker II. This figure did not distinguish between civilians not taking a direct part in the hostilities and civilians killed while working in lawful targets or taking part in the conflict. Nor does it take into account those people killed by SAMs or AAA projectiles which, having missed their targets or lost guidance control, plummeted to the ground. Over one thousand SAMs were launched against Linebacker II forces, and the area around Hanoi and Haiphong became an impact zone for falling North Vietnamese high-explosive ordnance.[18] Also, a number of the B-52s shot down crashed in populated areas of Hanoi, some causing fires that consumed entire neighborhoods. Regardless, the fairly low number of civilian casualties reported provides the evidence that the raids were certainly not the "terror attacks" against civilians as reported by some members of the media. Had the U.S. considered the kinds of raids conducted against enemy cities in World War II, Hanoi and Haiphong would have ceased to exist. As it was, except in accidental cases (as the case when a B-52 was hit by SAMs while dropping its bomb load), almost all of the bomb damage was limited to the designated target areas. As noted in previous chapters, U.S. aircrews placed themselves at great risk to ensure that their bombs were being directed only at military targets.

Overall, Linebacker II was deemed a success, both in the sense that the targets selected were destroyed, the stalled peace talks were jarred back into motion, and the final agreements were signed in January 1973. However, the results of the campaign did not go without cost to U.S. air power. During Linebacker II thirty aircraft were lost.

B-52 Losses

All B-52 losses were due to SAM shoot-downs (ten over North Vietnam, four which made it to Laos or Thailand before crew bailout, and one which crashed at Utapao), a result of more than one thousand SA-2 SAM firings over a twelve-day spread.[19] Considering that the SA-2 was specifically designed to kill B-52s at the altitudes that the bombers were operating from, the SAM effectiveness was remarkably low due to the American measures employed by the use of ECM and SAM-suppression tactics.

SUMMARY OF B-52 AIRCREW LOSSES[20]

Total SAC B-52 crewmembers involved	92
Recovered	26
Missing in Action (North Vietnam)	23
Missing in Action (Laos)	1
POWs (later recovered)	33
Killed in Action/Died of Wounds	5
Total	180

USAF Tacair Losses

Of the seven USAF Tacair craft lost, one was hit by AAA, two were downed by MIGs, one was lost to unknown causes, and three were lost due to accidents. One helicopter (HH-53 Jolly Green) was downed by small-arms automatic-weapons fire during the unsuccessful search-and-rescue effort for the crew of Jackel-33, the F-111 downed by AAA.[21] The helicopter managed to fly to Laos, where the crew was successfully recovered by another Jolly Green helicopter while under fire. Another F-111 (Snug 40) was lost to unknown causes (probable AAA), and the two crew members are still MIA. Two F-4Es were downed by Atoll missiles fired by MIGs. All four F-4 crew members ejected successfully and became POWs.

The three accidents claimed an A-7, 0-2, and EB-66. The A-7 (Slam 04) and 0-2 (Raven 21) collided and crashed over Laos while attacking North Vietnamese gun sites. The A-7 pilot was captured and later recovered, and the 0-2 pilot is still MIA. The EB-66 crashed on Christmas Eve while on approach to Korat RTAFB, when it lost both engines. All three crew members were killed. The two mission controllers died when the aircraft struck the ground, since they were too low to successfully eject. The pilot ejected when the aircraft was in a near-inverted position, and his seat blasted him through a Thai officer's quarters, killing him.[22]

SUMMARY OF USAF TACAIR AIRCREW LOSSES[23]

Total crew members involved (includes helicopter)	17
Recovered (includes helicopter)	5
Missing in Action (North Vietnam)	2
Missing in Action (Laos)	1
POWs (later recovered)	6
Killed in accident	3

Navy/Marine Tacair Losses

Of the six Navy and one Marine aircraft lost, three were hit by AAA (two A-6 and one F-4J), one was downed by a MIG (RA-5C), one was hit by a SAM (A-7C), and two were lost to unknown causes (one A-7E and one Marine A-6A).

SUMMARY OF NAVY/MARINE AIRCREW LOSSES[24]

Total crew members involved	12
Recovered	0
Missing in Action (North Vietnam)	3
POWs (later recovered)	6
Killed in action	3

Although the B-52s suffered the highest attrition during the campaign, the 15 losses still equated to only a 2.1 percent loss rate.[25] When the offensive was begun, the planners had estimated a B-52 loss rate of three percent. Of approximately 4000 combat sorties flown by all types of aircraft during Linebacker II, 27 were lost as a direct result of hostile action, an overall loss rate of 0.67 percent.

Lessons Learned

Even though the losses were lower than the three percent predicted by the JCS, many questions arose with regard to whether anything could have been done to prevent those losses that did occur.[26] It is difficult to assess how changes in tactics throughout the campaign would have influenced the loss rate had these changes been part

of the original planning factors. Just as in Linebacker I,
though, a number of significant lessons were learned during Linebacker II, which could have prevented the high
losses experienced by the B-52s early in the offensive.
Some of the more significant lessons are discussed below:

Countering Enemy Tactics.   North Vietnamese SAM
tactics were modified to lessen the effects of ECM. Sites
tracked and launched in the passive angle-track modes
using range data from T-8209 I-band radar to improve
their accuracy. Barrage firing of missiles toward the center of narrow chaff corridors using the B-52 ECM strobes
to determine a relative position of the aircraft caused
some attrition. To counter this technique, area chaff blankets were used instead of the stereotyped corridors which
pointed toward the target area. This increased the area
that could contain the aircraft causing the barrage technique to be less effective, chaff blankets apparently also
degraded acquisition by T-8209 range radars.

Chaff cloud density and corridor placement were
greatly affected by the high winds during the operation.
In future chaff operations, a thorough analysis of the
threat, wind conditions, and ingress/egress routes must
be undertaken prior to using chaff tactics developed during previous operations.[27]

Defense Suppression.   The only missile available to the
Wild Weasels for attacks against the T-8209 radar was
the AGM-78C, which was in short supply. This prompted
the emergency requisitioning and airlift of other types of
missiles. The Wild Weasels had five types of Shrike
(AGM-45) and AGM-78 missiles to use against threat-
band frequencies. Since the F-105G was limited to carrying only two Shrikes of any type and one AGM-78, it
was sometimes difficult to select the proper missiles for
a mission. This problem emphasized the need to *reduce*
the proliferation of antiradiation missiles employing
special-purpose seekers using instead wide-band cockpit-
selectable seekers.[28]

Another lesson was relearned from the previous offensive: the best way to destroy a SAM site was through the

use of the Hunter-Killer teams. It appears that concentrated efforts against SAM sites, radars, and other air-defense components by strike forces and Hunter-Killer teams prior to the B-52 attacks could have paid big dividends by minimizing the SAM threat.[29] This was shown during the third phase of Linebacker II, when the emphasis shifted toward concentration on enemy SAM sites and support facilities. After only three days of concentrated attacks against North Vietnamese air-defense networks, U.S. air power was able to fly virtually unopposed over the skies of North Vietnam. The basic doctrine of strategic air power employment requires that enemy defenses must be attacked or suppressed initially; then military and industrial targets can be concentrated on with little loss to the attackers.[30]

When considering strikes against enemy defenses such as airfields and SAM sites, the duration of the campaign is of prime importance. A short campaign of one or two days, should only try to suppress or harass defenses. Acceptable damage to enemy targets requires a large weight of effort, more than can be allocated in a short period of time if other targets are to be struck. However, during a long campaign, if the enemy has limited defense means, elimination of the defenses will better enable the strike force to achieve the campaign objectives. In conjunction with strikes on other lucrative targets, an early effort mounted against defenses would enhance the overall effort.[31]

B-52 Tactics. The enemy demonstrated he quickly understood the implications of stereotyped B-52 operations during the first few days of the offensive. In order to acquire knowledge concerning the flight routes to be used by follow-on cells, the North Vietnamese did not choose to engage the first cells over the target area with SAMs. Each B-52 cell followed the track of the first, flying at the same altitudes and airspeeds, and departing on the same course from the target area. The defenses were then probably aligned and committed after the approach routes and turn points were revealed by the initial strike cells. The North Vietnamese exploited the vulnerability of the B-52s in their post-target turns. These turns reduced the effects of the B-52 ECM protection and offered large radar cross-sections to the SAM tracking radars. Changes in B-52 routes, turn points, airspeed, and altitudes were necessary to overcome the vulnerable stereotyped tactics of the B-52 forces.[32]

Single Manager Theater Command. A major problem that continually hindered efficient targeting in air operations over North Vietnam again surfaced during Linebacker II. The need for a single command agency for air resources was even more apparent during Linebacker II because, for the first time in U.S. air operations over North Vietnam, a full range of weapon systems was available. The aircraft and ordnance were capable of all-weather operations, area bombing, or pinpoint bombing. These capabilities were made less effective by the lack of a single commander for air. In several instances less than optimal mixes of aircraft and ordnance were used, resulting in limited damage. For example, B-52s and F-111s were used against point targets without much effect and could have been better employed against area targets such as airfields or rail yards. In addition the isolation of Navy strikes in Route Package SixB and USAF strikes in Route Packages Five and SixA prevented the best integration of forces and weapons to maximize destruction in each of the areas.[33]

Target selection and the fixing of TOTs for all forces participating in strike missions should have been exercised by only one authority in the combat theater. Problems caused by MACV/7th AF and 8th AF [SAC] dual targeting served as an excellent example of the necessity for a single command authority. SAC picked the targets to be struck by its B-52s from the master-target list formulated by JCS. Meanwhile, 7th AF picked the targets for Tacair, including the F-111 strikes, and provided support packages for the B-52 strikes. Changes in B-52 targets or TOTs created enormous problems. A single authority for targeting and strike timing would have provided tremendous advantages in effectiveness as well as in improved force survivability. Regardless of military service, available assets should be committed by a single authority so that maximum advantage can be gained by scheduling strikes to be mutually supporting, to put total weight of effort where it is needed most, and to take advantage of the total protection available from the specialized equipment of the various component forces.[34]

Bomb Damage Assessment. There was an urgent need to obtain timely and accurate BDA to support strike planning in Linebacker II. The fact that strikes may be planned at two different headquarters, as was the case in Linebacker II, only served to highlight this need. There is always a chance that an aircraft will be lost during combat operations, but to lose an aircraft and crew while striking a target that has already been destroyed is senseless. Yet, because U.S. forces lacked adequate BDA during Linebacker II, some sorties were unnecessarily tasked against targets that may have been previously destroyed.[35] Often, the BDA reports reached most units days after strikes had been flown against targets. In this book to demonstrate the same kind of data, to demonstrate the kind of information that most aircrews had on the status of their targets, I purposely omitted from the day-to-day descriptions the overall bomb damage already inflicted on specific targets.

Post-strike BDA analysis indicated that guided ordnance, such as laser-guided bombs, is most effective in achieving damage to targets with a single essential element, for example, the boilerhouse of a thermal power plant, the switch control building of a transformer station, the transmitter and receiver building of a radio-communication facility, or a bridge, were significantly damaged only when LGBs were used. Marginal weather was a major factor in limiting the use of LGBs. Strikes by B-52s or F-4s and A-7s using LORAN generally resulted in very little damage to pinpoint targets. The F-111s effectiveness was limited by the use of single-ship flights with a relatively small bomb load. Basically, we fought the air war, with its long poor-weather periods, with systems that were primarily designed as "fair weather" systems. Such conditions are being better addressed today with the introduction of a number of all-weather systems such as the F-15E.[36]

MIGCAP Communications. Interference on the MIGCAP control frequency of 322.2 MHz. was due to harmonic radio interference in the 298–328 MHz. range, caused by EB-66 jamming in the 100–170 MHz. range and B-52 jamming in the 149–164 MHz. range. In addition, the MIGCAP control frequency was completely blocked out for five minutes on 21 December 1972, by an electronic signal emanating from Hainan Island (People's Republic of China). Having only two MIGCAP frequencies limited to the 300-MHz. range was unsatisfactory when operating in a heavy ECM environment. Additional frequencies should have been designated as backups to ensure a working frequency at all times. The selection of the control frequencies should be considered during premission planning, taking into account the effects of friendly ECM and its harmonic properties.[37]

Assessment of Tacair in Linebacker II

The Linebacker II operation demonstrated the effective use of Tacair both as a daytime strike force and as a B-52 support element. The use of the F-111 in concert with the B-52s illustrated the unique effectiveness of the F-111 to penetrate enemy defenses at low altitude and conduct attacks against targets in a heavily defended area. In the initial stages of Linebacker II, the F-111 was principally targeted against the airfields in an attempt to minimize North Vietnamese use of the MIGs at night. As a result, MIG reactions during the offensive were noted to be far less than experienced in previous campaigns. During the final phase of Linebacker II, F-111s were targeted against SAM sites that constituted a major threat to the B-52s.[38] The nightly F-111 attacks served to keep Hanoi's technical warfare people on twenty-four-hour alert and probably contributed to general fatigue that could have had great importance in breaking down the defenses.[39]

The daily F-4 and A-7 strike attacks, using either visual or LORAN techniques for bombing, served to maintain the pressure on the North Vietnamese. For the first time in the Vietnam War, they were subjected to around-the-clock attacks. The short periods of good weather that allowed the use of laser-guided ordnance again proved the worth of terminally-guided weaponry against point targets near congested living areas.

The support forces, which included the SAM suppression teams, MIGCAPs, escorts, chaff bombers and ECM aircraft, provided superb protection to the B-52 forces. Although problems such as high winds for chaff, stereotyped chaff corridors, and new SAM radars and tactics within the first several days of Linebacker II degraded this protection, the Tacair support forces adjusted quickly to counter the problems. During the final phase of the campaign the SAMs had been thoroughly defeated, and numerous B-52s can probably attribute their survival to Tacair support. The MIGCAP and escort flights also did their part to counter the threat. Throughout the offensive only thirty-two MIG aircraft managed to mount attacks against the strike forces, and for the most part were effectively blocked by the scores of patrolling F-4s.[40] The North Vietnamese lost five MIGs during their attempts to attack U.S. forces, two to B-52 gunners and the remaining three to USAF F-4s. The MIGs had been considered the primary danger by the B-52 crews, but the MIG threat turned out to be minimal.

In short, the Tacair contribution to the accomplishment of Linebacker II was a coordinated, mutually-supported team effort that effectively used airpower to attain the objectives of the campaign.

Campaign Impact Summary

Despite poor weather and a diversified North Vietnamese logistic system, Linebacker II achieved its objective—maximum sustained pressure on the Hanoi and Haiphong complexes. The large and concentrated strike effort on the relatively small area around Hanoi in such a limited time was completely unprecedented in Southeast Asia air operations. The impact of the campaign was obvious in the severe damage to the North Vietnamese logistic and war-support capability. Coupled with the results of Linebacker I, the overall air campaign against NVN resulted in the complete disruption of rail traffic within ten miles of Hanoi and a serious degradation of rail movement on the northeast rail line and the Thai Nguyen rail loop. The major rail-associated warehouse complexes were all seriously damaged, adding to the disruption of logistic movement, while strikes on other key storage facilities seriously impaired North Vietnamese efforts to restock necessary supplies.[41]

Post-strike analysts speculated that the damage and disruption could have been even more significant if the targets had been struck with the short-duration concentrated effort applied at the start of Linebacker I, before the enemy shifted to truck movement and dispersed storage. The large-scale destruction of rail and storage facilities in the immediate Hanoi and Haiphong areas followed by the extensive interdiction campaign of Linebacker I would undoubtedly have hindered NVN efforts far more effectively than the strategy actually employed. Because of the low force levels employed and the restricted Linebacker I operations, the North Vietnamese were able to make adjustments to maintain vital supply lines for operational requirements. Our efforts in Linebacker I seriously disrupted the enemy at first, but the development of a truck-oriented supply system for the heartland area, along with an expanded logistics system, made viable targeting extremely difficult. If a renewed strike effort in NVN had commenced during good weather, as in Linebacker I, and had been concentrated like Linebacker II, North Vietnam might have been deprived of vital war supplies for a much longer period than that achieved.[42]

The psychological impact of Linebacker II is extremely hard to measure. There were indications that the North Vietnamese had anticipated a renewed bombing of the homeland, as evidenced by a government evacuation of school children, nonessential civilian workers, and government offices in early December. The intensity of U.S. air operations, however, was surely greater than expected, and some reports indicated that for the first time in the war, people were anxious to leave the cities. Undoubtedly, the population suffered a decline in morale as a result of the intensity of the strikes. Despite the decline in morale, no evidence indicated that North Vietnam's leadership could not maintain control of the situation.[43]

However, it should be pointed out that the North Vietnamese did return to the peace-conference table following Linebacker II. In fact, Sir Robert Thompson, a noted British expert on Asian wars, pointed out the significance of the offensive:

> In my view, on 30 December 1972, after eleven days of those B-52 attacks on the Hanoi area, *you had won the war. It was over!* They had fired 1242 SAMs; they had none left, and what would come in overland from China would be a mere trickle. They and their whole rear base at that point were at your mercy. They would have taken any terms. And that is why, of course, you actually got a peace agreement in January, which you had not been able to get in October.[44]

Many high-ranking U.S. officials also felt that the Linebacker II offensive should be credited with ending the U.S. participation in the war. One member of the U.S. delegation to the Paris peace talks stated simply:

> Prior to Linebacker II, the North Vietnamese were intransigent, buying time, and refusing to discuss even a formal meeting schedule. After Linebacker II, they were shaken, demoralized, and anxious to talk about *anything.*[45]

The renewed negotiations yielded tangible results in a short time. On 23 January 1973, the Paris negotiators signed the cease-fire agreement that would take effect on 28 January. The most important aspect of the agreement provided for the return of all American and Allied POWs within sixty days.[46] Dr. Henry Kissinger, the chief U.S. negotiator, had his assessment of the offensive's effects on the North Vietnamese:

> . . . there was a deadlock . . . in the middle of December, and there was a rapid movement when negotiations resumed on 8 January. These facts have to be analyzed by each person for himself. . . .[47]

The defeat of North Vietnamese defenses by Tacair and

SAC forces, added to the psychological impact of the intensity of the day-and-night strikes, had most certainly helped to convince the North Vietnamese to once again resume serious negotiations. The talks swiftly produced an agreement that ended the role of the U.S. in the Vietnam conflict and brought the POWs home. One can only speculate on what the outcome would have been had these same forces been available during the 1975 invasion of South Vietnam by large concentrations of North Vietnamese soldiers and tanks operating on the open roads.

APPENDICES

Appendix 1: Linebacker II Targets

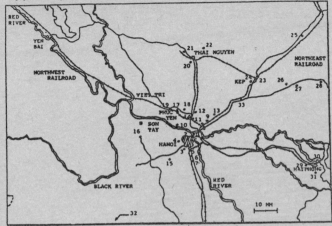

Figure 16. Linebacker II B-52 Targets

B-52 TARGETS	SORTIES FRAGGED AGAINST TARGET	TOTAL BOMBS DROPPED
1. Gia Thuong Storage	21	1176
2. Hanoi RR Yard	57	2371
3. Hanoi Storage/Bac Mai	12	560
4. Hanoi Radio	36	2016
5. Giap Nhi RR Yard	17	952
6. Van Dien Vehicle Storage	39	2184
7. VN-243 SAM Site	3	168
8. Yen Vien RR Yard	60	2751
9. Trung Quan RR Yard	12	682
10. VN-266 SAM Site	3	168
11. Duc Noi RR Yard	8	448
12. Duc Noi Storage	21	1176
13. VN-158 SAM Site	3	168
14. Kinh No RR Yard	71	3220
15. VN-549 SAM Site	3	168
16. Hoa Lac Airfield	6	300
17. VN-234 SAM Site	3	168
18. Phuc Yen Airfield	6	336
19. Phuc Yen SAM Support	42	2352
20. Thai Nguyen RR Yard	36	1656
21. Thai Nguyen Thermal Power	42	2185
22. Trai Ca SAM Support Facility	15	870
23. Kep RR Yard	12	672
24. Kep Airfield	9	524

B-52 TARGETS	SORTIES FRAGGED AGAINST TARGET	TOTAL BOMBS DROPPED
25. Lang Dang RR Yard	86	3480
26. VN-537 SAM Site	2	112
27. VN-563 SAM Site	2	112
28. VN-660 SAM Site	2	112
29. Haiphong PPS	18	1008
30. Haiphong RR Siding	27	1512
31. Haiphong Transformer Station	14	840
32. Quang Te Airfield	6	336
33. Bac Giang Trans-shipment Pt.	30	1761
LINEBACKER II TOTALS	734	35,544

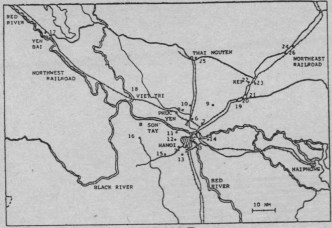

Figure 17. Linebacker II F-111 Targets

F-111 TARGETS	SORTIES FRAGGED AGAINST TARGET	TOTAL BOMBS DROPPED
1. Bac Mai RADCOM Center	10	120
2. Hanoi RADCOM Facilities	22	264
3. Hanoi Port	11	132
4. Hanoi Transformer Station	6	72
5. Gia Thong Storage	3	36
6. Duc Noi RR Yard	1	12
7. Trung Quan RR Yard	2	24
8. Phuc Yen Airfield	10	120
9. VN-119 SAM Site	1	12
10. VN-226 SAM Site	1	12
11. VN-159 SAM Site	2	24
12. VN-014 SAM Site	1	12
13. VN-186 SAM Site	1	12
14. VN-004 SAM Site	1	12
15. VN-549 SAM Site	1	12
16. Hoa Lac Airfield	7	84
17. Yen Bai Airfield	11	92
18. Viet Tri Trans-shipment Pt.	6	72
19. Bac Giang TPP	8	96
20. Bac Giang Trans-shipment Pt.	4	48
21. Bac Giang RR Siding	6	72
22. Kep Airfield	14	164
23. Kep RR Yard	4	48
24. Coa Nung RR Bridge	3	36
25. Thai Nguyen TPP	1	12
26. Lang Lau Bridge	2	24
LINEBACKER II TOTALS	139	1424

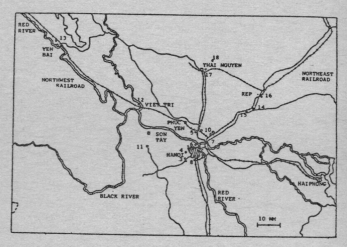

Figure 18. Linebacker II F-4 Targets

F-4 TARGETS	SORTIES FRAGGED AGAINST TARGET	TOTAL BOMBS DROPPED
1. Hanoi RR Yard	4 (LGB)	8
2. Quinh Loi Storage	8 (LORAN)	54
3. Hanoi RADCOM Facilities	84	1062
4. Hanoi Radio	8 (LGB)	16
5. Hanoi Transformer Station	28	245
6. Hanoi TPP	4 (LGB)	8
7. Hanoi RR/HWY Bridge	4 (LGB)	8
8. Giap Nhi RR Yard	4 (LORAN)	24
9. Trung Quan RR Yard	16	191
10. Duc Noi RR Yard	12	132
11. Hoa Lac Airfield	4 (LORAN)	54
12. Viet Tri Trans-shipment Pt.	4 (LORAN)	35
13. Yen Bai Airfield	4 (LORAN)	8
14. Bac Giang RR Siding	16	96
15. Bac Giang TPP	15	90
16. Kep RR Yard	16	96
17. Thai Nguyen TPP	15	90
18. Trai Ca SAM Support Facility	8 (LORAN)	54
LINEBACKER II TOTALS	254	2271

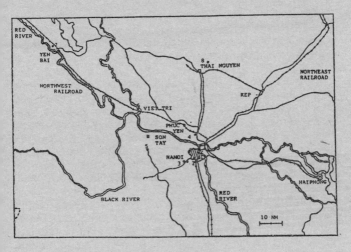

Figure 19. Linebacker II A-7 Targets

A-7 TARGETS	SORTIES FRAGGED AGAINST TARGET	TOTAL BOMBS DROPPED
1. Quinh Loi Storage	32	394
2. Giap Nhi RR Yard	16	30
3. Hanoi RADCOM Transmitters	26	240
4. Hanoi Transformer Station	32	348
5. Hoa Lac Airfield	24	48
6. Viet Tri Trans-shipment Pt.	24	48
7. Yen Bai Airfield	40	200
8. Trai Ca SAM Support Facility	32	394
LINEBACKER II TOTALS	226	1702

Appendix 2. Cobalt 01, 26 and 27 December 1972

The events of the Cobalt 01 mission were clearly recollected by the pilot, Frank Lewis, and a detailed transcript provided to this author recalled his crew's harrowing experience of the shootdown and their captivity:

On 26 December 1972, I was the aircraft commander of a B-52D that was targeted on a rail yard north of Hanoi. My crew members were: Capt. Sam Cusimano, copilot; Maj. Allen Johnson, EWO; Lt. Col. Jim Condon, radar navigator; First Lt. Bennie Fryer, navigator; and SMSgt. Jim Gough, gunner. We were armed with eighty-four, 500-pound bombs internally and twenty-four 750-pound bombs under the wings. We took off from Anderson AFB, Guam, about 1800 local time. It was still not quite dark.

Takeoff and climb-out were routine. We were number Two in a three-ship cell code-named Cobalt. En route to our refueling north of the Philippines, both Lead and Three experienced problems with their electronic-warfare equipment. We assumed lead in the cell because our equipment was operating normally. Refueling was routine, with all ships taking a maximum offload of fuel.

At about 1045 (Guam time) we coasted in over South Vietnam and began rendezvous with about fifty other aircraft. After establishing Cobalt cell correctly in this long linear stream of aircraft, the entire formation turned north off the coast of South Vietnam. As we proceeded north about ten to fifteen miles off the coast of North Vietnam, I did not observe any activity over Dong Hoi or Vihn as we passed abeam of these two North Vietnamese coastal cities. As we passed Haiphong, still several miles off the coast, I saw a considerable amount of AAA activity over the city. Additionally, two SAMs were launched in an almost vertical trajectory. They were, of course, no threat to us. We were now at an altitude of 35,000 feet, running at about 350 KIAS, and beginning to make small timing corrections to put us over target plus or minus thirty seconds, which guaranteed us safe separation.

We proceeded north of Haiphong, making landfall, but continuing north almost to the Chinese border. At this time we made a large turn to the southwest and established our run-in heading to Hanoi. Cobalt cell was on time and on heading, with Two and Three each a mile and a half in trail, stacked five hundred feet up. All running lights were extinguished. The time was about 2330 (Guam). Shortly after turning inbound on Hanoi, I authorized the cell to go to independent bombing mode, which means that each aircraft used its own radar to locate and attack the target which was just across the Red River north of Hanoi.

I was handling UHF communication with the rest of the cell as well as any HF traffic. The copilot was talking to our support package on the second UHF radio. Of some concern to me was the likelihood of not seeing SAMs targeted against us. I had the copilot run his seat full up to give himself the best chance of clearing right. I also reiterated to the gunner that his primary responsibility was to clear for SAMs from behind. In order to help in this process, I was making shallow turns left and right of course. I could now see considerable AAA activity in the distance around Hanoi. There was a lot of 37mm AAA which I could see coming up through a milky undercast in their characteristic seven-round sequence before detonating. I estimated this undercast at about ten thousand feet, based on observing it in relation to the 37mm rounds. There was also a considerable amount of heavier-caliber AAA detonations in front of us and nearer to our altitude, but still low. We were getting lots of AAA signals and SAM signal activity. At about this time I saw SAM launches beginning. Under the undercast, their launch was evident as a diffused orange glow. As they broke through the undercast they looked like fast-moving white lights. These initial SAMs were not a threat.

Cobalt Two and Three kept up a constant radio chatter, calling out every SAM they saw. I ordered Cobalt cell to cease SAM calls unless they appeared to be an immediate threat. As we continued inbound, the SAM activity increased. I think I may have seen as many as ten SAMs in the air at one time. The radar navigator acquired his offset aimpoint (I believe it was the Hanoi railroad highway bridge). Offsets were reconfirmed with the navigator. Everything was go. My bomb direction indicator (BDI) was centered. We were about two minutes from the bomb release. At this time the EWO called SAM guidance signals at ten o'clock. At almost the same time I saw two SAMs break through the undercast. They stabilized on my windscreen at about ten o'clock low. I made a slight turn into them and back to my bomb-run heading. They moved with me and restabilized. I confirmed to the EWO that two SAMs were locked-on and tracking us. We were within sixty seconds of bomb release.

At this point there was nothing to do except allow the SAMs to get closer. I waited until I could stand it no longer, until the twin SAMs looked like huge train lights bearing down on us, counted to three, and broke hard left into them. They began to move up and right on the windscreen, and I immediately started a hard turn back right to get back on my bomb-release heading. The two SAMs passed immediately high in front of us. I did not see them detonate. From this point things began to happen very fast. We were probably inside thirty seconds to bomb release.

Amazingly, I remember, the BDI was centered after my rather violent SAM evasive turn and recovery. The EWO said, "Pilot, we are going to get it!" In that split second I started to tell Al that they had just missed. Before I could say a word, we were hit with a tremendous concussion. The only similar experience I've had was running into a telephone pole at fifty mph in a small car. Everything went into slow motion. My forward and side windscreens turned to opaque sugar and disappeared. I felt a hot burning across my shoulder. The warm, red glow of the safe cockpit lighting was replaced with the harsh white of the emergency floodlights. My oxygen mask blew off my face from the force of the air rushing out of my lungs. White sparks were coming out of the instrument panel in front of me. After what seemed like a long time, the torrent of air coming out of my mouth stopped and I reconnected my oxygen mask. The control yoke I was holding was like a wet noodle. All pitch-and-roll authority were gone from my position. I do not recall whether I had any rudder control.

The aircraft had pitched over slightly into a descent, but we were wings level. I couldn't tell this from my ADIs which were tumbling, but I could see the outside horizon created by the undercast and the sky in the distance. There was a bright orange glow out my left window. I remember mentally kicking myself for having missed seeing the SAM which I assumed had hit us on the left side of the aircraft. From this orange glow I knew that we were burning.

I reached across to grab my copilot's control yoke. He was still holding it. Pushing and pulling on it as hard as I could, I couldn't get it to move, and there was no aircraft response. The wind blast and noise were tremendous. The copilot's ADI was frozen in an incorrect steep climb indication. We were gathering speed in the shallow descent and were up to about 400 KIAS. I immediately pulled the throttles back to cut our speed but felt the nose of the aircraft drop abruptly. I firewalled all eight engines and saw two red fire-warning lights blink on for the two right inboard engines. I remember at the time pausing momentarily to wonder how come my right engines were on fire when the SAM had hit us on the left side. Going to max power on all engines caused the aircraft to dish out of the dive and almost, but not quite, come level. I never touched the throttles again.

I knew that we had taken a fatal hit and were going down. I knew we were burning and potentially riding a bomb with over 60,000 pounds of ordnance and 200,000 pounds of JP-4. We were still, as near as I can judge, inside our thirty seconds to bomb release. I never did feel the bombs drop, if they did. At this point I determined to get my crew out. I hit the abandon switch and ordered bailout into what seemed to be a dead intercom. I gave the same bailout order over my UHF radio but heard no feedback. I looked at my copilot and pointed up to the ejection hatch.

Sam looked around and then began fiddling with a panel on his right. I took off my oxygen mask, reached over and hit him, and having gotten his attention, yelled for him to bail out. He again looked around quizzically. I remember hearing a dull thump behind me and thinking that someone ejected. Sam was still looking around. I assumed the ejection position and reached down and rotated my seat-arming handles exposing the ejection triggers. Again I looked at Sam. He was watching me. I

pointed to my now-stowed control yoke and then up at
the large hole left above me where the ejection hatch had
blown off. I remember thinking how bright and beauti-
fully clear the stars looked. I pointed up to Sam's still-
in-place ejection hatch and both yelled and motioned for
him to eject. Still no response. I assumed an ejection
position and squeezed the ejection triggers.

The next thing I remember was the curious sensation
of falling, of the decreased wind, and of nothing around
me. It was dark. I was falling facedown. I rolled over to
try to see the plane but could not see it. I realized that
my oxygen mask was still dangling loose, and reconnected it only to be surprised that I could not breathe.
Then I remembered my emergency oxygen and pulled the
green apple to activate it. I was rewarded with a blast of
high-pressure oxygen, and had to loosen my mask to allow some of it to escape around my cheeks. And I was
tumbling. I recall thinking that this was a poor time to
learn to skydive. I oriented myself to fall facedown. I
could see the undercast a long ways below me. I was
witness to the grandest fireworks display I have ever seen.
SAMs were in the air, red AAA tracer rounds lit the sky
above the milky undercast, and white-orange explosions
blossomed around but not too close to me. I could feel
their dull concussions. One SAM passed me in an instant, and I could feel its engine vibration. As I freefell
through the air, I slowly began to spin. I corrected this
effect by curling into a ball and then spread-eagling again.
I determined to open my parachute, if it had not automatically opened, before I went into the undercast. I fell
for some time.

Parachute opening came as a surprise as I was strug-
gling to locate again my manual D-ring. I was unfortunately again wound up in a flat spin. I felt the parachute
risers pulling out, but there was only a slightly reassuring
bump. When I looked above me, I saw that the parachute
risers had wound up almost to the parachute canopy,
which was not fully open. I was too scared to do anything, which was probably the best thing to do. I slowly
began to be turned as the torsion in the corkscrewed risers caused them to begin to, slowly at first and then ever
faster, unwind. As they came fully unwound, the canopy

fully deployed and I felt a welcome soft deceleration. All this occurred just above the undercast. I floated down into the undercast. If freefalling had seemed to take a long time (probably a little over two minutes), the slow parachute descent in the milky clouds seemed to take an eternity. It probably lasted about ten minutes. Since I couldn't see the ground, I couldn't tell in what direction to maneuver.

Unhappily, now I began a slow swinging oscillation which slowly built up to the point that it felt as though I would swing up and over my parachute canopy. I deployed my survival kit, which dropped below me on a long lanyard and automatically inflated my life raft. This fairly quickly stopped the giant pendulum effect. I estimated that I broke out of the clouds about a thousand feet above the ground. There were scattered, smaller clouds, but I could just barely make out the ground below. I had earlier pulled off all my name tags and insignia, taken out my Geneva Convention card and military I.D. card and thrown them to the wind. I got ready to land. I made an unexpectedly soft stand-up landing, rolled to the ground, took off my helmet and looked around.

I was in a partially dried-up rice paddy about twenty yards from an elevated road. Around me were a large number of people with flashlights who were moving, shouting, and talking in that alien discordant dialect. The nearest was maybe fifty yards away, but they apparently had not seen me. About this time a guy on a bicycle came down the road behind me. I didn't move as he peddled past, but I was in a hurry to pull in my chute, which had strung out across the paddy, before it was spotted. As I was doing so, a flashlight beam fell on it.

Any enthusiasm for running I had was quickly dampened by the unmistakable low, gruff bark of several AK-47s on full automatic, the soft thunking of bullets near me, and the concentration of numerous flashlights on me. I put up my hands and stood up.

I was set upon by a crowd of unpleasant villagers or farmers. They were not in military dress. They knocked me down and proceeded to beat and kick me with fists, feet, and bamboo poles. Curiously, I felt no pain. As they were stripping me, one short, ugly, bow-legged fellow pulled out my service Smith & Wesson .38 and pointed it down at me. As he started pulling the trigger I recall thinking that the characteristic counterclockwise cylinder rotation of a Smith & Wesson revolver was actually clockwise when viewed from this end. The hammer fell and clicked on an empty chamber. He looked surprised, I laughed, and he began rapidly clicking the trigger, all on empty chambers. I never carried my revolver loaded. Instead I kept six rounds in a small ziplock bag in the lower leg pocket of my flight suit.

At about this same time, the first fellow's brother opened up my big, razor-sharp Buck knife and started at me with it. I had no trouble coming off the ground, although about six of them were hanging on me. There was a sharp military order yelled, and all the villagers fell back as four uniformed soldiers appeared carrying AK-47s. They had been there all the time, I think.

They tied my arms behind me, barefoot and in my skivies; and the crowd encouraged me with sharp bamboo spears to run through the rice paddies for, I think, a couple of miles back to a small village. Everytime I fell down I got several jabs. I don't remember falling very often, and I cruised the distance without even thinking of being winded.

At the village I was hustled into a central, stucco-type building and into a fairly large room (twenty by thirty feet). It seemed like everyone else was trying to get into the room, and there was a lot of yelling, pushing, and shoving. Once things settled down, my belongings were laid out on a table in front of me. Across the table sat what I figured was the mayor, a civilian in better clothes. He couldn't speak English but began reading to me from what I took to be *Directions on What to Do with American Prisoner*. He began going over a litany of what aircraft I was from. I identified myself as a Navy A-4 pilot after a while, when I could see that he was running out of his list of airplanes. He was pleased, and got up and left the room. I could hear him in the corridor, hand cranking a phone. There followed a long discussion in which I clearly heard A-4 repeated several times. The reason I misrepresented myself as an A-4 pilot was to not alert them that there might be other crew members nearby besides myself.

He came back and we went through another couple of hours of his reading and my responding. Such things as sit down, turn around, stand up. I knew how my dog must feel. But everyone seemed real pleased with all this. Finally, they took me to a single-room jail building and locked me in, still tied, still in my underwear. I was cold. I crawled underneath a two-by-five-foot sleeping board and went right to sleep.

I awoke to someone knocking on my board. It was early morning and the whole village was trying to see me through the two barred windows of the cell. The knocking had been large rocks which they were throwing off the board to wake me up. As I got up, another large rock hit me in the back. I spent the next couple of hours dodging rocks and bricks thrown through the windows at me. As I ran along the walls, I began scraping the ropes that bound my arms behind me. Finally, I could feel them come apart, although I still kept my arms behind me. I was angry. I quickly reached down, picked up a large brick, and threw it hard right through the bars of a window at one particularly nasty fellow who had so seemed to enjoy stoning me. It hit him a terrific blow in the face, and he went down, and the crowd drew back. From then on they only tried to stone me from a distance, so it was easy to avoid their rocks.

Eventually I was ushered out of the cell by an armed guard. He stopped me on the small concrete porch. The whole village seemed to be gathered for some sort of ceremony. About twenty small children were in front. Before I could think about this, someone smashed a brick down on my foot, which split open and caused me to yell and jump about on one foot. Everyone got a big laugh out of this. When things quieted down, the same mayor began a long dialogue. I couldn't understand it, but the gist of it was apparent. He was showing me off to the kids as the very bad enemy. As this went on, my mind drifted. I thought about my young daughter, Kelly. Kids are good everywhere. I began to catch the eye of some of the littlest kids and wink slyly at them. They started giggling. Pretty soon they were trying to stifle laughs.

This stopped whatever ceremony was going on, and I was locked up again.

I suppose it must have been about 1000 local time that I was again taken out of the cell. This time I could see a military truck parked in the road. It looked like the professionals had arrived. They even had a photographer. I was marched into the road and my arms were again tied very tightly behind me. In broken English the photographer told me he wanted to take my picture. Well, I thought this over and agreed. Although I didn't laugh, it was funny because it wasn't as though I had a choice. He then apologetically told me that I must bow my head. I said no. The soldiers, the photographer, and I spent about thirty minutes each trying to do what we wanted. The soldiers would hold me bent over while the photographer got ready. They would then release me and try to jump back out of the picture before I could snap straight up. The photographer either gave up or ran out of film or got what he wanted. I don't know which. The soldiers were pretty mad.

They then blindfolded me and threw me into the back of the open truck. Two guards got in with me. I could also sense someone else in the truck. In fact, it was Lt. Col. Jim Condon, my radar navigator. He was also bound and blindfolded like me. I could tell this because I could just peer out from underneath my blindfold while looking toward my feet. The next three to four hours were pretty uncomfortable. When I tried to talk to Jim, the guards beat me. The road was full of potholes, and the driver seemed to get a kick out of hitting them at full clip. We were constantly tossed into the air and slammed back down on the steel bed of the truck on which we were laying. The guards periodically beat me with their rifle butts to their chant of "Nixon, Nixon, Kissinger, Kissinger." Although I saw lots of stars, I was never really knocked unconscious. I did feign unconsciousness just to get the beatings to cease. We made two stops at villages, where the locals were allowed to see us, poke us, and hit us to the extent that they could reach us in the truck. Eventually the guards began to get a little excited, from which I figured we were approaching our destination, which had to be Hanoi.

I believe that we drove across the Red River just north of Hanoi on a submerged pontoon bridge. We went down a fairly steep embankment. I could hear the water and feel the up and down shifting of bridge sections as we slowly crossed. Then up a steep embankment, and I could hear city traffic noise around me. This lasted for a short while, until we came to a stop. I could hear heavy metal bolts sliding and the creaking of a heavy metal door swinging open. We then drove slowly forward through a dark tunnel back into light. I heard the really depressing clang of the doors shutting and being bolted behind us. Although I couldn't see it, I knew that I had arrived at the infamous Hoi Lo prison, better known as the Hanoi Hilton.

I was abruptly jerked out of the truck onto the concrete drive and stood up. I was guided across an apparent courtyard, along a dark corridor, and into what I figured was the torture chamber. When you cannot see, your own imagination is your worst enemy. Although talking was going on around me, it was not in English. A new and much better blindfold was put over my old blindfold and I lost my last visual cue of the world around me, my feet. The ropes were taken off me, but as I was flexing and rubbing my numb arms, I was knocked down by an unexpected rifle butt to my head and rolled onto my stomach. Someone stood on my back and pinned my arms up behind me. Then what later turned out to be clear, thin monofilament plastic line was used to tightly bind my arms from about two inches below to two inches above my elbows. I could feel it cut into my skin as each winding was pulled tight. They kept pulling my arms up behind me, until I guessed they were going to dislocate my shoulders. I think three or four guards did this. They were workmanlike, with little talk. They finished and pulled me to my feet. I stood for an indeterminable length of time. Eventually I sensed some movement and anticipation from the guards. Someone was approaching.

He was an interrogator and spoke fairly good English. The next few hours were not pleasant. He wasn't satisfied with name, rank, and serial number. He told me that I was from a B-52 and not an A-4. Maintaining this facade became untenable for me after the third beating, so I had to give in and admit that he was correct. It became easy to rationalize talking to him, although I knew it was a mistake. He wanted to know my crew position, and I told him that I flew B-52s. We spent some time on this issue, until I finally had to agree that I was the pilot, which I maintained was what I had told him in the first place. By this time I think that I was about ready to tell him anything. I knew that I was slowly losing this encounter, and I was ashamed. At one point I heard a man scream not too far away. I thought that it was my EWO, Maj. Allen Johnson. The thought that he was alive helped me for a while. But I was losing my power to resist. What next occurred is something that I will never be able to explain.

After I had admitted to being a B-52 pilot, the interrogator concentrated on finding out who my crew members were. For some reason, at that time, I refused to give him this information. There was more abuse by the guards. I would have told him whatever he wanted to know about myself, but the one and probably only thing I would not tell him was who my crew members were. By focusing on this single issue, I think that I got stronger. The interrogator became angrier. Eventually he told me that unless I gave him one name, he would kill me. He pointed out to me that no one knew that I was alive anyway. As far as the outside world was concerned, I would just have died from wounds suffered when I was shot down. Well, I believed him, although I sure hoped he was bluffing. The end came when he put what I think was a revolver to my right temple and cocked the hammer. He said that I had until the count of ten to give him just one name, and then he began slowly counting. My mind was in chaos. It was sure easy to rationalize giving him a name, maybe a fictitious name. To this day I don't know why I said what I did. At the count of six I told him to go ahead and pull the trigger because even if I gave him a name, I figured he would either shoot me anyway or torture me to death. I don't know if I meant it. I don't know what I would have done if he had continued counting. There was a long silence.

Then, in an apologetic voice, he said, "Oh no, Captain Lewis, you have very wrong idea of North Vietnamese

people. We are very humane.'' I almost laughed with the
gun at my head. He did not continue counting. To my
immense relief he removed the gun. I heard him talking
to the guards. Then he told me that he already had the
names of all my crew members anyway. He named all of
us by position. Then he read back to me what sounded
like a copy of our TDY orders, which listed us all by
name and crew position. He said, ''Major Johnson is a
black man.'' He declared that he had just been trying to
determine if I were honest and cooperative. He said that
I had been very uncooperative and dishonest. He said
that I was a criminal and must change my attitude. This
one-sided dialogue went on for some time.

Finally, he asked if I would not like to go on the radio
to tell my friends and family that I was okay. I said that
I would like to do this. He talked to the guards some
more, and then I heard him leave. The guards removed
the blindfold. I was at the middle of a long dusty corridor. At one end I could see the light from the outside. It
was late in the afternoon. The guards began removing
the plastic line from around my arms, which had gone so
numb that they had ceased to be a part of me. I was
concerned because I couldn't move them or feel them at
first. The line had cut pretty deeply into them, and they
were purple and swollen from lack of circulation. After
a few minutes the sensation in them began to return. The
guards were not nearly as formidable as I had imagined
them. There were four of them. Only two had rifles.
Three left and one with a rifle remained with me.

Pretty soon a young man in civilian clothes came down
the corridor, looked at me and said something to the
guard, then walked back out. He immediately returned
with two stools. In English he told me that he was here
to help me and to find out what I would like to say on
Radio Hanoi.

I told him that I just wanted to give my name, rank,
and serial number, and tell my family that I was okay.
Then he read to me what he thought I wanted to say. He
also sat on a stool and motioned for me to do likewise
across from him. With my apprehension again returning,
I did so. The gist of what I was supposed to say was that
I was a criminal who had attacked the peace-loving North

Vietnamese people, who nevertheless were treating me kindly. As a B-52 pilot who had indiscriminately bombed Hanoi, I was sorry for being a tool of my government's criminal and inhumane war against the peaceful North Vietnamese people. I figured that my chances of going on the radio were slim to none when I told him that I could not say these things. Surprisingly, we spent the next hour dickering over what I would say.

He had a pot of tepid tea brought for me. It was the first drink that I had had since after refueling north of the Philippines. That seemed like a long time ago. I drank the whole thing down at once, delicious. Eventually I agreed to say who I was, that I was a B-52 pilot, that I was being treated well, that I hoped the war would end soon, and that I was sorry for what I had done. He wrote it all out for me and had me memorize it. Additionally, he said that I must bow and only look at the floor. I agreed. When he was satisfied, he left.

A guard came with a basin and some water and a rag. With this I cleaned myself up as best I could. My foot and my arms were bloody. The guard had me clean my face. I felt a lot better. The guard took the basin away and returned with a set of the infamous maroon-and-gray striped pajamas, some socks, and Ho Chi Minh sandals. I was glad to put these on. By now it was about dusk.

The same young man returned. He had the guard blindfold me. Again I could see my feet. I was led outside and helped, not thrown, into the back of a truck and sat down on a wooden bench. My prompter told me we were going to the radio station. The truck started up. I could hear the metal doors of the prison open. We drove through the short tunnel. We drove for perhaps ten minutes through the city before pulling into a long driveway. My prompter asked if I were ready, and I said yes. He got out of the truck. He returned about ten minutes later. I was helped out of the truck. From under my blindfold I could see other trucks parked. He led me past these and into a building. As I came in, I think that another prisoner was being led out. I sensed a large room with lots of people, by the undercurrent of murmuring that I was now hearing. He took off my blindfold.

I was in a side corridor which opened into a large room.

I could see that it was full of people. I could see a dais with a microphone. He led me out into the large room, onto the dais, and in front of the microphone. He whispered for me to say what we had rehearsed, and got off the dais to squat about eight feet to my right in front of me with what I guess was our speech in his hand.

I stood the straightest I have ever stood in my life and slowly let my gaze pass across the audience. The floodlights were blinding and I could see little except shadowy forms, my little prompter squatting out there, and what I suppose were North Vietnamese military officers in uniform at a table off to my right and out of the glare of the floodlights. The shadowy forms, I supposed, were journalists, and although I could not see them, I could see their feet. I remember recognizing the typical French-cut shoes, and so assumed there were probably French and East European reporters present. I was glad to be alive. I was prouder then to be an American than I ever had been. It was electric. I felt the hair on my neck rise, and I forgot my speech.

I said, "Good evening, gentlemen. I am Captain Frank D. Lewis. My serial number is ----------. I am a B-52 pilot. Unfortunately, as you can see, I was shot down. I want you to tell my country and my family that I am alive. I am okay except for some wounds and a twisted leg which have not yet been treated. I do not know what has happened to my other crew members. Do you have any questions?"

During these short remarks my prompter got very agitated. At this point he jumped up, almost ran to the dais and started to pull me away. I resisted slightly, said, "Thank you," and then turned and exited in as military a fashion as I could with him pulling me. He was very upset and didn't remember to blindfold me until the truck started up. I just told him that in all the light and with all the people, I forgot what I was supposed to say. I reminded him that he hadn't prepared me for this, and told him I thought I said about what he wanted. He said that we were both in a lot of trouble.

We returned to the prison. He and three guards took me to a solitary cell. Before they locked me in, he told me that because of my bad attitude I was not going to be allowed to join the other prisoners. I was sorry to hear this, but otherwise I was feeling pretty pleased with myself. They closed the door and I heard the padlock snap shut. I never saw him again.

I was alone in a ten-by-ten-foot tiled-floored cell. It was illuminated by a bare, harsh light bulb. A waist-high empty shelf was in one corner. One wall had a five-foot-high barred window opening. There was no glass in the window, but heavy, green, wooden shutters were closed over it outside the bars. I couldn't see outside. In the opposite corner was a mysterious door that had been heavily nailed shut and bricked in across the bottom. By now it was pitch-dark outside and I estimated it to be about 2100 local. After exploring my new home, I lay down on the floor and fell asleep.

I think that it must have been a couple of hours later when I was awakened by the sound of air-raid sirens. I had completely forgotten that the old USAF would be back to bomb these turkeys again tonight. I was elated! The sirens went on for about fifteen minutes and then stopped. It was dead quiet. None of the background prison sounds I had heard earlier were present. Then the AAA started and began picking up in intensity. I could hear close and distant reports. It was all over the place. And then I heard two of the most beautiful sounds I have ever heard. Kablamm! And a few seconds later another, kablamm! I instinctively knew that the two F-111s had just passed close by, low and supersonic. The shutters shook. Dust and plaster fell off the ceiling onto me. A few seconds later there followed, boom, boom, boom, boom, boom, boom, boom, boom . . . I could hear their bombs going off. I couldn't keep quiet, and danced around my cell like a fool, yelling and cheering. The sounds of AAA firing died off in the distance. Everything was quiet again. I knew what would be coming pretty soon.

About ten minutes later the sirens went off again and the AAA started up. The sirens quit, but the AAA continued intermittently. I could hardly wait. Then a new sound occurred. It was a low-level whoosh. It had to have been a SAM. Then there were more whooshes and heavy-caliber AAA explosions. And then the sound came, off in the distance, faint at first, but louder as it approached. The overlapping explosions of B-52D strings were marching across the ground in the distance around what must have been the outskirts of Hanoi. Each separate B-52D bomb string lasted a long time. They seemed to be coming nearer. It sounded like Godzilla was crunching around the city. Three of these bomb strings started pretty close and came in my direction. Their overlapping explosions became so intense that the walls of the cell shook; the bars and shutters shook so violently that I thought they would fall out; plaster and debris fell all around me. It was absolutely the most awesome sound show I had ever heard. I recall hoping that the navigators had remembered to set their offsets. The AAA reports were intense and the whooshes of SAMs came more frequently. I jumped around and yelled with delight. As quickly as it had come, it began to subside. The whooshes of SAMs ceased. The sound of the AAA began to lessen in intensity. Finally, I heard the last long string recede off in the distance. The silence that followed was overwhelming. I remember that I cried with pleasure. I didn't feel alone anymore. Never again in the next three months did I ever feel alone. It was the ultimate deux ex machina. I prayed for the men, the crews, and the aircraft they flew. To me they had become the hand of God that had reached out to bring me an inner peace and strength with which I would endure this cruel land.

This concludes my recounting of two momentous days in my life. What followed was never again as frighteningly intense as these two days had been. Things gradually became better. I remained in this solitary cell for a month before being moved to the Zoo and allowed to be among the other prisoners. I existed by getting through a day at a time, never dwelling on a future much more distant. And I counted a day as good if I could somehow laugh at or somehow confound my captors. These are other stories, and most of them are good. I was able to break out of my cell clandestinely. I secretly contacted other prisoners. I wrecked a prison truck. I told my interrogators outrageous lies and never cracked a smile. I constructed a secret cigarette lighter and confounded my guards when they discovered me passively smoking a cigarette in my cell without any apparent way to have lit it. I figured out how to lock my cell door from the inside so that the guards could not enter. I delighted in blowing out the prison electrical system at night when the guards were all gathered in the courtyard watching war movies for entertainment. These were all highs. And I made these highs far outweigh the lows.

It was an honor for the short time that I was in prison to be associated with the old guys. My brief baptism gave me just a little insight into the fear, pain, and heartache that they had suffered for years. Their courage and their endurance and their overwhelming love of America are a simple bright memorial to the miracle that has given our country the ability to bear and nurture such sons. But more miraculous than this is that they are not special. They were just like you and I, normal, average Americans with hopes and dreams, but thrown abruptly into the abyss.

After the first month in solitary, I was moved to the Zoo, where I was reunited with three of my crew members. We tried to piece together what had happened to us.

We believe that the SAM that hit us struck our aircraft at about the *right* wing root or right forward wheel well. This is just below and behind the crew compartment. Senior Master Sergeant Gough, our gunner who rides in the very tail of the B-52D, said that as soon as we were hit we caught fire. The fire was burning along the entire right side of the fuselage and extended about half a mile behind the aircraft. Later reports by Cobalt Two and Three also confirmed this.

Cobalt Two and Three also reported that we were struck by two SAMs that came up directly underneath us. None of us in the aircraft actually felt a second impact, however. Our radar navigator, Lt. Col. Jim Condon, believes that the bombs released. He felt them go. He was closer to them than anyone else, so perhaps is correct. Although I did not feel them release, I hope that he was right. Lieutenant Colonel Condon also believes that he heard the three thumps of ejection seats going above him before he ejected. These would have been the EWO, pilot, and copilot positions. Capt. Sam Cusimano, my copilot, was trying to figure out what I was yelling at him when he said that I just disappeared. He said that he ejected instantly thereafter.

Senior Master Sergeant Gough heard no communications. He estimates that he rode the aircraft down to about 12,000 to 14,000 feet. He said that the plane was burning ferociously and that he was reluctant to jump through it, which he had to do to bail out since he had no ejection seat. He determined to leave the aircraft before the undercast which I have previously mentioned. He said that the aircraft remained pretty much in a wings-level descent up until he jettisoned his tail-gun turret and jumped through the flames and chunks of debris now coming off the aircraft. His chute opened instantly, automatically, which coincides with my estimates of the top of the undercast. Gough saw a brilliant, huge flash of light diffusing through the clouds a short time after his chute opened. He believes that this was the aircraft either exploding in the air or hitting the ground.

Our navigator, Lt. Bennie Fryer, was apparently killed in the explosion of the SAM that hit us. Lt. Col. Jim Condon, who sat next to him downstairs at the navigator crew positions, said that Ben collapsed forward on the nav table and was bleeding profusely. His seat was the closest of any crew member to the point of impact of the SAM that we think was in the right, forward wheel well. Lieutenant Colonel Condon was wounded in the leg by shrapnel. Jim tried shaking Ben and yelling at him to get him to regain consciousness and eject, but could get no response. He believes that Ben went down with the aircraft. I escorted his body home after it was returned by the North Vietnamese in 1978, and named my first son after him.

The fate of our EWO, Maj. Allen Johnson, is still a mystery. My second son is named for him. We believe that Al ejected from the aircraft. I believe that Al was alive and in the hands of the North Vietnamese for two reasons. First, I still believe that it was Al who I heard scream nearby while I was undergoing interrogation and also, by the way, doing my own screaming. Second, and evidence stronger, is the fact that my interrogator told me that Al was a black man. Neither I nor any of us who survived ever told them this fact. Of course, the North Vietnamese denied any knowledge of Maj. Allen Johnson up until the point that they returned his remains in 1986. Only then did I ever feel a measure of peace with myself. My crew had finally returned home to the country we loved.

BIBLIOGRAPHY

A. References Cited

BOOKS

Burbage, Major Paul, et al. "The Battle for the Skies Over North Vietnam." *USAF Southeast Asia Monograph Series*, Volume 1, Monograph 2, U.S. Government Printing Office, Washington, DC, 1976.

Doglione, Colonel John A., et al. "Airpower and the 1972 Spring Invasion." *USAF Southeast Asia Monograph Series*, Volume II, Monograph 3, U.S. Government Printing Office, Washington, DC, 1976.

Drendel, Lou. *The F-111 in Action.* Squadron/Signal Publications, Inc., Carrollton, Texas, 1978.

Futrell, Frank, et al. *Aces and Aerial Victories: The United States Air Force in Southeast Asia 1965–1973.* Office of USAF History, HQ USAF, 1976, U.S. Government Printing Office, Washington DC, 1977.

Hopkins, Charles K. *SAC Tanker Operations in the Southeast Asia War.* Office of the Historian, HQ SAC, 1979.

McCarthy, Brigadier General James R. and Lt. Col. George B. Allison, USAF. *Linebacker II: A View From the Rock.* Published under the auspices of the Airpower Research Institute, Air War College, Maxwell AFB, AL, 1979.

Mersky, Peter B. and Norman Polmar. *The Naval Air War in Vietnam.* The National and Aviation Publishing Company, Annapolis, MD, 1981.

Momyer, General William W., USAF (Ret.). *Airpower in Three Wars.* U.S. Government Printing Office, Washington DC, 1978.

ARTICLES AND PERIODICALS

"B-52s Make Heaviest Raids of War." *Pacific Stars & Stripes*, 27 Nov. 1972, p. 6.

Branham, David M. "Former Navigator Recalls Close Call," *Capital Flyer* Newspaper, Andrews AFB, MD, Vol. 22, No. 1, 8 Jan. 1987, p. 14.

Brownlow, Cecil. "North Viet Bombing held Critical." *Aviation Week & Space Technology*, 5 March 1973.

Drenkowski, Dana. "Operation Linebacker II: Part 1." *Soldier of Fortune*, Vol. 2, No. 3, September 1977, pp. 32–37, 60–61.

———. "Operation Linebacker II: Part 2." *Soldier of Fortune*, Vol. 2, No. 4, November 1977, pp. 48–59.

Duffner, Robert W. "Pilot and POW, A Vietnam Experience." *Airman Magazine*, Vol. XXVIII, No. 10, October 1984, pp. 42–45.

Eschmann, Major Karl J. "Spirit and Surge." *Air Force Magazine*, Vol. 67, No. 7, July 1984, pp. 94–98.

Manning, First Lt. Stephen O. "Something Big Coming!" *Airman Magazine*, Vol. 17, September 1973, pp. 24–32.

Mize, John D. "Linebacker." *NAM-The Vietnam Experience 1965–75*, No. 17, 1987, pp. 513–517.

Parks, Hays W. "Linebacker and the Law of War." *Air University Review*, Vol. 34, No. 2, January–February 1983, pp. 2–30.

"Rescuers Lift Thud Crew Off NV Ridge." *Sawadee Flyer*, Korat RTAFB Newspaper, Thailand, 2 Dec. 1972, p. 5.

Thomis, Wayne. "Whispering Death: The F-111 in SEA." *Air Force Magazine*, Vol. 56, June 1973, pp. 22–27.

Wolff, Captain Robert E. "Linebacker II: A Pilot's Perspective." *Air Force Magazine*, September 1979, pp. 86–91.

OFFICIAL DOCUMENTS

"Air Defense Reactions to F-111 Aircraft." *Air Intelligence Review*, HQ PACAF, 30 Jan. 1973. SECRET, declassified 31 Dec. 1981.

Baker, Colonel Coleman L. *End of Tour Report: 432d Tactical Recon Wing, August 1972-73.* Corona Harvest Program, 23 July 1973. SECRET, declassified 31 Dec. 1981.

Beaton, Col. Clifford M. *End of Tour Report: 7th AF Intelligence, April 1971-April 1973.* Corona Harvest Program, 20 July 1972. SECRET, declassified 31 Dec. 1980.

Bellamy, Major General Jack. *End of Tour Report: MACV/7th AF HQ, September 1972-April 1974.* Corona Harvest Program. SECRET, declassified 31 Dec. 1982.

"Chaff Effectiveness in Support of Linebacker II Operations." Briefing to SAC Director of Operations, Offutt AFB, NE, April 1973. SECRET, declassified 31 Dec. 1981.

"Command and Control Lessons Learned." PACAF Report, Director of Operations, undated. SECRET, declassified 31 Dec. 1981.

Corona Harvest: USAF Air Operations against North Vietnam, 1 July 1971–30 June 1972. HQ PACAF, 8 June 1973. TOP SECRET, declassified 31 Dec. 1981.

Depuer, Sidney G. *History of the 354th TFW, October–December 1972.* Ninth Air Force. SECRET, declassified 31 Dec. 1981.

"Electronic Warfare Lessons Learned." PACAF Report, Director of Operations, October 1973. SECRET, declassified 31 Dec. 1981.

History of the 17th Wild Weasel Squadron, July–September 1972. 388th Tactical Fighter Wing, PACAF. SECRET, declassified 31 Dec. 1980.

History of the 17th Wild Weasel Squadron, October–December 1972. 388th TFW, PACAF. SECRET, declassified 31 Dec. 1980.

History of the 42nd Tactical Electronic Warfare Squadron (TEWS), July–September 1972. 388th TFW, PACAF. SECRET, declassified 31 Dec. 1980.

History of the 42nd TEWS, October–December 1972. 388th TFW, PACAF. SECRET, declassified 31 Dec. 1980.

Historical Report, 354th TFW, October–December 1972. 354th TFW Director of Operations, Ninth Air Force. SECRET, declassified 31 Dec. 1981.

History of the 388th TFW, October–December 1972. 388th TFW, PACAF. SECRET, declassified 31 Dec. 1980.

History of the 432d Tactical Recon Wing, October–December 1972. 7th/13th AF, PACAF. SECRET, declassified 31 Dec. 1981.

Hudson, Col. Eugene L. *End of Tour Report: MACV/7th AF Intelligence, February 1972–May 1973.* Corona Harvest Program, 20 April 1973. SECRET, declassified 31 Dec. 1981.

Hurst, Lt. Col. John F. *End of Tour Report: 42nd TEWS, August 1972–April 1973.* Corona Harvest Program, 4 April 1973. SECRET, declassified 31 Dec. 1981.

Johnson, Calvin R. *Linebacker Operations: September–December 1972.* Project CHECO Report, HQ PACAF, 31 December 1978. SECRET. Classified by HQ PACAF, downgraded at 12-year intervals, not automatically declassified. [Only unclassified information used]

"Linebacker II B-52 Summary." 43rd Strategic Bomb Wing Report, 22 Jan. 1973. SECRET, declassified 31 Dec. 1981.

"Linebacker Study." MACV Report, 20 Jan. 1973. TOP SECRET, declassified 31 Dec. 1983.

"Linebacker II Talking Paper." HQ USAF Report, Daily Briefings 18–30 Dec. 1972. SECRET, declassified 31 Dec. 1980.

"Linebacker II USAF Bombing Survey." HQ PACAF Report, April 1973. SECRET, declassified 31 Dec. 1981.

Merkling, Col. Richard E. *End of Tour Report: Commander, 388th TFW, November 1971–January 1973.* Corona Harvest Program, 7 Feb. 1973. SECRET, declassified 31 Dec. 1976.

Message, "F-111 Operations." CINCPACAF to 7th A.F. D.O., 23/0330Z Dec. 1972. SECRET, declassified 31 Dec. 1982.

Message, "Linebacker Conference Oscar IV and Papa IV." 7th AF to CINCPACAF, 23/0834Z Aug. 1972. SECRET, declassified 31 Dec. 1980.

Message, "Linebacker Conference Bravo V." AFSSO Udorn to AFSSO 7th AF, 04/0800Z Sept. 1972. SECRET, declassified 31 Dec. 1980.

Message, "Linebacker Conference Victor VI and Whiskey VI." AFSSO Udorn to AFSSO 7th AF, 30/1905Z Sept. 1972. SECRET, declassified 31 Dec. 1980.

Message, "Management and Control of Air Warfare in SEASIA." CINCPAC to CINCPACAF, 06/2200Z Oct. 1972. TOP SECRET, declassified 31 Dec. 1982.

Message, "Linebacker Conference Kilo VII and Juliet VII." 7th AF to CSAF, 13/1333Z Oct. 1972. SECRET, declassified 31 Dec. 1980.

Message, "Mission Analysis of B-52 Strike in North Vietnam on 21 Dec." 388th TFW to 7th AF, 22/1330Z Dec. 1972. SECRET, declassified 31 Dec. 1980.

Message, "Linebacker Conference 24 Dec. 1972." 7th/13th AF AFSSO to 7th AF AFSSO, 24/1715Z Dec. 1972. SECRET, declassified 31 Dec. 1980.

Message, "Linebacker Critique 26 Dec. 1972." AFSSO Udorn to 7th AF AFSSO, 26/1355Z Dec. 1972. SECRET, declassified 31 Dec. 1980.

Message, "Linebacker II Foxtrot." 7th AF to CINCPACAF, 27/0756Z Dec. 1972. SECRET, declassified 31 Dec. 1980.

Message, "Linebacker II India Critique." AFSSO Udorn to AFSSO 7th AF, 27/1115Z Dec. 1972. SECRET, declassified 31 Dec. 1980.

Message, "Linebacker Conference 22 Dec. 1972." 7th AF to CSAF, 28/0405Z Dec. 1972. SECRET, declassified 31 Dec. 1980.

Message, "Linebacker II Juliet Critique." 7th AF to CSAF, 31/1034Z Dec. 1972. SECRET, declassified 31 Dec. 1980.

Message, "Linebacker II Kilo Critique." AFSSO Udorn to AFSSO 7th AF, 30/0400Z Dec. 1972. SECRET, declassified 31 Dec. 1980.

Message, "Linebacker II Lima Critique." 7th AF to CSAF, 01/1040Z Jan. 1973. SECRET, declassified 31 Dec. 1980.

Message, "MIJI Weekly Summary 01-73." AFSPCOMMCEN to AIG 8557, 04/2242Z Jan. 1973. SECRET, declassified 31 Dec. 1980.

"Ops Analysis: Analytical Notes on Support/Strike Ratios." HQ PACAF Report, 11 Oct. 1972. SECRET, declassified 31 Dec. 1980.

Porter, M. F. *Linebacker: Overview of the First 120 Days.* Project CHECO Report, HQ PACAF, 27 September 1973. TOP SECRET, declassified September 1984.

Smith, Col. Scott G. *End of Tour Report: Commander, 432d TRW, April 1972–March 1973.* Corona Harvest Program, 31 May 1973. SECRET, declassified 31 Dec. 1981.

U.S. Congress, House, Committee on Appropriations. "DOD, Hearings on Bombing of North Vietnam," 9 Jan. 1973. Witnesses: Admiral Thomas H. Moorer and Col. Robert M. Lucy.

"U.S. Navy, Marine Corps, and Air Force Fixed-Wing Aircraft Losses and Damage in Southeast Asia (1962–73)." Center for Naval Analysis, January 1977.

UNPUBLISHED MATERIALS

Clement, Major Robert A. "A Fourth of July in December: A B-52 Navigator's Perspective of Linebacker II." Unpublished Air Command and Staff College Research Study, Air University, Maxwell AFB, AL, March 1984.

Giroux, Major Peter J. "Fifty-two Days in Hanoi: A B-52 Pilot's Perspective." Unpublished Air Command and Staff College Research Study, Air University, Maxwell AFB, AL, March 1982.

Geloneck, Major Terry M. "At the Hands of the Enemy: A Bomber Pilot's View." Unpublished Air Command and Staff College Research Study, Air University, Maxwell AFB, AL, May 1981.

Lennard, Lt. Col. William R. "Policy Options of Linebacker II." Unpublished Air War College Research Study, Air University, Maxwell AFB, AL, April 1983.

Lewis, Lt. Col. Frank. "The Events of 26 and 27 December 1972 as Recalled by Lt. Col. Frank D. Lewis." Personal narrative of the Cobalt 01 mission in Linebacker II, 1988.

Matson, Major Arthur R. "Linebacker II." Unpublished Armed Forces Staff College Research Study, May 1983.

Shackelford, Col. William F., et al. "Eleven Days in December: Linebacker II." Unpublished Air War College Research Study, Air University, Maxwell AFB, AL, 1977.

B. Related Sources

BOOKS

Bonds, Ray. *The Vietnam War.* Crown Publishers, Inc., New York, 1979.

Boyne, Walter. *Boeing B-52: A Documentary History.* Jane's Publishing Company, London, 1981.

Drendel, Lou. *Air War Over Southeast Asia, Volume 3, 1971–1975.* Squadron/Signal Publications, Inc., Carrollton, Texas, 1984.

———. *The B-52 in Action.* Squadron/Signal Publications, Inc., Carrollton, Texas, 1975.

Esper, George, and the Associated Press. *The Eyewitness History of the Vietnam War,* 1961–1975. Ballantine Books, New York, 1983.

ARTICLES AND PERIODICALS

Allison, Geroge B. "The Bombers Go to Bull's-eye." *Aerospace Historian,* Winter, December 1982, pp.227–30.

Frisbee, John L. "The B-52: The Phoenix That Never Was." *Air Force Magazine,* February 1973, p. 4.

Giusti, Frank. "Linebackers of the Sky." *Bee-Hive,* Summer 1973, pp. 12–17.

Hopkins, Charles K. "Linebacker II—A Firsthand View." *Aerospace Historian,* Vol. 23, Fall, September 1976, pp. 128–35.

Hotz, Robert. "B-52s Over Hanoi." *Aviation Week & Space Technology,* Vol. 98, 2 Feb. 1973, p. 7.

Ostrow, Martin M. "The B-52's Message to Moscow." *Air Force Magazine,* Vol. 56, April 1973, pp. 2–3.

Ulsamer, Edgar. "USAF Prepares for Future Contingencies." *Air Force Magazine,* Vol. 56, June 1973, pp. 34–40.

OFFICIAL DOCUMENTS

Chain, Col. John T. *End of Tour Report: 388th TFW, August 1972–August 1973.* Corona Harvest Program 7 Sept. 1973.

Davis, Col. Reginald R. *End of Tour Report: 8th TFW, July 1972–March 1973.* Corona Harvest Program, 29 Aug. 1973. SECRET, declassified 31 Dec. 1981.

Humphreys, Col. Francis A. *End of Tour Report: 8th TFW, November 1972–January 1974.* Corona Harvest Program. SECRET, declassified 31 Dec. 1982.

"Minutes of the 7th AF Commanders Conference." HQ PACAF Report, 18–19 July 1972. SECRET, declassified 31 Dec. 1980.

FOOTNOTES

Introduction

1. "Linebacker II USAF Bombing Survey." HQ PACAF Report, April 1973. SECRET, declassified on 31 Dec. 1981, p. 1.
2. Eschmann, Major Karl J. "Spirit and Surge." *Air Force Magazine*, Vol. 67, No. 7, July 1984, pp. 95–96.
3. Burbage, Major Paul, et al. "The Battle for the Skies Over North Vietnam." *USAF Southeast Asia Monograph Series*. Volume 1, Monograph 2, U.S. Government Printing Office, Washington DC, 1976, p. 177.

Chapter One

1. Porter, M. F. *Linebacker: Overview of the First 120 Days*, Project CHECO Report, HQ PACAF, 27 Sept. 1973. TOP SECRET, declassified Sept. 1984, p. 1.
2. Ibid., p. 2.
3. Ibid.
4. Ibid., pp. 3–4.
5. Ibid., p. 6.
6. Ibid.
7. Ibid., p. 7.
8. Hudson, Col. Eugene L. *End of Tour Report: MACV/7th AF Intelligence, Feb. 1972–May 1973*. Corona Harvest Program, 20 April 1973. SECRET, declassified 31 Dec. 1981, p. 2.
9. Doglione, Col. John A., et al. "Airpower and the 1972 Spring Invasion." *USAF Southeast Asia Monograph Series*, Volume II, Monograph 3, U.S. Government Printing Office, Washington, DC, 1976, p. 1.
10. Parks, Hays W. "Linebacker and the Law of War." *Air University Review*, Vol. 34, No. 2, Jan.–Feb. 1983, p. 2.

11. Hudson, p. 3.
12. Doglione, p. 15.
13. Hudson, p. 4.
14. Ibid., p. 5.
15. *Corona Harvest: USAF Air Operations Against North Vietnam, 1 July 1971–30 June 1972.* HQ PACAF, 8 June 1973. TOP SECRET, declassified 31 Dec. 1981, p. 3. Hereafter cited as *USAF AIROPS.*
16. Porter, p. 9.
17. Ibid., p. 13.
18. Hudson, pp. 10–11.
19. *USAF AIROPS,* p. 63.
20. "Linebacker Study," MACV Report, 20 Jan. 1973. TOP SECRET, declassified 31 Dec. 1983, pp. 3–6.
21. *USAF AIROPS,* p. 71.
22. Ibid., p. 72.
23. Ibid., p. 75.
24. Ibid., pp. 75–76.
25. Porter, pp. 13–14.
26. Drenkowski, Dana K. "Operation Linebacker II: Part 1." *Soldier of Fortune.* Vol. 2, No. 3, Sept. 1977, pp. 32–33.
27. *USAF AIROPS,* p. 80.
28. Ibid., pp. 81–82.
29. Ibid., pp. 82.
30. *USAF AIROPS,* pp. 82–83.
31. Ibid., p. 88.
32. Ibid.
33. Momyer, General William W., USAF (Ret.) *Airpower in Three Wars,* U.S. Government Printing Office, Washington DC, 1978, p. 91.
34. Hudson, p. 14.
35. Momyer, pp. 93–94.
36. *USAF AIROPS,* p. 94.
37. Ibid., p. 97.
38. Ibid., pp. 98–100.
39. Ibid., p. 101.
40. Porter, p. 44.
41. Momyer, p. 118.
42. Ibid., p. 119.
43. Porter, pp. 44–45.
44. *USAF AIROPS,* p. 121.
45. Ibid., p. 122.
46. Ibid.
47. Ibid., p. 123.
48. Ibid.
49. Ibid., p. 124.

50. Ibid.
51. "Linebacker Study" pp. 15–16.
52. *USAF AIROPS*, p. 132–133; "Linebacker Study," p. 15.
53. Ibid., p. 133.
54. Ibid., p. 135.
55. Ibid., p. 134.
56. Ibid., pp. 136–37.
57. Ibid., p. 131.
58. "Ops Analysis: Analytical Notes on Support/Strike Ratios," HQ PACAF Report, 11 Oct. 1972. SECRET, declassified 31 Dec. 1980, p. 11.
59. *USAF AIROPS*, p. 148.
60. Message, "Linebacker Conference Bravo V," SSO Udorn to 7th AF, 04/0800Z Sept. 1972. SECRET, declassified 31 Dec. 1980.
61. *USAF AIROPS*, p. 150.
62. Johnson, Calvin R. *Linebacker Operations: September–December 1972*, Project CHECO Report, HQ PACAF, SECRET, declassified 31 Dec. 1978, p. 19.
63. Ibid., p. 11.
64. Ibid., p. 8.
65. "Linebacker Study," pp. 7–8.
66. Ibid., pp. 8, 11.
67. Burbage, Major Paul, et al. "The Battle for the Skies Over North Vietnam." *USAF Southeast Asia Monograph Series*. Volume 1, Monograph 2, U.S. Government Printing Office, Washington DC, 1976, p. 164.
68. "Linebacker Study," pp. 7–8.
69. Porter, p. 47.
70. Ibid., pp. 47–48.
71. Porter, p. 25.
72. "Linebacker Study," p. 25.
73. Porter, p. 64.
74. *History of the 432d Tactical Reconnaissance Wing October–December 1972*, 7th/13th AF, PACAF. SECRET, declassified on 31 Dec. 1981, pp. 23–24. Hereafter cited as *432d History*.
75. Porter, p. 52.
76. "Linebacker Study," pp. 51–53.
77. Ibid., p. 30.
78. Ibid.
79. Ibid., pp. 57–58.
80. *USAF AIROPS*, pp. 120–21.
81. "Linebacker Study," p. 36.
82. Porter, p. 51.
83. "Linebacker Study," p. 36.

250 Karl J. Eschmann

84. Ibid., p. 37.
85. Ibid., p. 38.
86. *USAF AIROPS*, p. 126.
87. "Linebacker Study," p. 38.
88. Ibid., p. 41.
89. Ibid., pp. 41–43.
90. Message, "Linebacker Conference Oscar IV and Papa IV," 7th AF to CINCPACAF, 23/0834Z Aug. 1972. SECRET, declassified 31 Dec. 1980.
91. "Linebacker Study," p. 46.
92. *432d History*, p. 31.
93 *USAF AIROPS*, pp. 141–42.
94. Baker, Col. Coleman L. *End of Tour Report: 432d TRW, Aug 1972–73*, Corona Harvest Program, 23 July 1973. SECRET, declassified 31 Dec. 1981, p. 3.
95. "Linebacker Study," p. 45.
96. Johnson, p. 46.
97. Ibid.
98. "Linebacker Study," p. 46.
99. Johnson, p. 46.
100. Ibid.
101. Message, "Linebacker Conference Kilo VII and Juliet VII", 7th AF to CSAF, 13/1333Z Oct. 1972. SECRET, declassified 31 Dec. 1980.
102. Message, "Linebacker Conference Victor VI and Whiskey VI," AFSSO Udorn to AFSSO 7th AF, 30/1905Z Sept. 1972. SECRET, declassified on 31 Dec. 1980.
103. "Linebacker Study", p. 37.
104. McCarthy, Brigadier General James R. and Lt. Col. George B. Allison, USAF. *Linebacker II: A View From the Rock*. Published under the auspices of the Airpower Research Institute, Air War College, Maxwell AFB, AL, 1979, pp. 55, 140.
105. Momyer, p. 222.
106. *USAF AIROPS*, p. 129.
107. Ibid., p. 128.
108. Momyer, p. 127.
109. *432d History*, p. 56.
110. Baker, p. 11.
111. Momyer, p. 233.
112. "Linebacker Study," pp. 53–56.
113. Momyer, p. 228.
114. Hopkins, Charles K. *SAC Tanker Operations in the Southeast Asia War*. Office of the Historian, HQ SAC, 1979, p. 106.
115. "Linebacker Study," p. 48.
116. Hopkins, p. 98.

117. *USAF AIROPS*, p. 143.
118. Momyer, p. 152.
119. *USAF AIROPS*, p. 143.
120. "Linebacker Study," pp. 48–50.
121. *USAF AIROPS*, p. 162.
122. Ibid., pp. 162–66.
123. Ibid., pp. 103–104.
124. Porter, p. 24.
125. *USAF AIROPS*, p. 106.
126. Ibid., pp. 106–107.
127. Ibid., p. 110.
128. Ibid., pp. 113–14.
129. Ibid., pp. 117–18.
130. Lennard, Lt, Col. William R. "Policy Options of Line-backer II," Unpublished Air War College Research Study, Air University, Maxwell AFB, AL, April 1983, p. 12.
131. Parks, p. 17.
132. *USAF AIROPS*, p. 106.
133. Porter, p. 42.
134. Ibid, pp. 42–43.
135. "Linebacker Study," p. 59.
136. Ibid., p. 60.
137. Ibid., p. 62.
138. Ibid., p. 63.
139. Ibid., p. 65.
140. Johnson, p. 29.
141. Ibid., p. 27.
142. Ibid., p. 29.
143. Ibid., p. 35.

Chapter Two

1. Clement, Major Robert A. "A Fourth of July in December: A B-52 Navigator's Perspective of Linebacker II." Unpublished Air Command and Staff College Research Study, Air University, Maxwell AFB, AL, March 1984, p. 21.
2. Ibid., p. 22.
3. Parks, W. Hays. "Linebacker and the Law of War." *Air University Review*, Vol. 34, No. 2, Jan.–Feb. 1983, p. 17.
4. Ibid.
5. Momyer, General William W., USAF (Ret.). *Airpower in Three Wars*. U.S. Government Printing Office, Washington DC, 1978, p. 99.
6. Johnson, Calvin R. *Linebacker Operations: September–December 1972*, Project CHECO Report, HQ PACAF, SE-CRET, declassified 31 Dec. 1978, p. 19.

7. Shackelford, Colonel William F., et al. "Eleven Days in December: Linebacker II." Unpublished Air War College Research Study, Air University, Maxwell AFB, AL, 1977, p. 5.

8. Hurst, Lt. Col. John F. *End of Tour Report: 42nd Tactical Electronic Warfare Squadron, August 1972–April 1973*, Corona Harvest Program, 4 April 1973. SECRET, declassified 31 Dec. 1981, p. 18.

9. *History of the 17th Wild Weasel Souadron (WWS), October–December 1972*, 388th Tactical Fighter Wing (TFW), PACAF. SECRET, declassified 31 Dec. 1980, p. 8.

10. McCarthy, Brigadier General James R. and Lt. Col. George B. Allison, USAF. *Linebacker II: A View From the Rock*. Published under the auspices of the Airpower Research Institute, Air War College, Maxwell AFB, AL, 1979, p. 30.

11. Beaton, Col. Clifford M. *End of Tour Report: 7th AF Intelligence, April 1971–April 1973*, Corona Harvest Program, 20 July 1972. SECRET, declassified 31 Dec. 1980, p. 19.

12. *History of the 42nd Tactical Electronic Warfare Squadron (TEWS), October–December 1972*, 388th TFW, PACAF. SECRET, declassified 31 Dec. 1981, pp. 8–9.

13. *History of the 42nd TEWS, July–September 1972*, 388th TFW, PACAF. SECRET, declassified 31 Dec. 1980, p. 23.

14. *History, 42nd TEWS, Oct–Dec. 1972*, p. 10.

15. Ibid., pp. 23–24.

16. Ibid., p. 9.

17. *History of the 17th Wild Weasel Squadron, July–September 1972*, 388th TFW, PACAF. SECRET, declassified 31 Dec. 1980, p. 3.

18. Ibid., p. 4.

19. *History. 17th WWS, Oct.–Dec. 1972*, p. 7.

20. Ibid., p. 8.

21. Ibid.

22. "B-52s Make Heaviest Raids of War." *Pacific Stars & Stripes*, 27 Nov. 1972, p. 6.

23. McCarthy, pp. 34–35.

24. *History, 17th WWS, Oct.–Dec. 1972*, p. 9.

25. Johnson, p. 29.

26. "Rescuers Lift Thud Crew off NV Ridge." *Sawadee Flyer*, Korat RTAFB Newspaper, 2 Dec. 1972, p. 5.

27. Giroux, Major Peter J. "Fifty-two Days in Hanoi: A B-52 Pilot's Perspective." Unpublished Air Command and Staff College Research Study, Air University, Maxwell AFB, AL, March 1982, p. 25.

28. "Rescuers . . .," p. 5.

Chapter Three

1. Wolff, Capt. Robert E. "Linebacker II: A Pilot's Perspective." *Air Force Magazine*, September 1979, p. 87.
2. Drendel, Lou. *Air War Over Southeast Asia, Volume 3, 1971–
   1975.* Squadron/Signal Publications, Inc., Carrollton, Texas,
   1984, p. 21.
3. Futrell, Frank, et al. *Aces and Aerial Victories: The United
   States Air Force in Southeast Asia 1965-1973.* Office of
   USAF History, HQ USAF, 1976, U.S. Government Printing
   Office, Washington, DC, 1977, p. 16.
4. Lennard, Lt. Col. William R. "Policy Options of Linebacker II." Unpublished Air War College Research Study,
   Air University, Maxwell AFB, AL, April 1983, p. 16.
5. Ibid., p. 16.
6. Clement, Major Robert A. "A Fourth of July in December:
   A B-52 Navigator's Perspective of Linebacker II." Unpublished Air Command and Staff College Research Study, Air
   University, Maxwell AFB, AL, March 1984, p. 23.
7. Parks, W. Hays. "Linebacker and the Law of War." *Air
   University Review*, Vol. 34, No. 2, Jan.-Feb. 1983, p. 18.
8. Ibid., p. 16.
9. Shackelford, Colonel William F., et al. "Eleven Days in
   December: Linebacker II." Unpublished Air War College
   Research Study, Air University, Maxwell AFB, AL, 1977,
   p. 2.
10. Clement, p. 28.
11. Matson, Major Arthur R. "Linebacker II." Unpublished
    Armed Forces Staff College Research Study, May 1983,
    p. 2.
12. Parks, pp. 16-17.
13. Ibid., p. 17.
14. Message, "Management and Control of Air Warfare in
    SEASIA," CINCPAC to CINCPACAF, 06/2200W Oct.
    1972. TOP SECRET, declassified 31 Dec. 1982.
15. "Linebacker Study," MACV Report, 20 Jan 1973. TOP SE-
    CRET, declassified 31 Dec. 1983, p. 35; Shackelford, p. 25.
16. Hudson, Col. Eugene L. *End of Tour Report: MACV/7th AF
    Intelligence, Feb. 1972–May 1973,* Corona Harvest Program,
    20 April 1973. SECRET, declassified 31 Dec. 1981, p. 19.
17. Drenkowski, Dana. "Operation Linebacker II," *Soldier of
    Fortune.* Vol. 2, No. 3, September 1977, p. 34.
18. Ibid., p. 36.
19. Hudson, p. 19.
20. Bellamy, Major General Jack. *End of Tour Report: MACV/*

    7th AF HQ, September 1972–April 1974, Corona Harvest Program. SECRET, declassified 31 Dec. 1982, p. 3.

21. Ibid., p. 4.
22. Ibid., p. 12.
23. Shackelford, p. 33.
24. Ibid., p. 34.
25. Ibid.
26. Matson, p. 3.
27. McCarthy, Brigadier General James R. and Lt. Col. George B. Allison, USAF. *Linebacker II: A View From the Rock.* Published under the auspices of the Airpower Research Institute, Air War College, Maxwell AFB, AL, 1979, pp. 46–47.
28. Shackelford, p. 35.
29. Clement, p. 28.
30. Shackelford, p. 35.
31. Ibid., p. 32.
32. Ibid.
33. Bellamy, p. 3.
34. Eschmann, Major Karl J. "Spirit and Surge," *Air Force Magazine*, Vol. 67, No. 7, July 1984, p. 95.
35. Drenkowski, p. 37.
36. Bellamy, p. 4.
37. Drenkowski, p. 37.
38. Ibid.
39. Eschmann, p. 95.
40. Smith, Col. Scott G. *End of Tour Report: Commander, 432d TRW, April 1972–March 1973*, Corona Harvest Program, 31 May 1973. SECRET, declassified 31 Dec. 1981, p. 8.
41. Ibid.
42. "Chaff Effectiveness in Support of Linebacker II Operations." Briefing to SAC Director of Operations, Offutt AFB, NE, April 1973. SECRET, declassified 31 Dec. 1981, p. 31.
43. Message, 7th AF to CSAF, "Linebacker Conference 22 Dec. 72," 28/0405Z Dec. 72. SECRET, declassified 31 Dec. 1980, p. 2.
44. "Chaff Effectiveness," p. 35.
45. *History of the 388th TFW, October–December 1972.* 388th TFW, PACAF. SECRET, declassified 31 Dec. 1980, p. 31.
46. Merkling, Col. Richard E. *End of Tour Report: Commander, 388th TFW, November 1971–January 1973.* Corona Harvest Program, 7 Feb. 1973. SECRET, declassified 31 Dec. 1976, p. 7.
47. Drenkowski, Dana. "Operation Linebacker II," *Soldier of Fortune.* Vol. 2, No. 4, November 1977, p. 49.

48. Smith, p. 8.
49. Ibid., p. 27.
50. Ibid., p. 28.
51. Ibid., p. 35.
52. Ibid., p. 38.
53. Ibid., p 35.
54. *History, 42nd TEWS*, Oct.–Dec. 1972, p. 11.
55. Smith, p. 9.
56. Eschmann, p. 95.
57. Smith, p. 9.

Chapter Four

1. Drenkowski, Dana. "Operation Linebacker II," *Soldier of Fortune*, Vol. 2, No. 4, November 1977, p. 48.
2. "Linebacker II Talking Paper." *HQ USAF Report*, Daily Briefings 18–30 Dec. 1972. SECRET, declassified 31 Dec. 1980, p. 12.
3. Thomis, Wayne. "Whispering Death: The F-111 in SEA," *Air Force Magazine*. Vol. 56, June 1973, p. 26.
4. *History of the 42nd Tactical Electronic Warfare Squadron (TEWS), October–December 1972*, 388th TFW, PACAF. SECRET, declassified 31 Dec. 1981, p. 14.
5. Message, "Linebacker Conference 22 Dec. 1972," 7th AF to CSAF 28/0405Z Dec. 1972. SECRET, declassified 31 Dec. 1980, p. 2.
6. "Linebacker II Talking Paper," p. 8.
7. Message, "Linebacker Conference 22 Dec 1972," p. 1.
8. "Chaff Effectiveness in Support of Linebacker II Operations," Briefing to SAC Director of Operations, Offutt AFB, NE, April 1973. SECRET, declassified 31 Dec. 1981, p. 11.
9. Ibid., p. 13.
10. Shackelford, Col. William F., et al. "Eleven Days in December: Linebacker II." Unpublished Air War College Research Study, Air University, Maxwell AFB, AL, 1977, p. 42.
11. "Linebacker II B-52 Summary." 43rd Strategic Bomb Wing Report, 22 Jan. 1973. SECRET, declassified 31 Dec. 1981, p. 18.
12. Shackelford, pp. 38–40.
13. McCarthy, Brigadier General James R. and Lt. Col. George B. Allison, USAF. *Linebacker II: A View From the Rock*. Published under the auspices of the Airpower Research Institute, Air War College, Maxwell AFB, AL, 1979, p. 65.
14. Message, "Linebacker Conference 22 Dec. 1972," p. 2.

15. *History of the 388th TFW, October–December 1972*, 388th TFW, PACAF. SECRET, declassified 31 Dec. 1980, p. 37.
16. Ibid.
17. Ibid., p. 38.
18. Message, "Linebacker Conference 22 Dec. 1972," pp. 2–3.
19. Ibid., p. 3.
20. Baker, Col. Coleman L. *End of Tour Report: 432d TRW, August 1972–August 1973*, Corona Harvest Program, 23 July 1973. SECRET, declassified 31 Dec. 1981, p. 9.
21. Merkling, Col. Richard E. *End of Tour Report: Commander, 388th TFW, November 1971–January 1973*, Corona Harvest Program, 7 Feb. 1973. SECRET, declassified 31 Dec. 1976, p. 9.
22. Message, "Linebacker Conference 22 Dec 1972," p. 3.
23. Baker, p. 9.
24. Message, "Linebacker Conference 22 Dec 1972," p. 3.
25. Smith, Col. Scott G. *End of Tour Report: Commander 432d TRW, April 1972–March 1973*, Corona Harvest Program, 31 May 1973. SECRET, declassified 31 Dec. 1981, p. 28.
26. Message, "Linebacker Conference 22 Dec 1972," p. 3.
27. Ibid., pp. 3–4.
28. "Linebacker II B-52 Summary," p. 22.
29. McCarthy, pp. 61–63.
30. Shackelford, pp. 45–47.
31. McCarthy, pp. 64–65.
32. Message, "Linebacker Conference 22 Dec 1972," p. 5.
33. Ibid.
34. Shackelford, p. 48.
35. Duffner, Robert W. "Pilot and POW—A Vietnam Experience," *Airman Magazine*, Vol. XXVIII, No. 10, October 1984, pp. 42–45.
36. "Linebacker II B-52 Summary," p. 1.
37. Shackelford, pp. 34–35.
38. Message, "Linebacker Conference 22 Dec. 1972," pp. 5–6.
39. Shackelford, p. 64.
40. Shackelford, p. 49.
41. McCarthy, p. 67.
42. Shackelford, pp. 49–50.
43. "Linebacker II Talking Paper," p. 17.
44. "Linebacker II USAF Bombing Survey," HQ PACAF Report, April 1973. SECRET, declassified 31 Dec. 1981, p. 24.
45. "Linebacker II Talking Paper," p. 28.
46. Ibid., p. 30.

47. Shackelford, p. 51.
48. Message, "Linebacker Conference 24 Dec. 1972," 7/13 AF AFSSO to 13th AF AFSSO, 24/1715Z Dec. 72. SECRET, declassified 31 Dec. 1980, p. 6.
49. McCarthy, p. 68.
50. Ibid., p. 77.
51. Shackelford, p. 52.
52. "Linebacker II Talking Paper," p. 19.
53. Shackelford, p. 52
54. Message, "Linebacker Conference 22 Dec. 1972," p. 6.
55. McCarthy, p. 75.
56. Shackelford, p. 53.
57. "Linebacker II B-52 Summary," p. 31.
58. McCarthy, p. 77.
59. "Linebacker II B-52 Summary," p. 28.
60. Shackelford, pp. 53–54.
61. Ibid., p. 55.
62. Message, "Linebacker Conference 22 Dec. 1972," p. 9.
63. McCarthy, p. 77; "Linebacker II B-52 Summary," p. 16.
64. "Linebacker II Talking Paper," pp. 32, 40.
65. History of the 432d TRW, October–December 1972, 7th/13th AF, PACAF. SECRET, declassified 31 Dec. 1981, pp. 56–57.
66. Shackelford, p. 57.
67. Ibid., pp. 57–58.
68. Geloneck, Major Terry M. "At the Hands of the Enemy: A Bomber Pilot's View." Unpublished Air Command and Staff College Research Study, Air University, Maxwell AFB, AL, May 1981, pp. 23–27.
69. Shackelford, p. 58.
70. "Linebacker II B-52 Summary," p. 35.
71. "Linebacker II Talking Paper," p. 45.
72. Clement, Major Robert A. "A Fourth of July in December: A B-52 Navigator's Perspective of Linebacker II." Unpublished Air Command and Staff College Research Study, Air University, Maxwell AFB, AL, March 1984, pp. 35–42.
73. Shackelford, p. 58.
74. "Linebacker II B-52 Summary," p. 37.
75. Shackelford, p. 59.
76. Message, "Linebacker Conference 22 Dec. 1972," pp. 9–10.
77. Ibid., p. 14.
78. Ibid., p. 10.
79. Ibid., p. 14.
80. Ibid., pp. 83–84.
81. Ibid., p. 86.

82. Shackelford, p. 59.
83. McCarthy, p. 86.
84. "Linebacker II B-52 Summary," p. 39.
85. Shackelford, p. 60.
86. Branham, David M. "Former Navigator Recalls Close Call," *Capital Flyer* Newspaper, Andrews AFB, Vol. 22, No. 1, 8 Jan. 1987, p. 14.
87. Ibid.
88. McCarthy, p. 86.
89. Shackelford, pp. 60–61.
90. "Linebacker II B-52 Summary," p. 45.
91. "Linebacker II Talking Paper," p. 34.
92. Shackelford, p. 62.
93. Ibid., pp. 62–63.
94. Shackelford, p. 62; McCarthy, p. 83.
95. McCarthy, p. 89.

Chapter Five

1. Message, "Linebacker Conference 22 Dec. 1972," 7th AF to CSAF 28/0405Z Dec. 72. SECRET, declassified 31 Dec. 1980, p. 12.
2. *History of the 388th TFW, October–December 1972*, 388th TFW, PACAF. SECRET, declassified 31 Dec. 1980, p. 32.
3. *History of the 17th Wild Weasel Squadron (WWS), October–December 1972*, 388th Tactical Fighter Wing (TFW), PACAF. SECRET, declassified 31 Dec. 1980, p. 10.
4. Hurst, Lt. Col. John F. *End of Tour Report: 42nd TEWS, August 1972–April 1973*. Corona Harvest Program, 4 April 1973. SECRET, declassified 31 Dec. 1981, p. 17.
5. Ibid.
6. Message, "Linebacker Conference 22 Dec. 1972," p. 13.
7. "Chaff Effectiveness in Support of Linebacker II Operations," Briefing to SAC Director of Operations, Offutt AFB, NE, April 1973. SECRET, declassified 31 Dec. 1981, p. 24.
8. Ibid., p. 25.
9. Burbage, Major Paul, et al. "The Battle for the Skies Over North Vietnam." *USAF Southeast Asia Monograph Series*, Volume 1, Monograph 2, U.S. Government Printing Office, Washington DC, 1976, p. 184.
10. McCarthy, Brigadier General James R. and Lt. Col. George B. Allison, USAF. *Linebacker II: A View From the Rock*. Published under the auspices of the Airpower Research Institute, Air War College, Maxwell AFB, AL, 1979, p. 91.
11. Ibid., pp. 91–92.
12. "Electronic Warfare Lessons Learned," PACAF Report,

Director of Operations, October 1973. SECRET, declassified 31 Dec. 1981, p. 6.

13. Burbage, p. 184.
14. "Electronic Warfare Lessons Learned," pp. 2–3.
15. Burbage, p. 184.
16. "Linebacker II Talking Paper," *HQ USAF Report*, Daily Briefings 18–30 Dec. 1972. SECRET, declassified 31 Dec. 1980, p. 50.
17. Ibid., pp. 59–61.
18. "Linebacker II USAF Bombing Survey," HQ PACAF Report, April 1973. SECRET, declassified 31 Dec. 1981, p. 12.
19. "Linebacker II Talking Paper," p. 61.
20. Shackelford, Col. William F., et al. "Eleven Days in December: Linebacker II." Unpublished Air War College Research Study, Air University, Maxwell AFB, AL, 1977, p. 65.
21. McCarthy, p. 91.
22. "Linebacker II Talking Paper," p. 50.
23. "Electronic Warfare Lessons Learned," p. 2.
24. Message, "Linebacker Conference 24 Dec. 1972," 7th/13th AF/AFSSO to 7th AF/AFSSO, 24/1715Z Dec. 72. SECRET, declassified 31 Dec. 1980, p. 1.
25. *388th TFW History*, p. 28.
26. Ibid., p. 33.
27. Shackelford, p. 66.
28. "Linebacker II Talking Paper," p. 56.
29. Shackelford, p. 67.
30. Ibid., p. 67.
31. Giroux, Major Peter J. "Fifty-two Days in Hanoi: A B-52 Pilot's Perspective." Unpublished Air Command and Staff College Research Study, Air University, Maxwell AFB, AL, March 1982, pp. 35–37.
32. Ibid., p. 39.
33. McCarthy, pp. 93–94.
34. Shackelford, pp. 68–70.
35. "Linebacker II B-52 Summary," 43rd Strategic Bomb Wing Report, 22 Jan. 1973. SECRET, declassified 31 Dec. 1981, p. 49.
36. Parks, W. Hays. "Linebacker and the Law of War." *Air University Review*, Vol. 34, No. 2, January–February 1983, p. 25.
37. Message, "Linebacker Conference 24 Dec. 1972," p. 1.
38. Futrell, Frank, et al. *Aces and Aerial Victories: The United States Air Force in Southeast Asia 1965–1973*. Office of

    USAF History, HQ USAF, 1976, U.S. Government Printing
    Office, Washington DC, 1977, pp. 112–113.
39. Ibid.
40. Message, "Linebacker Conference 24 Dec. 1972," p. 2.
41. Message, "Mission Analysis of B-52 Strike in North Viet-
    nam on 21 December," 388th TFW to 7th AF, 22/1330Z
    Dec. 72. SECRET, declassified 31 Dec. 1980, pp. 1–3.
42. Ibid., p. 7.
43. *388th TFW History*, p. 33.
44. Mersky, Peter B. and Norman Polmar. *The Naval Air War
    in Vietnam*, The National and Aviation Publishing Com-
    pany, Annapolis, MD, 1981, p. 203.
45. McCarthy, pp. 97–98.
46. Message, "Linebacker II Foxtrot," 7th AF to CINCPA-
    CAF, 27/0756Z Dec. 1972. SECRET, declassified 31 Dec.
    1980, p. 1.
47. Ibid., p. 3.
48. Futrell, pp. 113–114.
49. Message, "Linebacker II Foxtrot", pp. 1–2.
50. Ibid., p. 2.
51. Shackelford, p. 74.
52. "Linebacker II Talking Paper," p. 65.
53. Drendel, Lou. *The F-111 in Action*, Squadron/Signal Publi-
    cations, Inc., Carrollton, Texas, 1978, p. 30.
54. "Chaff Effectiveness," pp. 6–7.
55. McCarthy, p. 100.
56. "Linebacker Conference 24 Dec. 1972," pp. 4–5.
57. Ibid., p. 6.
58. Ibid.
59. Ibid.
60. Ibid., p. 7.
61. Shackelford, pp. 76–77.
62. McCarthy, p. 107.
63. Shackelford, pp. 76–77.
64. Message, "Linebacker Critique 26 Dec. 1972," AFSSO
    Udorn to 7th AF AFSSO, 26/1355Z Dec. 72. SECRET, de-
    classified 31 Dec. 1980, p. 2.
65. McCarthy, p. 110.
66. "Linebacker II Talking Paper," p. 81.
67. Shackelford, pp. 77–78.
68. Message, "Linebacker Critique 26 Dec. 1972," p. 4.
69. Ibid., p. 5.
70. Depuer, Sidney G. *History of the 354th TFW, October–
    December 1972*. SECRET, declassified 31 Dec. 1981, no
    page number references.
71. Shackelford, p. 80.

72. Ibid., p. 81.
73. Message, "MIJI Weekly Summary 01-73," AFSPCO-MMCEN to AIG 8557, 04/2242Z Jan. 73. SECRET, declassified 31 Dec. 1980.
74. Message, "F-111 Operations," CINCPACAF to 7th A.F.D.O., 23/0330Z Dec. 72. SECRET, declassified 31 Dec. 1982.
75. Shackelford, pp. 81-82.
76. Eschmann, Major Karl J. "Spirit and Surge," *Air Force Magazine*, Vol. 67, No. 7, July 1984, p. 98.
77. McCarthy, p. 132.

Chapter Six

1. McCarthy, Brigadier General James R. and Lt. Col. George B. Allison, USAF. *Linebacker II: A View From the Rock.* Published under the auspices of the Airpower Research Institute, Air War College, Maxwell AFB, AL, 1979, p. 122.
2. Message, "Linebacker II India Critique," AFSSO Udorn to AFSSO 7th AF, 27/1115Z Dec. 72. SECRET, declassified 31 Dec. 1980.
3. Shackelford, Col. William F., et al. "Eleven Days in December: Linebacker II." Unpublished Air War College Research Study, Air University, Maxwell AFB, AL, 1977, pp. 83-84.
4. Ibid., p. 83.
5. "Chaff Effectiveness in Support of Linebacker II Operations," Briefing to SAC Director of Operations, Offutt AFB, NE, April 1973. SECRET, declassified 31 Dec. 1981, p. 26.
6. McCarthy, p. 125.
7. Shackelford, pp. 83-84.
8. Ibid., p. 85.
9. McCarthy, pp. 134-137.
10. "Linebacker II USAF Bombing Survey," HQ PACAF Report, April 1973. SECRET, declassified 31 Dec. 1981, p. 16.
11. Shackelford, pp. 90-91.
12. McCarthy, p. 137.
13. Shackelford, pp. 85-86.
14. Ibid., pp. 86-88.
15. Drenkowski, Dana. "Operation Linebacker II: Part 2." *Soldier of Fortune*, Vol. 2, No. 4, November 1977, p. 55.
16. Shackelford, p. 89.
17. Ibid., pp. 80-91.
18. Ibid., p. 92.
19. Giroux, Major Peter J. "Fifty-two Days in Hanoi: A B-52 Pilot's Perspective." Unpublished Air Command and Staff

College Research Study, Air University, Maxwell AFB, AL, March 1982, p. 41.

20. McCarthy, p. 141.

21. Clement, Major Robert A. "A Fourth of July in December: A B-52 Navigator's Perspective of Linebacker II." Unpublished Air Command and Staff College Research Study, Air University, Maxwell AFB, AL, March 1984, pp. 45–46.

22. Ibid., p. 46.

23. McCarthy, p. 140.

24. Message, "Linebacker II Juliet Critique," 7th AF to CSAF, 31/1034Z Dec. 72. SECRET, declassified 31 Dec. 1980, p. 1.

25. Ibid.

26. 354th TFW Historical Report, October–December 1972. 354th TFW Director of Operations, Ninth Air Force. SECRET, declassified 31 Dec. 1981, no page references.

27. "Linebacker II USAF Bombing Survey," p. 35.

28. Drenkowski, p. 52.

29. History of the 388th TFW, October–December 1972, 388th TFW, PACAF. SECRET, declassified 31 Dec. 1980, p. 38.

30. Message, "Linebacker II Juliet Critique," p. 3.

31. Author's personal recollections of the incident on 27 Dec. 1972 while assigned to the 388th TFW at Korat RTAFB, Thailand.

32. Message, "Linebacker II Juliet Critique," p. 2.

33. Ibid., pp. 3–5.

34. Shackelford, pp. 94–95.

35. "Linebacker II B-52 Summary," 43rd Strategic Bomb Wing Report, 22 Jan. 1973. SECRET, declassified 31 Dec. 1981, p. 59.

36. The events of the last moments of Cobalt 01 were derived from the author's discussion of that night with the former aircraft commander, Lt. Col. Frank Lewis, in 1988.

37. McCarthy, p. 149.

38. Manning, First Lt. Stephen O. "Something Big Coming!" Airman Magazine, Vol. 17, September 1973, p. 30.

39. Burbage, Major Paul, et al. "The Battle for the Skies Over North Vietnam." USAF Southeast Asia Monograph Series, Volume 1, Monograph 2, U.S. Government Printing Office, Washington DC, 1976, p. 186.

40. Manning, p. 30.

41. Burbage, p. 186.

42. Mize, John D. "Linebacker." NAM—The Vietnam Experience 1965–75, No. 17, p. 515.

43. Manning, p. 32.

44. Ibid.

45. Burbage, p. 186.
46. Mize, p. 516.
47. Manning, p. 32.
48. Ibid.
49. Shackelford, p. 96.
50. Message, "Linebacker II Kilo Critique," AFSSO Udorn to AFSSO 7th AF, 30/0400Z Dec. 72. SECRET, declassified 31 Dec. 1980, pp. 1–2.
51. Ibid., p. 1.
52. *388th TFW History*. p. 39.
53. Message, "Linebacker II Kilo Critique," p. 3.
54. Shackelford, p. 96.
55. "Chaff Effectiveness," p. 28.
56. Futrell, pp. 114–115.
57. McCarthy, p. 159.
58. Message, "Linebacker II Lima Critique," 7th AF to CSAF, 01/1040Z Jan. 73. SECRET, declassified 31 Dec. 1980, pp. 1–2.
59. Shackelford, pp. 97–98.
60. McCarthy, p. 166.
61. Shackelford, p. 99.

Chapter Seven

1. Shackelford, Col. William F., et al. "Eleven Days in December: Linebacker II." Unpublished Air War College Research Study, Air University, Maxwell AFB, AL, 1977, p. 101.
2. "Linebacker II USAF Bombing Survey," HQ PACAF Report, April 1973. SECRET, declassified 31 Dec. 1981, pp. 1–2.
3. Ibid., p. 2.
4. U.S. Congress, House, Committee on Appropriations. "DOD, Hearings on Bombing of North Vietnam," 9 Jan. 1973. Witnesses: Admiral Thomas H. Moorer and Col. Robert M. Lucy, pp. 6–7.
5. Ibid., p. 7.
6. "Linebacker II USAF Bombing Survey," pp. 5–6.
7. U.S. Congress, pp. 7–8.
8. "Linebacker II USAF Bombing Survey," pp. 5–10.
9. Ibid., p. 40.
10. Ibid., p. 10.
11. Ibid., pp. 12–14.
12. Ibid., pp. 14–16.
13. Ibid., p. 16.

14. *History of the 388th TFW, October–December 1972,* 388th TFW, PACAF. SECRET, declassified 31 Dec. 1980, p. 23.

15. "Linebacker II USAF Bombing Survey," p. 18.

16. Ibid., pp. 18, 20.

17. Bellamy, Major General Jack. *End of Tour Report: 7th AF Director of Operations. September 1972–February 1973.* Corona Harvest Program, undated. SECRET, declassified 31 Dec. 1982, p. 4.

18. Parks, W. Hays. "Linebacker and the Law of War." *Air University Review,* Vol. 34, No. 2, January–February 1983, pp. 25–26.

19. Hudson, Col. Eugene L. *End of Tour Report: MACV/7th AF Intelligence, February 1972–May 1973,* Corona Harvest Program, 20 April 1973. SECRET, declassified 31 Dec. 1981, pp. 20–21.

20. Shackelford, p. 100.

21. Hudson, p. 21.

22. Author's personal recollection of the accidents while assigned to the 388th TFW at Korat RTAFB, Thailand, during the Linebacker II operation.

23. "U.S. Navy, Marine Corps, and Air Force Fixed-Wing Aircraft Losses and Damage in Southeast Asia (1962–73)," Center for Naval Analyses, January 1977, pp. 488–492.

24. Ibid., pp. 191–94, 223.

25. Hudson, p. 21.

26. Shackelford, p. 107.

27. Electronics Warfare Lessons Learned," PACAF Report, Director of Operations, October 1973. SECRET, declassified on 31 Dec. 1981, p. 1–3.

28. Ibid., pp. 3–4.

29. Merkling, Col. Richard E. *End of Tour Report: Commander, 388th TFW, November 1971–January 1973.* Corona Harvest Program, 7 February 1973. SECRET, declassified 31 Dec. 1976. p. 8.

30. McCarthy, Brigadier General James R. and Lt. Col. George B. Allison, USAF. *Linebacker II: A View From the Rock.* Published under the auspices of the Airpower Research Institute, Air War College, Maxwell AFB, AL, 1979, p. 149.

31. "Linebacker II USAF Bombing Survey," p. 33.

32. "Electronic Warfare Lessons Learned," pp. 6–7.

33. "Linebacker II USAF Bombing Survey," p. 35.

34. Bellamy, p. 12.

35. Ibid., p. 13.

36. "Linebacker II USAF Bombing Survey," p. 34.

37. "Command and Control Lessons Learned," PACAF Re-

port, Director of Operations, Undated. SECRET, declassified 31 Dec. 1981, p. 2.

38. "Air Defense Reactions to F-111 Aircraft," Air Intelligence
   Review, HQ PACAF, 30 Jan. 1973. SECRET, declassified
   31 Dec. 1981, p. 17.

39. Thomis, Wayne. "Whispering Death: The F-111 in SEA,"
   Air Force Magazine. Vol. 56, June 1973, p. 27.

40. Brownlow, Cecil. "North Viet Bombing Held Critical,"
   Aviation Week & Space Technology. March 5, 1973, p. 13.

41. "Linebacker II USAF Bombing Survey," p. 37.

42. Ibid., p. 34.

43. Ibid., p. 37.

44. McCarthy, p. 173.

45. Clement, Major Robert A. "A Fourth of July in December:
   A B-52 Navigator's Perspective of Linebacker II." Unpub-
   lished Air Command and Staff College Research Study, Air
   University, Maxwell AFB, AL, March 1984, p. 45.

46. Ibid., p. 46.

47. McCarthy, p. 173.

GLOSSARY

AAA—Antiaircraft Artillery

ABC—Airborne Commander, the senior officer aboard a B-52 in a wave, responsible for inflight decisions and the conduct of the wave

Abort—Cancellation of an aircraft mission for any reason other than enemy action, at any time from takeoff to mission completion

AFB—Air Force Base

Afterburner—An auxiliary burner attached to the tailpipe of a jet engine for injecting fuel into the hot exhaust gases and burning it to provide extra thrust

AGM—Air-to-ground missile

AGM-45—Shrike air-to-ground missile, antiradiation type (enemy radars had to be operating continuously for the missile to home in on the site)

AGM-78—Standard ARM air-to-ground missile, antiradiation type (this missile seeker contained a computer memory that would "remember" the enemy radar site location even if the radar was turned off)

AIM-7—Sparrow air-to-air missile, semiactive radar type

AIM-9—Sidewinder air-to-air missile, passive infrared type

Aircrew—The full complement of air officers and airmen who man an aircraft in the air; also applied to the pilot of a single place aircraft; often shortened to "crew"

Arc Light—Conventional bombing of selected targets in Southeast Asia by SAC B-52s, exclusive of those targets associated with Linebacker II

A-7—"Corsair II," single-engine fighter bomber

Atoll—Soviet-built air-to-air missile, infrared seeker type, similar to the US AIM-9 IR-homing missile (outright copy)

Ballistic—Unguided, that is, follows a ballistic trajectory when thrust is terminated

Bandit—Term for an enemy aircraft

BARCAP—Barrier combat air patrol; fighter cover between the strike force and an area of expected threat; a MIG screen for one or more missions (see CAP)

BDA—Bomb Damage Assessment

Beeper—Emergency radio in crew member's parachute pack, automatically activated upon ejection or bailout

B-52—"Stratofortress"; heavy jet bomber. Two model series, the D and G, were used in the Linebacker II operations.

Bingo (fuel)—Minimum fuel quantity reserve established for a given geographical point to permit aircraft to return safely to its home base, an alternate base, or an aerial refueling point

Break—An emergency turn in which maximum performance is desired instantly to destroy an attacker's tracking solution

Brigham—Radar Control and Reporting Center, which was located at Udorn RTARB

BRL—Bomb Release Line, that point on the bomb run where bomb release is initiated. The "bombs away" point

BUFF—Informal nickname and acronym for the B-52, derived from "Big Ugly Fat Fella"

Bull's-eye—A reference point in North Vietnam (Hanoi)

Burn Through Point—That point near the SAM sites where its radiated power exceeds that of the aircraft's jamming power, enabling the site to "see through" the electronic jamming

CAP—Combat Air Patrol; an aircraft patrol provided over an objective area, over the force protected, or over an air-defense area, for the purpose of intercepting and destroying hostile aircraft before they reach their target

Capt.—Captain

CBU—Cluster Bomb Unit; antimaterial munition with clam-shell dispenser and incendiary lined bomblets. Bomblets are spin-armed and detonate on impact

CBU-52—CBU with 220 2.7-pound bomblets, designed to destroy personnel and material targets

CBU-58—CBU with 650 one-pound bomblets, for use against soft targets

Cell—Unit of airborne military aircraft, usually bombers or tankers, made up of a number of individually organized cells or teams which may operate independently of one another to provide flexibility; that is, three B-52 aircraft flying in a designated formation, thereby providing mutual ECM support

Centerline tank—A fuel tank carried externally on the centerline of the aircraft

Chaff—A type of confusion reflector, which consists of thin, narrow metallic strips of various lengths to provide different frequency responses, used to create false signals on radar scopes and confuse enemy defenses

CHECO—Contemporary Historical Examination of Current Operations

CINCPACAF—Commander-in-Chief, Pacific Air Forces

CINCSAC—Commander-in-Chief, Strategic Air Command

Col.—Colonel

Combat Apple—Nickname for reconnaissance operations performed by RC-135s

Compression—Mission where several aircraft launch during a short time interval to provide for a massive bombing force over a target area in a brief time period

COMUSMACV—Commander, U.S. Military Assistance Command, Vietnam

CONUS—Continental United States

CSAF—Chief of Staff, U.S. Air Force

CVA—Attack aircraft carrier (U.S. Navy)

DISCO—Radio call sign for the EC-121 aircraft, which provided airborne navigational assistance, border warnings, and MIG warnings

DMZ—Demilitarized Zone (between North and South Vietnam)

D.O.—Director of Operations

Dogfight—An aerial battle, especially between opposing fighters, involving considerable maneuvering and violent aerobatics on both sides

Downlink—Beacon signal transmitted from a surface-to-air missile to the command guidance radar site

EA-6—"Intruder," U.S. Navy and Marine attack bomber modified for ECM operations

EB-66—"Destroyer," a light reconnaissance bomber that had several configurations for gathering electronic intelligence data or for radiating jamming to provide protection for strike forces

EC-121—Early-warning, fighter-control, and recon aircraft derived from the Super Constellation transport

EC-135—Modified version of KC-135 Stratotanker, used in communications/command and control

Echelon—A formation in which flight members are positioned sequentially on one side of the lead aircraft

ECM—Electronic Countermeasures: various defensive tactics using electronic and reflecting devices to reduce the military effectiveness of enemy equipment or tactics

ECM pod—Pylon or fuselage-mounted container which houses multiple transmitters and associated electronic devices; a self-protection device for aircraft penetrating an electronically-controlled ground-to-air defense system

Element—USAF term for the basic fighting unit (two aircraft)

ELINT—Electronic intelligence

Engagement—An encounter that involves hostile or aggressive action by one or more of the participants

Envelope—A volume of airspace within which a particular weapon or weapon system must operate, be expended, or be employed in order to achieve maximum effectiveness

EOGB—Electro-optical guided bomb

E.W.—Electronic warfare; early warning (radar)

EWO—Electronic Warfare Officer, the crew member on an aircraft (such as B-52 and EB-66) responsible for detecting enemy electronic signals and initiating appropriate defensive electronic/chaff actions

F-4—"Phantom II," USAF and Navy tactical all-purpose, two-engined jet fighter with two-man crew (pilot and WSO)

F-105—"Thunderchief," USAF tactical fighter bomber; version used during Linebacker series was the G-model, or Wild Weasel

F-111—Variable geometry (wing sweep) tactical fighter bomber able to fly at very low altitudes to penetrate enemy airspace by use of terrain-following radar

FAC—Forward air controller

Fan Song—Name designated for ground-based guidance radar used with the Soviet designed SA-2 SAM missile

Feet Wet—Crossing hostile coastline outbound

Fighting Wing—A formation by which the wingman can provide optimum coverage and maintain maneuverability during maximum performance maneuvers

First Lt.—First Lieutenant

Flight—USAF term for a tactical fighter unit, usually consisting of two elements, each element of two aircraft

Fluid-four—A tactical formation having the second element spread in both the vertical and horizontal planes to enhance maneuverability, mutual support, and lookout ability

Fragged—Mission directed by fragmentary operational order from higher headquarters

Frag Order—A fragmentary operations order; the daily supplement to standard operations orders governing the conduct of the air war in Southeast Asia; directs a specific military mission (usually shortened to "Frag")

Freedom Train—Nickname for JCS-directed USAF strikes against targets in North Vietnam as far as 20 degrees N. latitude during the period April-May 1972; replaced by Linebacker I

g—Force of gravity

GCI—Ground-controlled intercept

g-load—The force exerted upon a pilot and his aircraft by gravity or a reaction to acceleration or deceleration as in a change of direction

Guide—With respect to a missile: to follow the course intended when fired

Haiphong—Major coastal port city of North Vietnam

Hanoi—Capital city of North Vietnam

HH-3E—"Jolly Green Giant," rescue helicopter developed originally to penetrate deep into North Vietnam on rescue missions

HH-53B—"Super Jolly," helicopter designed to supplement the HH-3E mission (faster and larger with greater range)

Home(d)—Of a missile: to direct itself toward a target by guiding in on heat waves, radar, radio waves, or other radiation emanating from the target

Hunter-Killer—An Iron Hand mission against SAM sites, flown by a flight of two specially-equipped F-105s and two F-4s

IFF—Identification, friend or foe: aircraft transponding beacon receiving radar information distinguishing friend from foe

IP—Initial Point; a well defined point, usually distinguishable visually and/or by radar, used as a starting point for a bomb run to a target or for other tactical purposes

IR—Infrared

IR missile—An infrared (heat-seeking) missile

Iron Hand—Nickname for a flight with special ordnance and avionics equipment, with a mission of seeking and destroying enemy SAM sites and radar-controlled AAA sites

JCS—Joint Chiefs of Staff

JCS target—A target appearing on the JCS target list

KC-135—"Stratotanker," provides aerial refueling for all types of tactical and strategic aircraft. Also used as long-range passenger or cargo aircraft

KIA—Killed in Action

Kill—An enemy airplane shot down or otherwise destroyed by military action while in flight

Lead—The lead aircraft in a flight or element, or the lead element of a flight

Laser—Light amplification by stimulated emission of radiation

LGB—Laser-guided bomb

Linebacker—A series of JCS-directed USAF/Navy strikes against targets in North Vietnam; Linebacker I began 9 May 1972 and ended 22 Oct. 1972; Linebacker II ran from 18 to 29 Dec. 1972

LOC—Lines of communication

Lock-on—To follow a target automatically in one or more dimensions (range, bearing, elevation) by means of a radar beam or heat seeker

LORAN—Long-range navigation

Lt. Col.—Lieutenant Colonel

M-117—750-pound class, general purpose conventional bomb

MK-82—500-pound, general purpose conventional bomb

MIA—Missing in Action

MHz.—Megahertz

MIG—The name for the Mikoyan/Gurevich series of Soviet jet fighter aircraft

MIGCAP—Combat air patrol directed specifically against MIG aircraft

Missile tone—Audio signal indicating an AIM-9 is locked onto an infrared source

MR—Military Region; the Republic of Vietnam was divided into four military regions

MSgt—Master Sergeant

NM—Nautical mile; 6,076.1 feet

NVA—North Vietnamese Army

NVN—North Vietnam

Olympic Torch—Nickname for U-2 high-altitude recon operations

Orbit—A circular or elliptical pattern flown by aircraft to remain in a specified area

PACAF—Pacific Air Forces

Pave Knife—Nickname for F-4s equipped for laser-guided bombing

Phantom—Nickname for F-4 type aircraft

Pod formation—A formation of two or more aircraft flown in such a way that ECM pods installed on each aircraft offer mutual and maximum protection

POL—Petroleum, oil, and lubricants

POW—Prisoner of War

PPS—Petroleum products storage

PRC—People's Republic of China

Press-on—A mission where aircraft continue their attack regardless of the nature or intensity of defensive reaction

PTT—Post-target turn

Pylon—A projection under an aircraft's wing, designed for suspending ordnance, fuel tanks, or pods

RC-135—Modified version of KC-135 Stratotanker, used for recon operations

Recce—Reconnaissance

Recon—Reconnaissance

Red Crown—U.S. Navy cruiser on station in the northern part of the Gulf of Tonkin for radar surveillance

RHAW—Radar homing and warning; on-board aircraft equipment to warn pilot of active enemy defenses

Ripple fire—Rapid sequential firing of two or more missiles

R.N.—Radar Navigator, primarily responsible for bomb release, assists in navigation to and from the target

ROE—Rules of engagement

Rolling Thunder—Nickname for JCS-directed USAF air strikes against targets in North Vietnam; began as gradual reprisals rather than hard-hitting military campaigns but gradually escalated into major air strikes as the war continued

Route Package (RP)—One of seven geographical divisions of North Vietnam assigned for air strike targeting (RP 1 through 5, 6A and 6B)

RR—Railroad and associated rail equipment

RTAFB—Royal Thai Air Force Base

RTB—Return to base

RVN—Republic of Vietnam (South Vietnam)

SAC—Strategic Air Command, parent command of the B-52

SAM—Surface-to-air missile

SAR—Search-and-rescue

SA-2—Soviet-built SAM system, designed to counter the B-52 at high altitude, but used extensively against all U.S. aircraft in Southeast Asia

SEA—Southeast Asia

7th AF—Seventh Air Force

Shrike—Nickname for the AGM-45 air-to-ground radar-seeking missile

Sidewinder—Nickname for AIM-9 heat-seeking missile

SIGINT—Signal intelligence

Sortie—A single flight by one aircraft (a single aircraft mission)

Sparrow—Nickname for AIM-7 radar-guided missile

Splash—Term meaning that destruction of the target has been verified by visual or radar means

Standard ARM—Nickname for the AGM-78 air-to-ground missile, antiradiation type

Stream—A flow of aircraft following approximately the same route

Strike—An attack upon a surface target, intended to inflict damage on or to destroy an enemy objective

TAC—Tactical Air Command

Tacair—Tactical Air (a generalized collective term for tactical aircraft employed in an operation)

TD—Time delay (LORAN)

TDY—Temporary Duty; the status of being on TDY

Teaball—A weapons control center at Nakhon Phanom RTAFB which used radar and "all source" information transmitted from U.S. aircraft to plot the locations of friendly and enemy aircraft in order to prevent MIGs from surprising U.S. aircraft.

TFR—Terrain following radar

TFW—Tactical Fighter Wing

Thud Ridge—Nickname for a mountain range beginning about 20 nautical miles north-northwest of Hanoi and extending about

25 nautical miles northwest, used for navigational and terrain masking

TOT—Time over target, the time of bomb impact (planned or actual)

Trail Formation—Aircraft directly behind one another

TTR—Target-tracking radar; used to identify the maneuver flown to counter the threat and deny tracking information to the hostile radar

TSP—Transshipment point

U-2—High altitude recon and intelligence gathering aircraft

Uplink—Command guidance signal transmitted from a ground radar site to a launched SAM missile

U.S.—United States

USAF—United States Air Force

USMC—United States Marine Corps

USN—United States Navy

USSR—Union of Soviet Socialist Republics

U-Tapao—Royal Thai Airfield, south-southeast of Bangkok, Thailand, also called U-T

VN-xxx—Designation of a North Vietnamese SAM missile launch site

Wave—A succession of aircraft formations which move across or against a target or other point

Weapons System—Refers to the combination of aircraft, crew, ordnance, avionics, etc

Wild Weasel—F-105G aircraft equipped with RHAW and antiradiation missiles, enabling them to home on SAM radar guidance signals and to mark the location of missile sites

Wingman—Pilot or aircraft who flies at the side and to the rear of an element leader

WSO—Weapon systems officer; backseater in the F-4

Yaw—Rotation of an aircraft about its vertical axis so as to cause the longitudinal axis of the aircraft to deviate from the line of flight

Z-time—Zulu time; a term for Greenwich Mean Time

ABOUT THE AUTHOR

Karl J. Eschmann is an Air Force officer (lieutenant colonel). He holds a Bachelor of Science degree in Aerospace Engineering from Texas A&M University and a Master of Science degree in Logistics Management from the Air Force Institute of Technology. He served as an aircraft maintenance officer on flightline and in staff positions in Pacific Air Forces, Tactical Air Command, and Air Force Logistics Command. During 1972–73 he was an F-4E maintenance officer in Southeast Asia. Between 1980 and 1984 he was the chief integration engineer for the Strategic Air Command's Air-Launched Cruise Missile program at Wright-Patterson AFB, Ohio. Lieutenant Colonel Eschmann is a graduate of Squadron Officers School, a Distinguished Graduate of the Air Command and Staff College, a graduate of the Air War College, and a Distinguished Graduate of the Naval War College.